CHRISTMAS
Unwrapped

Publications International, Ltd.

Contributing Writers: James Duplacey, Mary Fons-Misetic, Dave Gerardi, Heidi King, Yi Shun Lai, Laura Pearson, Michael C. Riedlinger, Russ Roberts, Lawrence Robinson, Paul Seaburn, Ken Sheldon, Don Vaughan, Kelly Wittmann

Factual Verification: Kathryn Holcomb

Cover Illustration: Adrian Chesterman

Interior Illustrations: Erin Burke, Adrian Chesterman, Robin Humer, Jupiterimages, Nicole H. Lee, Robert Schoolcraft, Shutterstock, Jen Torche

Louis Weber, CEO
Publications International, Ltd.
7373 North Cicero Avenue
Lincolnwood, Illinois 60712

ISBN-13: 978-1-60553-913-3
ISBN-10: 1-60553-913-9

Manufactured in USA.

8 7 6 5 4 3 2 1

CONTENTS

It's the Best Time of the Year!..9

How Do You Say That?: Merry Christmas!..................................10
Santas, Santas Everywhere: Santa Conventions............................11
Mmmmm…Christmas Treats..13
Antebellum Greased Lightning...16
Mistletoe: It's Not Just About Making Out 18
Peace in the Midst of War...21
Christmas Around the World: Italy 22
Santa Who?: La Befana...23
A Toy Story: The History of Toys for Tots 24
Holiday Horrors! 26
Go Hang It on the Mantel: The Christmas Stocking....................28
Christmas Movie Anagrams...29
Following Yonder Star...30
Frank Capra's *It's a Wonderful Life* 32
It's a Blunderful Life 33
What You Always Wanted to Know but Forgot to Ask
About "The Twelve Days of Christmas"..34
'Tis the Season to Have More Holidays 36
Fast Facts..40
Mum's the Word...41
The Trouble with Tiny Tim...42
Christmas Games of Yore..44
They Were Born on Christmas Day 46
Indelible Christmas..49
The "Wrap" on Wrapping Paper...50
Christmas Around the World: Poland 52
Santa Who?: Ded Moroz..53
Christmas Around the World: Russia 54

What Does Xmas Really Mean? 56
Top Grossing Films on Christmas Day 57
Bad Santa!...58
Christmas Island..59
Getting Carded..60
Fast Facts..62
Smoking Bishop...63
A Cup of Good Cheer 64
Crunching the Christmas Numbers 67
Every Day Can Be Christmas.......................................68
Mr. Christmas 70
How Do You Say That?: Merry Christmas!...................72
That's Myrrh-riffic! 73
School of Yule 74
"Deck the Halls with Boughs of Holly…"....................76
Christmas Movie Quiz 77
Christmas Around the World: Canada 78
Christmas Carols: A Timeline......................................80
A Thanksgiving Tradition 83
Fast Facts..85
Deck the Halls: Christmas Decorations 101 86
Tamale Time!...88
Lord of Christmas Cheer! 89
Spice Up Your Christmas…..90
They Died on Christmas Day 92
Toys That Caused a Christmas Riot.............................95
Finding Hope in Sorrow 98
Christmas Around the World: Australia 100
Christmas at the Crawfords 102
The Cola Claus 104
The Holiday Season?..105
When Christmas Was Canceled 106
Spin Mobsters...109

Christmas Windows: A Glimpse of Heaven (and Presents!) 110

This Verse Is Worse...112

Dead as a Doornail? Perish the Thought! 113

Christmas Around the World: Mexico......................................114

A Real American Hero...116

A Different Kind of Yule Log 117

Poinsettias...118

Christmas Hits Not Christmasy? 120

We Three (?) Kings 122

Santa, Baby 123

The Cost of Being Santa 124

Christmas Around the World: Sweden......................................126

Santa Who?: Jultomte 128

Mrs. Claus: The First Lady of Christmas 129

The Poetry of Christmas 130

Yes, Virginia, There Is a Santa Claus 132

Santa's Doppelganger? 134

How Do You Say That?: Merry Christmas!................................135

No Room at the Inn? 136

Liquid Christmas Dinner...137

Crunching the Christmas Numbers 138

Christmas in Alaska 139

Christmas Myths! 140

Favorite Christmas Traditions 142

The Warm Glow (and History) of the Advent Wreath 144

Sporting Santas..146

Christmas Around the World: France 147

Santa Who?: Pere Fouettard 149

Fast Facts..150

Sing a Song of Winter! 151

Why Is That on Your Tree?..152

Christmas Movie Quiz 154

Santa, Is That You?..155

The Snowflake Man...156
Christmas Around the World: The Netherlands.............158
Santa Who?: Zwarte Piet..159
Holiday Hope from Home...160
Rudolph's Roots...162
The Last Act of Christmas 164
Christmas in the Third Reich 166
Holiday Pet Dangers 169
Christmas Around the World: South Africa 170
What Carol Is This? 172
Ugly but Delicious: The Chocolate Truffle.....................173
A *Christmas Carol:* TV and Film Adaptations 174
Christmas Time Is Here...176
Fast Facts...178
All About Elfdom 179
More Than Just Children's Toys 182
Crunching the Christmas Numbers 183
Christmas Pantomime..184
Jive Turkey..187
The Art of Christmas..188
Poor Santa! 190
Christmas Around the World: Japan 191
Dickens Saves the (Christmas) Day! 192
Crazy Canadian Cuisine...194
An Alabama First! 195
Holy Days and Holidays..196
Very Special Christmas Episodes 198
What Carol Is This? 201
A Fairy Tale Come True...202
Kris Kringel Delivers! 204
Christmas Around the World: Turkey 205
Christmas in the White House 206
Christmas in the Big Apple..208

Ageless and Evergreen 211

From Germany to England 212

Going Out, Not Stressing Out 214

The Cinnamon Bear 215

Let It Snow! 216

More on Christmas Cards! 217

Baby, It's Cold Outside: Life at the North Pole 218

A Different Kind of Christmas Show! 220

Crunching the Christmas Numbers 221

Christmas Around the World: Greece 222

Santa Who?: Agios Vassilis 224

Fast Facts 225

These Crackers Aren't for Your Soup 226

Fake Forests 228

From Show Tune to Standard 230

How Do You Say That?: Merry Christmas! 232

Jingle Bells, Batman Smells! 233

Santa Is a New Yorker 234

Toymakers Toil at Christmas 236

Christmas Around the World: Brazil 238

The 20 Most Performed Modern Christmas Songs 239

Dickens Meets *Star Trek* 240

You'll Shoot Your Eye Out! 241

A Christmas Story House: Live the Dream 243

Nipping at Your Nose 244

Hopping Up the Wrong Tree 246

Christmas Around the World: England 247

Santa? Can I Have Your Autograph? 248

A "Deer" Gesture 251

How Do You Say That?: Merry Christmas! 252

Christmas Around the World: Iceland 253

Santa Who?: Yule Lads 254

Christmas in Space! 256

Christmas Movie Quiz 257
I'm Gettin' Nuttin' for Christmas 258
Christmas Jeers 260
The Giant Straw Goat of Gävle 261
Christmas Greetings from the White House! 262
Christmas Around the World: Ethiopia 265
The Boys in Blue 266
Depressing Holiday Returns! 268
More Reindeer Facts! 269
The Tremendous Tinkertoy 270
Zoot Suit Santa 272
Fast Facts 273
Hallmark Ornaments: Manufacturing Memories 274
Tree Thief 276
Funny Christmas Web Sites 277
This Verse Is Worse 278
Orson Welles in *Christmas Tails* 279
Ron Howard's *Grinch* 280
A Flintstones Christmas! 283
Tudor Tinsel 284
Away in a *Really Big* Manger: World's Largest Nativity Scene 287
Christmas Disasters! 288
23 Must-Have Toys from 1950 and Beyond 290
Strangest Christmas Movie Ever! 295
A Tree for All Americans 296
Letters to Santa Claus 298
Christmas Movie Quiz 299
Holiday Gifts for Pets 300
The Toll House Mystery 302
Toy Story 303
Aren't There Better Ways for Santa to Sneak into a House? 304

Index 306

It's the Best Time of the Year!

There's no time of the year that makes us feel so happy to be part of humanity as Christmas. We enjoy the sparkling ornaments, the shopping excursions, the merry music playing, the delicious aromas wafting from the kitchen. All is merry and bright... or is it?

There are plenty of lovely stories about Christmas, but there is also a lot of interesting information that you might never have heard about. Do you know about Pere Fouettard, the French "correction"? He travels with Father Christmas and is the snitch—so watch out all you bad French kids!

Read about Iceland's 13 Yule Lads. Among the brothers are Spoon Licker, Sausage Swiper, and Door Sniffer, who uses his enormous nose to search for baking bread. Apparently there's more to Iceland than erupting volcanoes and impish pop singers!

But it's not all about the creatures who visit us at Christmastime. There's also the customs, foods, and decorations. Want to try Canadian bangbelly? No, then how about flipper pie? Yes, it's made with real seal flippers! (Try finding those at your local grocery store.)

And then there are those holiday spirits, and we're not talking about Dickens's three ghosts. But he did mention Smoking Bishop in his classic tale *A Christmas Carol*. Now you can make your own brew, and you, Bob Cratchit, and Ebenezer Scrooge can all drink to Tiny Tim's health.

Explore the many Christmas traditions of different nations around the world, from the North Pole to the Land Down Under. There are these stories, and many, many more to explore in *Armchair Digest™: Christmas Unwrapped*. Christmas is the most wonderful time of the year, and now you can read about all the wonderful aspects of your favorite holiday!

How Do You Say That?

MERRY CHRISTMAS!

Afrikaans: Geseënde Kersfees

Afrikander: Een Plesierige Kerfees

Albanian: Gezur Krislinjden

Arabic: Milad Majid

Argentine: Feliz Navidad

Armenian: Shenoraavor Nor Dari yev Pari Gaghand

Azeri: Tezze Iliniz Yahsi Olsun

Basque: Zorionak eta Urte Berri On!

Binary: 01001101011001010111001001110010011110010010 000001 00001101101000011100100110100101011100110111 01000110 11010110000101110011!

Bohemian: Vesele Vanoce

Bovine: Moo moo moooo!

Brazilian: Feliz Natal

Bengali: Shubho borodin

Bulgarian: Tchestita Koleda; Tchestito Rojdestvo Hristovo

Canadian: Merry Christmas, eh?

Canine: Woof woof bark woof!

Catalan: Bon Nadal

Chile: Feliz Navidad

Santas, Santas Everywhere: Santa Conventions

If one Santa is good, thousands are way better, right? That's how participants of Santa Claus conventions feel. If you've ever had a yen to dress in your best red and whites and join a throng of like-minded Santa fans, you're not alone.

The roots of Santa chaos

Back in the early '90s, a loosely organized performance art group called The Cacophony Society (members of which helped found the annual bacchanalian Burning Man festival) decided to bring their brand of street prank/improv theater to the streets at Christmastime. The first SantaCon was held in San Francisco, and dozens of Santas gathered to roam the streets, interact with the public, and basically goof off. A fun time was had by all, so some of the Santas decided to make this "Santarchy" a tradition.

Santas round the world!

News of the fun of SantaCon traveled fast, and soon there were Cacophony Societies throwing SantaCons all over the place, including groups in Tokyo, London, Atlanta, Oklahoma City, Chicago, and plenty of places in between. After a while, other organizations were putting on mass Santa gatherings, apart from the originators of the event.

The gatherings continue to be popular: In London in 2007, over 1,000 Santas gathered for "Santarchy." More than 13,000 Santas set a Guinness World Record in Ireland on December 9, 2007, which is impressive, but there are other reports that claim an astonishing 70,000 Santas gathered in Moscow in 2006. (We didn't know that many red velvet Santa suits existed!)

Trouble in Santaland?

The rapid proliferation of Santa conventions has resulted in a few snags over the years as certain groups have strayed from the event's original purpose, which is to gather peaceably as a big bunch of Santas, play harmless pranks, and bring good cheer to the public at large. In some cases, Santa gatherings have turned into nothing more than costumed bar crawls that often result in run-ins with the police.

Many mass Santa groups make it clear they look down upon this behavior, distancing themselves from the notion that Santarchy is harmful in any way. New York City's SantaCon, for example, insists that it is definitely not a pub crawl, defining itself thusly: "SantaCon is a not-for-profit, non-political, non-religious & non-logical Santa Claus convention, attended for absolutely no reason." They provide tips for visting NYC and helpful information for Santas who are in it for the long haul.

Take That, Christmas!

Sometimes one more Christmas decoration is just one too many. In January 2008, a home security camera in Calgary, Alberta, captured footage of a man slashing through a couple's outdoor Christmas decorations with a machete. The huge inflatable Santa, polar bear, and train belonged to a mild-mannered couple. The camera didn't get a very good look at the grinch, who also destroyed the sound system playing holiday classics. The masked bandit responsible has yet to be brought to justice.

Mmmm . . . Christmas Treats

Cultures around the world mark special occasions with special foods, and Christmas is certainly no exception. In fact, the Western world probably has more special foods for Christmastime than any other holiday. Here are a few classic holiday treats that'll make your mouth water.

Eggnog

Made with milk, sugar, and frothy whipped egg, eggnog is a versatile holiday beverage. You can serve it hot or cold and with or without alcohol (rum and brandy being the favored liquors.) The word *eggnog* in old English literally means "egg in a little cup." It can be purchased at the store or made at home. Either way, take care: The presence of raw egg in eggnog makes it extremely important to refrigerate at all times before serving.

Panettone

This slightly sweet sourdough bread is a staple Christmas and New Year's food in Italy (where it originated) and across Latin America. The round loaf is dotted with candied orange, lemon zest, as well as dried raisins. Though panettone is delicious plain, often served with hot cider, tea, or coffee; some fans choose to eat it with chocolate or cream. Italian bakers produce over 100 million panettone loaves every year. Fruitcake had better watch out!

Roasted goose

Okay, so maybe you don't see too many Christmas geese on tables these days (turkey is today's go-to bird), but if you want classic Christmas fare, cook your goose. As you'll learn reading Dickens's *A Christmas Carol*, no Victorian table in England was without one come December 25, and goose is still common for Christmas in countries including Israel, Russia, France, and Germany. The meat of a goose has fewer unhealthy saturated fats than meats such as beef or lamb, and many prefer its flavorful meat over turkey.

Sugar cookies

Sure, you can make rolled-out sugar cookies any time of year, but there's something about the Christmas holiday that makes them taste even better. Kids love making sugar cookies, especially when the cookie cutters are in the shape of Santa, Rudolph, and Christmas ornaments, so clear space on the counter and preheat the oven: It's Christmas cookie time!

Peppermint bark

Christmas candies run the gamut from fudge to taffy and everything in between, but peppermint bark has become a favorite in modern times. There are many variations on the recipe, but the idea is the same: White chocolate is spread thinly on a flat wax paper surface. Crumbled peppermint stick candy is spread over the top. After it has set, the "bark" is broken up into pieces and either enjoyed on its own or stirred into hot cocoa.

Fruitcake

In 16th century Europe, cheap sugar arrived from the colonies and suddenly everything that could be sweetened was, including fruit. Pretty soon, there was a whole lot of candied fruit everywhere and nowhere to put it; thus, the fruitcake was born. These days, fruit-cake's popularity has flagged; many find the sticky sweetness and overabundance of nuts to be off-putting. But bakers swear they still do a steady fruitcake trade every year come December. We recom-mend dunking it in coffee at least—you don't want to chip a tooth!

Gingerbread

If you need a project for the kids that will take up the better part of the weekend, try building a ginger-bread house. Gingerbread is a molasses-flavored sweet dough that is baked and usually served either as gingerbread men cookies or as the basis for a charming gingerbread house. Both preparations give ample opportunity to dress up this nutmeg- and clove-spiced cookie with frosting and candies, making gingerbread both a tasty Christmas treat and a creative outlet for kids home for the holidays.

Mincemeat pies

In the Middle Ages, mincemeat pies were what they sounded like: pies containing minced meat, made in order to stretch out valuable protein. As people moved into the Renaissance era, it was common-place to spice up and stretch out meat with dried fruit such as cur-rants or raisins. Over time, fruits and nuts took over and meat was largely eliminated from the pies, though suet (animal fat) is still a key ingredient. Mince pie is an extremely popular holiday food in Great Britain, where kids leave little mince pies instead of cookies for Father Christmas.

Wassail (or spiced cider)

Wassail, a hot spiced wine, was said to have originated with the 5th century legend of the beautiful Saxon Rowena, who toasted the health of the English king with the words "Wass-hael!," which means "Your health!" The trend caught on, and wassail bowls were soon a staple of holiday gatherings. Many English wassail bowls were even-tually filled with ale rather than wine (it was cheaper) and flavored with nutmeg, cinnamon, grated ginger, cloves, and even cream. These days, many folks re-create the wassail bowl by heating spiced apple cider in a slow-cooker and serving it as a popular nonalcoholic holiday beverage option.

Marzipan

Many North Americans will most easily recognize marzipan as wedding cake decoration, but for much of the rest of the Christmas-celebrating world, marzipan is a traditional holiday treat. Made primarily of almond paste and sugar, marzipan is a dense, cakelike confection that is usually molded into shapes that include fruits, vegetables, eggs, or animals and then painted with brightly colored, edible paints. Although many scholars believe the Turks introduced marzipan to Europe, some Italians believe it belongs to them.

Antebellum Greased Lightning

When James Pierpont copyrighted "One Horse Open Sleigh" in 1857, there is no way he could have known that he had written one of the most popular Christmas songs of all time.

When Pierpont rechristened his song "Jingle Bells" two years later, the only part of the song he changed was the title, leaving us with lyrics that, today, are often misunderstood or forgotten altogether. In fact, the song has more to do with horse-drawn street racing and picking up antebellum babes than any holiday. The first two verses almost everyone knows:

> *Dashing thro' the snow,*
> *In a one horse open sleigh,*
> *O'er the hills we go,*
> *Laughing all the way;*
> *Bells on bob tail ring,*
> *Making spirits bright,*
> *Oh what sport to ride and sing*
> *A sleighing song tonight.*
>
> *A day or two ago*
> *I tho't I'd take a ride*
> *And soon Miss Fannie Bright*
> *Was seated by my side,*
> *The horse was lean and lank*
> *Misfortune seem'd his lot*
> *He got into a drifted bank*
> *And we—we got up sot.*

Hot date on a cold night

Most of us don't think much about those lyrics, but no one can deny that there isn't a single mention of Christmas. Pierpont describes his date with a young woman, wherein he speeds around in an open-top sleigh driven by a sleek horse with a stylishly bobbed tail. Further, the horse is decked out with jingling bells, so we know he has the pre–Civil War equivalent of a "hot ride." The holiday season isn't mentioned once. Even though he totals his pony-roadster in a snow-drift, he and his girl still have a great time.

Horse-powered roadster?

If the first two verses make you think of Sandy and Zuko going out for a night on the town, then surely the last two are Kenickie's ode to greaser life in the 19th century. Pierpont's oft-ignored next lyrics go,

> *A day or two ago,*
> *The story I must tell*
> *I went out on the snow*
> *And on my back I fell;*
> *A gent was riding by*
> *In a one horse open sleigh,*
> *He laughed as there I sprawling lie,*
> *But quickly drove away.*

> *Now the ground is white,*
> *Go it while you're young,*
> *Take the girls to night*
> *And sing this sleighing song;*
> *Just get a bob-tailed bay*
> *Two forty as his speed*
> *Hitch him to an open sleigh*
> *And crack, you'll take the lead.*

When he falls on his bum in the snow, a fellow roadster can't help but laugh and speed off. Then, as if to change the subject, he tells us that we should go out, pick up some girls, and try it ourselves. He spells out just how fast the horse should be, and what color and tail-style we should get! Translating for those who are nonequestrian-inclined, a "bob-tailed bay" is a reddish-brown horse whose tail has been cut short. This is Pierpont's version of purple taillights and 30-inch fins. Also, "two forty" refers to a mile in 2 minutes and 40 seconds. Burning up the quarter-mile might not have anything to do with Christmas, but "Jingle Bells" is still about enjoying the winter season and is one of the most loved holiday songs of all time.

Mistletoe: It's Not Just About Making Out

Ah, mistletoe. The little plant—hung on doorways across the land—conjures up quaint images of stolen kisses and blushing cheeks. The age-old tradition of kissing is what people think of when they consider the small green plant with white berries, but there's much more to mistletoe than just a peck on the cheek.

Kissing under the...parasite?

What you might think is a pretty little berry-producing plant is actually a bloodthirsty—okay, plant-thirsty—parasite. Mistletoes are hemi-parasitic flowering plants, or angiosperms, that obtain their nutrition by living off other plants. There are only a few of these class of plant in the plant world, so to that extent, mistletoe is special straight out of the gate.

In case you've never seen actual mistletoe, the plant sports smallish, dark to light green leaves and small, hard white berries. Mistletoe usually grows on oak or silver birch trees, as well as many varieties of shrubs. Mistletoe plants are found almost everywhere and actually first grew in the tropics. The hardy parasite traveled easily, however, and was soon found flourishing all over the West, where its lore was born.

Mythic mistletoe (say *that* three times fast!)

The ancient Greeks saw mistletoe as special, too, and incorporated it into their mythology from the start. Remember Aeneas' "Golden Bough"? Aeneas planned a trip through hell, and on his way he had to pass through a dark and creepy forest. Two doves led him to a mistletoe plant, and Aeneas took a branch with him. The mistletoe lit his way, and when he got to the river Styx, all he did was show his plant to the ferryman and he and his men were immediately transported to the netherworld. Not bad for a twig and some berries!

There is also a Norse legend that tells of the goddess Frigga and her son, Balder. Frigga petitioned the gods to keep her beloved child safe from fire, earth, air, and water. Thinking she had her bases covered, she relaxed. Then Loki, evil god that he was, made a poison-tipped arrow from mistletoe, since it grew in neither the earth nor the sea, but from the branches of other plants. He struck Balder down, and it was said that Frigga's tears turned into the white berries on the mistletoe plant.

The Celts start the trend

One of the earliest known examples of the importance of mistletoe, however, comes to us via the Druids, revered priests in the Celtic religious order. The Druids were big fans of trees, believing them to possess mystical properties. In fact, the word *Druid* means "oak-knower." Since mistletoe grows on oak trees, the Druids thought it had major significance, especially since oaks shed leaves in winter but the mistletoe (being, unbeknownst to them, a parasite) remained vibrant. There was also a summer ritual that involved slaughtering animals—and a few humans—that was begun by clipping mistletoe plants off the boughs of an oak tree. The word "mistletoe" meant "all-healing" in the ancient language of the Druids, which gives you a good idea of how important the little leafy green was.

Mistletoe: an idea that stuck

The Druids weren't the only ancient people to revere the trees. In ancient Europe (think several hundred years B.C.), trees were seen as life-giving sources and were used in medicines, rituals, and all types of ceremonies and holy goings-on. Once Christmas came into play, some of these leftover tree traditions held on, including the Christmas tree, the yule log, and yes, the mistletoe.

As the Middle Ages rolled into town, mistletoe hung on in people's minds as having special powers. Folks cut bunches to hang above their doors—not to inspire kissing but to ward off demons and bad spirits. Other uses included fire prevention (Sweden) and a cure for nightmares (Austria), as well as a poison antidote and an aphrodisiac. The idea that mistletoe could cure all ills was a widely held belief, and many tried it out in potions and other medicines in hopes that they could make barren animals conceive or epileptics cease to have seizures. In the third century A.D., mistletoe was incorporated into the traditions of Christianity as the faith became more and more widespread. This is where the origins of mistletoe as kissing cue may have begun. With all the powers mistletoe was believed to have, many thought it could help with fertility and conception. Therefore, kissing under a bough of the berries was sure to help bring a child into the world.

And remember Frigga, the Scandanavian goddess? Well, she was eventually able to bring her son Balder back to life. In her joy, the happy mother kissed everyone who passed beneath the now berry-filled tree that had caused her so much sorrow. Some believe that this is the reason we kiss under the mistletoe today.

Before you head off to a holiday party...

Mistletoe continues to be a typical holiday tradition, though it's more common to see plastic mistletoe plants than the real thing these days. The next time you find yourself in a house or office with mistletoe hanging, you should know that there's actually a bit of etiquette involved.

Traditionally, a man is supposed to kiss a woman under the branches—sorry gals, but that's the way it's supposed to go. Once a guy kisses a gal, he is to remove one of the berries from the plant. Once all the berries have been plucked, the plant should be removed and replaced with a fresh one, since all its "powers" have been used up.

If a couple kisses under the mistletoe, not only do they get that nice, just-kissed feeling, they'll also have good luck in the coming year and a long and happy marriage in general, according to legend. Conversely, the couple that's too cool to smooch under the doorway is in for bad luck. If you're a single woman lingering under the mistletoe and you don't get any takers, tradition says you'll be single for another year. If you do get kissed, you'll be lucky in love.

And if you don't want to deal with the whole kissing aspect of the tradition, you could always resort to fire. Burning a mistletoe plant is thought to foretell a woman's future in marriage. A mistletoe plant that burns slowly and steadily prophesies a healthy marriage, while spotty, smoky flames warn of a bad marriage or an ill-suited mate.

Pucker up!

Peace in the Midst of War

*Troops on both sides of the Western Front coincidentally
forgot to kill one another for one day.*

Stretching through Belgium and Northeastern France, the Western
Front of 1914 was a place of misery, death, and despair. On one side
were the armies of the German Empire and Austria-Hungary and on
the other were troops from the United Kingdom. Though they came
from different cultures, practiced different methods of Christianity,
and felt a fervent hatred for the cause of their respective enemies,
all the men on both sides of the Front had one thing in common: the
grinding, constant squalor of life in the trenches.

Not really diggin' the trenches

Few experiences are as harsh and filthy
as trench warfare. This form of fighting
came about because advances in firepower were not met with satisfactory
mobility solutions. Both sides in World
War I had plenty of weapons, but both
sides also had trouble figuring out how
to effectively haul these weapons from
one location to the next. This resulted in troops literally "digging in"
along the Western Front and living in the same trenches for months,
even years, on end. Living in these trenches was not only physically
unpleasant, but the mental torture could be absolutely excruciating.

On Christmas Eve 1914, both the British and German troops
along the front were cold, depressed, and homesick. The Germans
began setting candles on the edges of their trenches, then singing
Christmas carols. Soon they heard the British troops—who in some
areas were a mere 30 yards away—answering with their own carols.
Holiday greetings were shouted across no-man's land, and then the
soldiers came out of their trenches and actually exchanged gifts of
tobacco and liquor. Through Christmas Day, the guns were silent,
as both sides honored a common tradition. The next day, the hell of
war began again.

Christmas Around the World

ITALY

If you're tired of green bean casserole, over-crowded shopping malls, and Rudolph, escape to Christmas, Italian style. In Italy, Christmas is less about shopping and more about the food, fellowship, and spirit of the season.

Christmas, super-size

For Italians, Christmas is a lengthy affair. The season begins on the first Sunday of Advent, the period of excitement and preparation for the celebration of Christ's birth. The first Sunday happens four weeks before Christmas, and Italians start everything off with a bang—literally. Fireworks are set off and bonfires are lit, and families shop for trees, gifts, food, and decorations for the house at the popular Christmas markets set up just for the holiday.

As the weeks progress, kids take to the streets to sing carols, a tradition that began in Italy. Manger scenes are set up in yards, and children write down their Christmas wish lists on slips of paper in hopes that La Befana will take note.

La Befana is the Italian version of Santa (see page 23). She delivers gifts on Epiphany, the first week of January. Kids in Italy don't have to wait that long for gifts, though; Babbo Natale, aka Father Christmas, brings small gifts to children on Christmas Day too. But the wish lists youngsters write down on slips of paper are for La Befana.

Showtime

When Christmas Eve hits, it's all about the Nativity. Candles are lit, and the baby Jesus is passed from person to person in the family. After a meatless dinner, everyone heads to mass. On Christmas, traditional *panettone* (a sweetened bread with dried fruits—much lighter than fruitcake) is enjoyed, one small part of a feast large even by Italian standards.

By the time New Year's Eve rolls around, everyone's pretty exhausted, but the Italians take New Year's Day as an opportunity to exchange gifts and reflect on the enjoyment of the holiday. But don't worry, the season isn't over yet. La Befana still has to swoop down on her broom to deliver gifts on January 6.

SANTA WHO?

LA BEFANA

Step aside, Santa Claus: There's a new sheriff in town! In Italy, kids get gifts from a kindly old lady riding a broom—no reindeer necessary.

Many versions, one witch

As with most folktales, there are as many versions as there are people who pass them along. The same is true of the story of La Befana, a witch who delivers gifts to good little boys and girls at the end of the lengthy Italian Christmas season. Some say that the old, haggard woman was approached by the three wise men at the time of Christ's birth. They asked if she wanted to come along to visit the Christ child, but the old woman said she was too busy with housework to go along. She soon regretted her decision and took off to find the baby, but she could never find him. It's said that La Befana has flown on her broom ever since, searching for Jesus and bringing gifts to households with kids hoping she'll get the right place eventually.

Others believe that La Befana is a holdover from pagan rituals predating Christianity. Some believe her name comes from the Greek *epifania,* which translates to "epiphany"; others think it's a version of Strina, the Roman goddess of New Year's gifts.

Bringing home the bacon (or the candy)

No matter where you think she came from, if you're an Italian kid, you're all about La Befana. During the first weeks of the Christmas season, children write their Christmas lists on paper and throw them into the fire. The paper burns up and takes to the air, where La Befana catches them. On Epiphany Eve—the eleventh day of Christmas—the witch comes down the chimney and delivers candy and toys to the good children, onions and coal to the bad ones.

La Befana lives!

Similar to the SantaCon events held in North America, there is a 4-day festival for La Befana in Urbania, Italy. It is the biggest one for the legendary old lady and boasts a house for the witch, where kids can meet her in person. There is also a gondola race held in Venice where men dressed as La Befana race through the canals in her honor.

A Toy Story:
The History of Toys for Tots

For the past 62 years and counting, the U.S. Marine Corps Reserve's Toys for Tots program has distributed more than 400 million toys to more than 188 million needy kids every Christmas. One of the nation's most popular charities, Toys for Tots is a good example of how one spark of compassion can snowball into a whole lot of love—and cool toys!

If you want something done...

The idea for Toys for Tots came about in 1947 from a woman named Diane Hendricks. That fall, Diane made a doll that she wanted to give to a needy child and asked her husband, Bill, a Marine Reservist, if he knew where she should take it. Neither one of them could find any kind of facility or organization dedicated to giving toys to needy kids for Christmas, so Diane urged Bill to start one, using the power of the Marines to give it legs.

Bill did just that. That year, the Marines collected thousands of new and used toys to "bring the joy of Christmas to America's needy children." By the very next year, the Marines decided to go national with the idea, and by 1948, there were Toys for Tots programs all over the country.

A shiny coat of paint

It just so happened that in his civilian life, Bill Hendricks was a head public relations guy for Warner Bros. This put him in contact with high-profile celebrities, and Hendricks used his connections to garner support from famous faces, giving Toys for Tots major national attention. Bob Hope, John Wayne, and Doris Day all lent their support in those early days, and Walt Disney designed the logo that the organization still uses today. The program even got its own theme song, sung by Nat "King" Cole, Peggy Lee, and Vic Damone.

All the PR worked. Over the course of the next three decades, the Marines collected and distributed new and used toys for kids in every corner of the country. During the months of October, November, and December, Reserve Marines spent their drill weekends refurbishing the used toys that had been collected.

By 1979, however, the program was in need of some changes, mostly because it had simply gotten too big, which was a good thing.

To infinity and beyond!

Starting in 1980, Toys for Tots began accepting only new toys. Governmental changes meant that the Reservists were needed for duties more pressing than fixing broken toys during service weekends, and consumer awareness about safety and liability meant that redistributing old toys maybe wasn't such a great idea. Plus, the Marines felt that kids in need shouldn't feel like they were only good enough for hand-me-downs.

Later in the decade, in order to accommodate the size of the program as it stood—and to grow it for the future—a separate, nonprofit Toys for Tots Foundation was formed to work alongside the Marines. Still considered an official activity of the U.S. Marines, Toys for Tots regularly receives accolades for being one of the country's "Best Charities." Celebrities including Adam Sandler, Kenny Rogers, Courtney Cox, and Billy Ray Cyrus have all lent support to the cause.

"Christmas is doing a little something extra for someone."

—*Charles Schulz*

Holiday Horrors!

*Not all Christmas movies are about fun and
family. In some, the guy wearing the Santa
suit is definitely on the naughty list!*

Halloween is the traditional time for horror, but that hasn't stopped
Hollywood from finding thrills and chills in the yuletide season. The
number of Christmas-themed fright flicks isn't large, but the genre
has a devoted following. Here are some of the most infamous:

1. *Tales from the Crypt* (1972) This anthology of horrific
vignettes is based on tales originally published in the very successful
E.C. Comics of the 1950s. Only one of the segments has a Christmas
theme, but it's a humdinger. Titled "All Through the House," it stars
Joan Collins as Joanne Clayton, a less-than-loving wife who murders
her husband on Christmas Eve, then finds herself unable to dispose
of the body because a homicidal maniac wearing a Santa suit is
prowling around outside. Guess who Joanne's young daughter lets
in at the end? Yep, it's slay time at the Clayton home.

2. *Jack Frost* (1997) Not to be confused with the 1998 Michael
Keaton heart-warmer of the same title, this *Jack Frost* is a very
dark comedy about a soon-to-be-executed serial killer who, through
a freak accident, mutates into a real-life snowman a week before
Christmas. However, this Frosty isn't jolly—he wants revenge on the
sheriff who put him away. Don't look for good acting or expensive
special effects—there aren't any. But the film did well enough at
the box office to unleash *Jack Frost 2: Revenge of the Mutant Killer
Snowman* (2000).

3. *Silent Night, Deadly Night* (1984) This holiday slasher flick
caused a ruckus when it was first released during the Christmas
season, but it went on to become a cult favorite that spawned four
sequels. It's about a young boy who witnesses his parents' Christmas
Day murder at the hands of a man in a Santa suit. Of course, the kid
goes on to become a killer himself.

4. *Black Christmas* (1974) This odd little Canadian thriller has
the distinction of being produced and directed by Bob Clark, the

man who gave us another yuletide classic: *A Christmas Story* (1983). *Black Christmas* concerns a college student who confronts a serial killer prowling around her sorority house over Christmas break. Look for Margot "*Superman*" Kidder and Andrea "*SCTV*" Martin before they hit the big time. The film was remade in 2006 with Katie Cassidy and Michelle Trachtenberg.

5. *Christmas Evil* (1980) One of the more obscure yuletide horror films, *Christmas Evil,* aka *You Better Watch Out,* is yet another slasher flick about a murderous psycho in a Santa suit. It's a fave of cult movie director John Waters.

6. *Don't Open Till Christmas* (1984) This British entry is a reversal of sorts in that it's men in Santa suits who are the victims rather than the killers. It concerns a psycho who goes on a spree, killing department store Santas, and the detectives who try to catch him before he strikes again.

7. *Gremlins* (1984) Promoted as a comedy, this Steven Spielberg–produced movie, directed by Joe Dante, is extremely dark in places, especially considering that the story is set during

Christmas. It's about a young man who receives a cute little critter called a mogwai, which he names Gizmo. Instructions regarding its care and feeding are very specific: Don't feed it after midnight, and don't get it wet. Of course, both of these rules are broken, resulting in Gizmo producing dozens of offspring that transform into the titular gremlins. But unlike Gizmo, who's gentle and cuddly, the gremlins are ugly, mean, and very destructive. *Gremlins* was a box office smash, and a sequel was released in 1990.

"Santa Claus has the right idea. Visit people once a year."

—*Victor Borge*

Go Hang It on the Mantel: The Christmas Stocking

For many folks around the world, hanging an oversize, colorful sock on the fireplace (or stairwell or doorknob) is a beloved Christmas tradition. After all, by Christmas morning, the stockings are filled with little treats and gifts—who wouldn't want to get in on that? Here's some history behind the tradition.

A likely story

There are many theories behind why people hang Christmas stockings, but the one that seems to carry the most weight comes to us via an old folktale. In the story, a kindhearted but poor father had three daughters for whom he wished to find desirable husbands. The father was troubled, however, since he had no money for a dowry for even one of his sweet, loving daughters.

Then one day, St. Nicolas of Myra (aka Saint Nicholas, aka Santa Claus) was passing through town and heard about the plight of the kind father. Since he knew the man would be too proud to accept charity, St. Nicholas slipped down the chimney in the middle of the night (saints can do stuff like that) and dropped gold coins into the daughters' stockings, which they had hung on the fireplace to dry. They found the coins in the morning and voilà! A dowry for each, which led to a happy marriage for each, too. The story spread far and wide, and folks everywhere started hanging stockings on the mantel, hoping for a little love from St. Nicholas themselves.

Other sock stories

Clement Clarke Moore's famous poem "A Visit from St. Nicholas" (or

"'Twas The Night Before Christmas") was written in 1829, and as anyone who knows the poem will remember, Moore wrote:

*The stockings were hung by the chimney with care
in hopes that St. Nicholas soon would be there.*

The tradition was at least firmly entrenched by then, which suggests that it came to America long before. Stocking hanging might come from a Dutch tradition, which has children in Holland putting their wooden shoes out on Christmas Eve stuffed with straw for Saint Nicholas's donkeys. They'd put out a treat for St. Nick, too, and if he was pleased, St. Nick would leave them a little gift.

Regardless of the origin, stockings are found all over the Western world. In Italy, La Befana (the "good witch") put sweets and small gifts in stockings. In Puerto Rico, kids put flowers and tasty greens under their beds for the camels of the Three Kings. French kids put their shoes out, and in America, monogrammed stockings are put out well in advance of Christmas Day, serving as part of the decoration that fills the house with holiday cheer and goodwill.

Christmas Movie Anagrams

*Rearrange the letters of the phrases below to
find famous Christmas movie titles.*

1. FAST RUINED LOWLIFE
2. SHH, WARTIME TICS
3. RED NOSE HELPED HERD TO RIDE, RUN
4. 'TIS AS CHARCOAL, MR.

*Answers: 1. It's a Wonderful Life; 2. White Christmas;
3. Rudolph the Red-Nosed Reindeer; 4. A Christmas Carol*

Following Yonder Star

*In biblical times, earth-dwellers looked to the skies
for directions both literal and spiritual.*

The Gospel of Matthew tells us that shortly after Jesus was born,
King Herod was approached in Jerusalem by wise men from the
East, who asked him, "Where is the child who has been born King
of the Jews? For we have observed his star at its rising, and have
come to pay homage." Herod was upset but played it cool, and he
sent the men onward to Bethlehem, saying, "Go and search dili-
gently for the child; and when you have found him, bring me word
so that I may also go and pay him homage." (Of course, Herod did
not want to worship the infant; he wanted to kill him and thus nip
in the bud any threat to his power.) The wise men followed a star to
find Jesus and his mother, but they got a special message instructing
them to change their travel plans: "And having been warned of God
in a dream not to return to Herod, they left for their own country by
another road."

Three, twelve, whatever...

Though the word is not actually used in the biblical account (and
does not appear in English-language texts until around A.D. 1200)
Matthew's "wise men from the East" are commonly referred to
as the "Magi." It is a Latin word that comes from the Greek word
mago, which means "magician." But in those days, a "magician" was
not someone who pulled rabbits out of hats or sawed women in two.
He was a man who studied astronomy, astrology, and alchemy. Just
as the Gospel of Matthew does not actually use the word "magi,"
it also does not specify the number of wise men who came from
the East. Though most biblical scholars estimate that number to
be between two and twelve, it is tradition to display three in nativity scenes here in the western world, and they are commonly called
Caspar, Melchior, and Balthazar.

Most magi in biblical times were followers of Zoroaster, an
ancient Iranian prophet, philosopher, and poet. Though we cannot

even be sure when exactly he walked the face of the earth, many philosophers consider Zoroaster to be the inventor of the concept of Free Will, and his ideas and opinions greatly influenced Judaism, along with many other religions. But it was in his role as a sorcerer and astrologer that he most influenced the magi, and for centuries after he died—indeed, up until today—his followers have tried to emulate him in reading the stars.

Science or silliness?

These days, opinions on astrology run the gamut from "dangerous" to "silly." Some actually believe astrology to be satanic, but for most, it is simply a trivial entertainment, a blurb to be read in the daily paper and forgotten five minutes later. It has little or nothing to do with the science of astronomy. In Christ's time, however, astronomy and astrology were much more closely linked, almost indistinguishable from each another. There was, therefore, no shame in "reading the stars" or attempting to predict future events from celestial movements.

But what was the nature of the "star" that the wise men from the East followed? A Han-dynasty Chinese astronomical document notes what appears to be a nova or supernova around the time of Christ's birth, but it also could have been a comet or a planetary conjunction. There is evidence that Halley's comet may have made an appearance during the reign of King Herod, and there were planetary conjunctions of Venus and Jupiter in 3 B.C. and Jupiter and Saturn in 7 B.C. that could have caused great enthusiasm and speculation among the magi of the time.

In any case, the contemporaries of the "wise men from the East" would not have found it the least bit strange or silly that these respected astronomers were looking to the sky for directions.

Frank Capra's
It's a Wonderful Life

🕯 🕯 🕯

This movie went from box office flop to holiday
tradition. It's a great movie to wrap presents by!

On Christmas Eve, George Bailey stands on a bridge contemplating suicide. His life has gone all wrong. His dream of escaping the small town of Bedford Falls turns into the reality of taking over the family business and giving his college money to his brother once his father dies. George spends his life looking out for others first. He and his wife spend their honeymoon money averting a run on the bank. When his uncle misplaces $8,000, George figures he's worth more dead than alive. But his guardian angel, Clarence, intervenes, and when George sees what life would be like had he never lived, he changes his mind on the bridge and rushes home to his family, where the townspeople have chipped in to raise the missing money.

It's a wonderful flop

Although director Frank Capra had tremendous success with *It Happened One Night* and *Mr. Smith Goes to Washington*, *It's a Wonderful Life* was a flop by comparison. The film was nominated for several Academy Awards, including Best Actor for Jimmy Stewart and Best Picture, but it did not recoup its production costs. This led to the end of Liberty Films, Capra's independent production company. Capra's career declined sharply, and his reputation for bringing in big box office numbers was forever tarnished.

After making the film, Capra suffered constant headaches. He put a lot of his own money into Liberty Films and had trouble finding work again in Hollywood's crumbling studio system. His behavior was, by many accounts, arrogant, and he lost more friends than he made. Despite his rank of colonel in the army during World War II, he was dogged by the House Un-American Activities Committee.

Capra's postwar career suffered, but time smiled favorably on *It's a Wonderful Life*. The director's faith in the goodness of humankind resonates throughout the film, making it an enduring classic.

It's a Blunderful Life

*Frank Capra's Christmas classic contains
some noticeable bloopers.*

The Christmas season would not be complete without a viewing (or two or three) of *It's a Wonderful Life*. The 1946 film is wonderful, to be sure, but like many old films it's also chock-full of errors, anachronisms, and continuity mistakes! This year, while you're watching the redemptive story unfold, why not add some fun and see if you can also identify some of these goofs? Here are just a few:

- **Encore Performance:** During the dance, when people start jumping into the pool, the same person jumps in twice. Whoops!

- **Have I Seen You Before?:** In another repeat performance, a dark-haired female extra (holding the brim of her hat) crosses through a scene, where George is approaching Ernie's taxi, five times in 30 seconds!

- **Quitting Smoking?:** When George Bailey is a young man and Ol' Man Gower sends him to deliver a prescription, Gower's cigar disappears. Also, when George is talking to Violet in his office, his pipe disappears.

- **What's Your Name Again?:** In one scene, George addresses Violet (played by the actress Gloria Grahame) by the wrong name. He calls her Gloria.

- **Too Soon!:** The Coca-Cola thermometer on the wall of the drugstore (where young George is working in 1919) wasn't created until 1939!

- **Switcheroo:** The camera shows Clarence and George being thrown out of the bar, but in the next shot (when they land), they've switched places.

- **Accidental Snow:** George's car does not have much snow on it when he crashes it into a tree, but when he gets out to inspect his car, it is suddenly snow-covered.

What You Always Wanted to Know but Forgot to Ask About "The Twelve Days of Christmas"

It's the Christmas carol that goes on forever but everyone loves anyway: The one about the birds and the milkmaids and the drums and . . . what the heck is that song about? Sit back and relax with a cup o' nog, because your questions are about to be answered. Sort of.

The party that keeps on partying

In case you didn't know, the Twelve Days of Christmas begin the day *after* Christmas and go until the evening of the Twelfth Day, otherwise known as January 6. This block of days was first observed in the Middle Ages, when the Twelve Days were a time of merriment and gift-giving. In many parts of the world, the exact twelve days have been fiddled with a bit. (Many Americans are under the impression that the Twelve Days of Christmas *start* on Christmas Eve or Christmas Day, but now you know better.)

A partridge is born

The rousing carol, "The Twelve Days of Christmas" was first published in England in 1780, but many believe the song was born in France, where the particular kind of partridge mentioned in the first verse (or last verse, depending where you are in the song) could be found at the time. Long before it was put to paper, the tune appears to have been the structure for a game. The verses in "The Twelve Days of Christmas" build on each other and get longer as they go. In the game, the leader would recite a verse, then each player would repeat that verse; the leader added another verse, and the players sang the long list of verses until they stumbled, which meant lots of laughter and the loser giving everyone a treat or a kiss on the cheek.

Split decision

We don't really play the game anymore, but the song has stuck around, and over the years there has been some debate as to what the gifts in the song represent and what the song truly means. Many scholars maintain the items that "my true love gave to me" are literal: The partridge is a partridge, the turtledoves are turtle-doves, and so forth. These scholars believe that the secular song was intended simply to celebrate the bounty of the Twelve Days with images of typical presents, dancing, and general merriment. While the gifts might have had particular relevance at the time (i.e., swans were eaten as food back then and considered a special treat), they didn't hold hidden meanings.

But some Christians suggest there may be another layer to the popular song—though this theory does not have a real point in fact. They believe "The Twelve Days of Christmas" may have been a "catechism song" in England during times of persecution, a way for followers to observe their faith without writing anything down that could be used against them later. For the people who maintain this theory, each gift represents an aspect of Christianity or the Bible, i.e., the Old and New Testaments ("two turtledoves"), the apostles ("eleven pipers piping"), and the six days of creation ("six geese a-laying").

A few alterations

Whichever theory you hold to be true about the meaning of the song—which has been recorded by everyone from Sinatra to the Chipmunks—you should know that the version we sing today varies from the original. (Hint: There's no bling in the "five golden rings.") In the original version, it's "four colly birds," not "four calling birds," with colly birds being another name for blackbirds. The "pipers piping" are sometimes "fiddlers fiddling," depending on who you ask, and the "five golden rings" verse, which provides the song with a bridge that wasn't even arranged until 1909, actually refers to golden-necked pheasants, not jewelry.

There are various versions of "The Twelve Days of Christmas" around the world, and from France to Australia, Scotland to America, the words may differ slightly and the meaning may be up for debate, but the song that gives a total of 78 gifts to the recipient is a favorite the world over.

'Tis the Season to Have More Holidays

When does the Christmas holiday season officially start and end? Well, that's a more difficult question to answer than you'd think!

Black Friday (the day after Thanksgiving)

Many Thanksgiving Day parades, such as the Macy's parade in New York City, include the first appearance of Santa Claus—letting parents know it's time to open the pocketbooks! For most U.S. retailers, the Christmas shopping season begins on the day after Thanksgiving, a popular work holiday. It is generally the busiest shopping day of the year and the day when a retailer's profits may finally move into the black, although the first time the date was called Black Friday can be traced to a 1965 reference by the Philadelphia police department to the heavy traffic caused by shoppers.

Cyber Monday (the first Monday after Thanksgiving)

With so much shopping now being done via the Internet, a surge in buying activity is seen on the Monday after Thanksgiving when workers return to their jobs and use their companies' high-speed Internet to begin their Christmas shopping online. (Don't tell the boss!) The term "Cyber Monday" was invented in 2005 by Shop.org, a part of the National Retail Federation.

St. Nicholas Day (December 6)

Some historians believe that the origin of Santa Claus can be traced to St. Nicolas, a bishop in what is now Turkey, who died on

December 6, 346. Nicolas was known for giving anonymously to the needy and for secretly placing coins in the shoes of children who left them out for him. This tradition is continued on December 6 in Central Europe, Greece, Serbia, and in U.S. cities with large German communities. Children who have been good find candy or small toys in their shoes or socks, while those who have been bad find coal or nothing at all. This gives them time to change their behavior before the arrival of Santa Claus.

The Feast of the Immaculate Conception
(December 8)
Because it falls in the Christmas season, the Feast of the Immaculate Conception is often mistakenly thought to refer to the Christian and Islamic belief that Mary miraculously conceived Jesus while remaining a virgin. It actually celebrates the belief that Mary was conceived in divine grace and born without original sin, making her God's choice to be the mother of Jesus. It is a holy day of obligation (meaning mandatory church attendance) for Catholics, the patronal feast day of the United States, and a public holiday in Argentina, Austria, Chile, Italy, Ireland, Malta, Nicaragua, Paraguay, Peru, Portugal, and Spain.

St. Stephen's Day (December 26)
According to the popular Christmas carol, Good King Wenceslas looked out on the Feast of Stephen. That would be December 26, a day honoring St. Stephen, whose story is told in the Acts of the Apostles, who many regard as the first Christian martyr. St. Stephen's Day is a public holiday in historically Catholic, Anglican, and Christian countries in Europe and a bank holiday in parts of Spain and France. In England, it's also a nonreligious day known as Boxing Day.

Boxing Day (December 26, or the
Monday after if it falls on a weekend)
A popular holiday in the United Kingdom, Australia, Canada, New Zealand, Hong Kong, and other former members of the British Commonwealth, Boxing Day gets its name from the English tradition of giving gifts to laborers, servants, and those less fortunate on

the day after Christmas. The gifts were called "Christmas boxes," giving the holiday its name.

Holy Innocents Day (December 28)

The Gospel of Matthew tells the story of King Herod ordering the execution of all male babies in Bethlehem in a failed attempt to kill Jesus, whom Herod feared would someday take his throne. Holy Innocents Day, also called Childermas or Children's Mass, was started around the year 485 to remember the slain children. The religious holiday is celebrated by the Roman Catholic, Anglican, Lutheran, and Orthodox churches. In Spain and parts of Central and South America, it's also a day for pranks similar to April Fool's Day, and the pranksters are called "innocents."

Feast of the Circumcision (January 1)

The first day of the new year is also the Feast of the Circumcision of Our Lord, a Christian holiday celebrating the circumcision of Jesus according to Hebrew law eight days after his birth. It is also the day the child was formally given the name Jesus, which comes from the Hebrew word meaning "savior" or "salvation." For this reason, January 1 was also known as the Feast of the Holy Name of Jesus, but that holiday is now celebrated by Catholics on January 2 or on the Sunday between January 1 and Epiphany (January 6). The Feast of the Circumcision is a holy day of obligation for Catholics, but most other celebrations on that day are good luck traditions tied to it also being the beginning of the new year.

The Twelfth Night (January 5)

The arrival of the magi in Bethlehem is celebrated on January 6, making January 5 the eve of Epiphany, the traditional last day of the Christmas season. For this reason, it is the last day of Christmas partying for many cultures and the day that holiday decorations are taken down. In the times when Christmas wreaths were homemade, any parts made of food were eaten on the eve of Epiphany. This is also the twelfth night after Christmas and William Shakespeare's play of the same name was written to be performed as part of Twelfth Night partying.

Epiphany (January 6)

The Twelve Days of Christmas refer to the length of the journey of the magi (also known as the Three Kings or Three Wise Men) to Bethlehem. Epiphany is the Roman Catholic religious holiday that celebrates their arrival, bearing gifts for the child Jesus. In Eastern churches, Epiphany celebrates the baptism of Jesus in the Jordan River. In Louisiana, it marks the beginning of Mardi Gras season. One Mardi Gras tradition is the baking of King Cakes ("king" refers to the three kings), which sometimes have a tiny baby Jesus doll hidden in them. The person who finds the doll is supposed to supply the next cake.

Little Christmas (January 6)

In Ireland, the holiday of Little Christmas marks the end of the Christmas season and the last day before students go back to school. It is also known as Women's Christmas. It is tradition for the men to give their wives a day off from housework so they can go out and party with other women. The holiday is becoming popular in other countries with large Irish communities.

Chrismukkah and Festivus

While not tied to any formal dates, both Chrismukkah and Festivus are gaining popularity as alternatives to traditional Christmas celebrations. The name Chrismukkah comes from parts of the words Christmas and Hanukkah (the Jewish Festival of Lights that occurs during the Christmas season) and is often celebrated by families where one parent is Jewish and the other Christian. It has been popularized by television shows where the characters have both a Christmas tree and a menorah. Festivus was a holiday "for the rest of us" celebrated on an episode of the popular sitcom *Seinfeld* that was said to be for those jaded by the commercialism of the Christmas and Hannukah seasons. It was celebrated by erecting the festivus pole (an aluminum pole) and has since become a popular event during the Christmas season on college campuses.

Fast Facts

ALL ABOUT *RANGIFER TARDANDUS,* OTHERWISE KNOWN AS *REINDEER*

- *Behind every successful male is, well, a female, and in Santa's case, there are nine to be exact. Believe it or not, all of Santa's reindeer—including Rudolph—are probably of the feminine persuasion. According to the Alaska Department of Fish and Game, both male and females in the deer family Cervidae grow antlers, but most male reindeer drop their antlers at the beginning of winter, usually in late November to mid-December. Female reindeer, however, keep their antlers until after they give birth in the spring, meaning they are the only ones to have antlers during the holiday season. So much for the theory of a testosterone-powered sleigh!*

- *If you're ever lost in a snowstorm, make sure you're with a few reindeer. That's because these hooved holiday creatures have fur so insulated that when they lie down on snow, the snow underneath doesn't melt from their body heat. Furthermore, their fur can accommodate vast fluctuations in temperature, from 80 degrees below up to 115 degrees above 0.*

- *I say "caribow," you say "caribou." Either way, it's the name reindeer go by in North America. The name is derived from the Micmac Indian language and describes the way the animals dig and root around for food in the snow.*

- *Worldwide, there are 40 species of reindeer in existence today. Santa's reindeer are from Lapland, the place where the northern Scandinavian countries of Finland, Sweden, and Norway meet. In North America, reindeer/caribou live in Canada and Alaska.*

- *Reindeer aren't always brown. In fact, they come in various colors, including white and dark gray, depending on the time of year. Males can also have light-colored manes, necks, and shoulders.*

Mum's the Word

When there's more ham on the streets than on the table, the holiday mummers have come to call.

Stretching back to medieval times, the practice of mumming is a treasured holiday tradition in Britain, but many don't realize how prevalent it once was in the North American Colonies. Comic, crazy, and sometimes even chaotic, through the centuries this Christmas custom has been both loved and loathed by those who were either entertained or annoyed.

We know that mummers (sometimes also called "guisers" as in "disguise") were around as long ago as the Middle Ages, as the word appears frequently in manuscripts of the time. This early in its history, mumming seems to have been nothing more than visiting friends and acquaintances in identity-hiding masks. Over time, however, mumming became more elaborate. Music, dancing, and short comic sketches were added to the ritual, and mumming in many cases became a rehearsed performance rather than an impromptu lark. Most mummer plays involved a character dying and being restored to life by a doctor.

Mummers gone wild

In the American Colonies (and later the fledgling United States of America), mumming was more informal and definitely more boisterous and wild. Usually fortified by copious amounts of alcohol, Colonial mummers sometimes made their holiday mumming more "fun" with fireworks and gunplay. As the Temperance movement gained in influence and popularity, the outcry against mumming increased and antirevelry laws were put into place in most big cities. In rural areas, however, the practice was harder to curb, and mummers continued to roam the countryside every Christmas season well into the 20th century. In Kentucky, especially, the tradition of mumming died hard.

A Mummers Parade is held on New Year's Day in Philadelphia, and mummers participate in other U.S. parades, but the custom of door-to-door holiday mumming is essentially over in America.

The Trouble with Tiny Tim

Consider Tiny Tim. One of Charles Dickens's most memorable characters, the frail and infirm little son of Bob Cratchit serves to pull on the heartstrings of anyone who picks up A Christmas Carol. *But Dickens never said exactly what was wrong with Tiny Tim, which has led to much speculation by readers (and doctors) as to what it was the poor thing suffered from.*

Scene stealer

When Dickens introduces us to Bob Cratchit's youngest son, Tim, we see him through the window, as do Scrooge and the Spirit of Christmas Present. Scrooge sees that the boy walks with a cane, is small for his age, and is much too skinny. The meager meal the Cratchit family enjoys is far too little for anyone, least of all a child trying to fight disease. Still, Tiny Tim is full of life and love and seems to be everyone's favorite.

As Scrooge visits his various Christmas scenes, the Spirit of Christmas Future reveals that without intervention, Tiny Tim won't make it to see another Christmas. But (spoiler alert) Tim does live, which means that whatever he had was curable with proper medical attention. Based on those clues, some conclusions can be drawn.

According to the experts

Some doctors—who have published articles on the topic—believe that Tiny Tim may have suffered from a kidney disease. The disease, called type-I distal renal tubular acidosis (RTA), wasn't recognized at the time Dickens wrote *A Christmas Carol*, but doctors were able to treat its symptoms.

In a person with RTA, the kidneys fail to excrete acids into the urine, which causes the acid to then build up in the blood. This can result in stunted growth, kidney stones, bone disease, and progressive renal failure—symptoms that would result in someone pale, small, and in need of a cane, just like Tiny Tim. But RTA doesn't have to be fatal: With proper care and nutrition, people can overcome RTA. Thus, without the help of someone like Scrooge, Tim would have succumbed to the disease; with his help, he'd have a fighting chance of survival.

A second opinion

Others believe that Tiny Tim's environment was the culprit. In London in the 1800s, the smog from factories and other manufacturing areas lay like a blanket over the city, sometimes blocking out the sun itself. The smog caused many health problems, one of which was a lack of vitamin D, largely delivered to humans via the sun. Levels of vitamin D can go up and down somewhat, but if you suffer from an actual vitamin D deficiency, you'd be diagnosed with a disease known as rickets.

If you're unlucky enough to suffer from rickets, your body isn't able to absorb calcium, which makes it difficult to build and maintain strong bones and organ function. Muscle weakness, loss of bone tissue (aka osteoporosis), and joint pain are all symptoms of rickets and all jibe with a description of Tiny Tim. As with RTA, rickets is the kind of ailment that can be overcome with proper nutrition and attention. Plenty of people who live in places that don't get much sun keep rickets away by eating foods rich in vitamin D, such as fish, eggs, and cow's milk, all items that were surely hard to come by on Bob Cratchit's crappy salary. (Scrooge, we're looking at you!)

The message behind the character

Tiny Tim is a pathetic character that some feel is almost a cliché. That's easy for many modern people to say, but when Charles Dickens wrote his story, child morbidity was a very real thing. Acute poverty was epidemic in Victorian England, and countless children lost their lives as a result of inadequate shelter and food. There were also fewer cures for diseases at the time, so even if a needy child could get medical attention, the treatment they would've needed wasn't necessarily available. Tiny Tim serves as a way for Dickens to express his desire for those more fortunate to help those who were not, a theme that still resonates today.

Christmas Games of Yore

When many people gather together, games often abound. Whether it's a snowy round of capture the flag on the lawn, a board game marathon, or classic hide-and-seek with the kids, Christmas is a time for play. Here are some of history's traditional Christmas games you might consider adding to your family's holiday game repertoire.

Blindman's bluff

When the plain old game of tag got boring, someone came up with blindman's bluff, a fun variation. The game is simple: Whoever is "it" is blindfolded. That person then gropes around the room, trying to make contact with the other, nonblindfolded players—who try not to get caught. This game was popular during Henry VIII's reign and has been a holiday favorite for many years, especially for young people during the Victorian era.

Stoolball

In 1621, the governor of the British Colony of Massachusetts ordered the citizens of Plymouth to stop playing games on Christmas Day, deeming it an unholy way to observe the Lord's birthday. One of the rowdy games he put an end to was stoolball. The game went like this: A milking stool was used as a target, and a hard leather ball stuffed with either hair or feathers was thrown at it. One player pitched the ball; another defended the stool with a bat made of wood. Sound familiar? This game evolved over the years to something we call "baseball."

Pitching the bar

This was another Christmastime game Puritan leaders put a stop to, at least for awhile. "Pitching the bar" was essentially a game of strength, where the typically male players would heave a log over their shoulder, similar to events in logger games today. The guy who pitched the log the farthest won. Since there was lots of wood chopped for the winter season, this game was particularly popular during the colder months, and that meant it was a Christmas favorite.

Football, rugby, etc.

Football has been around since at least the Middle Ages, but as tough as it is today, it was nothing compared to what it was like back then. There were few rules, the "field" was usually the whole town, and games often dissolved into bitter fistfights and brawls. Basically, it was loosely organized chaos, which is maybe why it remained a popular sport through the ages. Many football games were organized around the Christmas holidays, since peasants and serfs had the rare opportunity to put down their work and spend time in leisure.

"Riding the stang"

The first colleges in America were the birthplace of plenty of games and pranks, and the Christmas holiday brought out the rowdiest of diversions. In addition to ballgames and pranks played on teachers, students at schools such as Cambridge would make a tiresome classmate "ride the stang." That meant he would have to sit on a pole that was carried by the rest of his class as they traveled throughout campus, laughing and poking fun at him. Not the nicest game in the world, but fun if you weren't the one on the pole.

Skits and plays

While you might not classify them as games exactly, it would be remiss not to mention the almighty Christmas play or skit—there are plenty of them every year. The tradition goes as far back as Christmas itself, as people reenact the Nativity or scenes from the Bible. Christmas plays are especially popular pastimes in schools. During the reign of Richard II, some traveling players on tour in London put on such a wildly popular Christmas show that they stole audiences from the school plays. A petition to protect the income of the school productions from such unsavory characters was put before the king in 1378.

Cat's cradle

This play-anywhere string game was originally known as "cratch cradle," referring to the Christ child's cratch, or manger. The shape of the strings, once intertwined between fingers, resemble the wooden crossbracing of the manger. The name of the game evolved to "cat's cradle," but its origin is definitely Christmas-based.

They Were Born on Christmas Day

. . . and it's, like, so totally not fair!

Ask any kid with a Christmas birthday and they'll inform you that no matter how much their parents try to make up for it, it just stinks. Even if they get twice as many presents, two days of celebration are reduced to one, and there's really no getting around it. These famous Christmas babies could tell you all about it:

- **Humphrey Bogart (1899)** Though he became famous playing tough guys with questionable backgrounds, Bogart was born into a world that was anything but rough. His father was a wealthy, WASP-y New York surgeon, and his mother was a well-known commercial illustrator. Young Humphrey grew up in the lap of luxury in his parents' beautiful Upper West Side apartment and was educated at the tony Delancy and Trinity schools. He was later expelled from the Phillips Academy prep school, which meant the Navy instead of Yale. Shocking!

- **Sissy Spacek (1949)** Mary Elizabeth Spacek was born in Quitman, Texas, the daughter of Edwin Arnold Spacek and Virginia Spilman Spacek, an agricultural agent and a homemaker. The Spaceks were of Eastern European descent, and her paternal grandfather, Arnold Spacek, had been the mayor of Granger, Texas. Though she loved her western upbringing, with its horses and vigorous outdoor activity, she longed to be a singer and actress and left Texas for New York City while still in her teens. Her cousin, actor Rip Torn, helped her get her start in the biz.

- **Rod Serling (1924)** Born in Syracuse, New York, Rodman Edward Serling was raised in Binghamton, which is about 66 miles to the south. Though brought up Jewish, as an adult, Serling converted to Unitarian Universalism and celebrated Christmas. One of the most memorable episodes of his brilliant and beloved science-fiction television show, *The Twilight Zone*, is "Night of the Meek," in which Art Carney gives a tour-de-force performance as Henry Corwin, a drunken Santa who is suddenly given the power to help the poor and downtrodden.

- **Annie Lennox (1954)** The daughter of a shipyard worker and a cook, singer Annie Lennox was born into humble circumstances in Aberdeen, Scotland. Though her parents struggled on the edge of poverty in a two-room flat, they recognized their daughter's talent when she was very young and always made sure to set aside money for music lessons. If Lennox ever felt bitterness about her Christmas birthday, she must have gotten over it by the time she recorded Eurythmics' popular version of "Winter Wonderland" in 1987 for the Special Olympics benefit album *A Very Special Christmas*.

- **Jimmy Buffett (1946)** Singer and businessman Buffett (no relation to Warren) was born in Pascagoula, Mississippi, but spent most of his childhood in Alabama. Famous for his laidback lifestyle of "island escapism" and his love of exuberant celebration, it's no surprise that he released an album called *Christmas Island* in 1996. Though there are a few traditional tunes on it, such as "Jingle Bells" and "I'll Be Home for Christmas," Buffett puts his own tropical stamp on the album with "A Sailor's Christmas," "Mele Kalikimaka," and "Ho Ho Ho and a Bottle of Rhum."

- **Anwar El Sadat (1918)** Egypt's third president was born in Mit Abu al-Kum, al-Minufiyah, Egypt, to an Egyptian father and a Sudanese mother. His Christmas birthday no doubt meant absolutely nothing to his large and impoverished family, as they were devout Muslims. Sadat idolized Mohandas Gandhi as a young man, and indeed he grew up to become famous as a peacemaker himself, along with Israeli Prime Minister Menachem Begin. But the peace he made with Israel enraged Islamic fundamentalists, a group of whom assassinated him on October 6, 1981.

- **Cab Calloway (1907)** On of the most popular entertainers of the big band era, singer and bandleader Cabell "Cab" Calloway III was born into a comfortable, middle-class home in Rochester, New York. His father was a successful lawyer and his mother was a teacher and church organist. A genius of jazz and "scat" music, Calloway left a lasting impression on generations of artists, including filmmaker Tim Burton. In his 1993 movie *The Nightmare Before Christmas,* Burton infused the villainous character Oogie Boogie with Calloway's wild performance style.

- **Conrad Hilton (1887)** The man who made millions of dollars as a hotel magnate and the patriarch who sired a thousand gossip columns began his life in a simple adobe hut in San Antonio, New Mexico Territory. His father, Augustus Halvorson Hilton, was a poor immigrant from Norway, and his mother, Mary Genevieve Laufersweiler, was a devoutly Catholic homemaker who taught young Conrad that prayer was the best investment he could ever make. He apparently asked for—and got—Zsa Zsa Gabor as one of his three wives, and Paris and Nicky Hilton are two of his great-grandchildren. (Paris and Nicky are descended from Hilton's second son by his first wife.)

- **Clara Barton (1821)** The youngest of five children, future nurse Clarissa Harlowe "Clara" Barton was born on her father's horse breeding farm in Oxford, Massachusetts. Her parents were deeply involved in the Unitarian Universalist movement that was popular in the area, and they brought Clara up to believe that a good Christian should serve her community and her country with all her heart. Clara certainly did not disappoint them, becoming famous as the "Angel of the Battlefield" during the Civil War and going on to found the American Red Cross.

Indelible Christmas

This body art leaves no doubt about the speaker's holiday cheer.

We all love Christmas. Okay, maybe not *all* of us, but if you bought this book, you must love Christmas, right? Well, even you probably don't love it enough to have a symbol of Christmas tattooed on your body. It's not for the faint of heart, and heaven knows how much alcohol is involved, but all it takes is a spin around the World Wide Web to know that some Christmas fans are more hardcore than most of us can even imagine.

Extended childhood

Some adults get Christmas tattoos that are... you know, adult. A beautiful Christmas tree with colorful ornaments on the back. A simple "Merry Christmas" in a cursive font on the shoulder. A sprig of mistletoe on the ankle. But these tasteful, mature Christmas tattoos are rare. It seems more common to use the Christmas tattoo as a means of expressing posttraumatic stress from childhood. Surfing tattoo sites on the Internet, one repeatedly sees characters from classic Christmas television specials twisted into nightmarish body brands: Rudolph the Red-Nosed Reindeer shot and mounted on the wall; Rudolph's long-eyelashed girlfriend Clarice portrayed as a busty sex symbol; Hermey the would-be-dentist elf holding a blood-dripping dental apparatus; Frosty the Snowman chasing children with a butcher knife in his hand; and little Ralphie from *A Christmas Story* coming at you with not a BB gun but a machine gun.

Wow... There was obviously a lot going on under the surface of those family-friendly Christmas shows, huh? Either that, or a lot of people with issues are doing a whole lot of projecting. In any case, Christmas tattoos have become so popular that the Australian country singer Darin Warner recorded a song called "Tattoo of Santa" for those who love Christmas so much it hurts.

The "Wrap" on Wrapping Paper

Because the three wise men gave gifts to the baby Jesus, gift giving became a favorite Christmas pastime. The ancient Greeks used to give gifts during their holy days, too. But neither the Greeks nor the wise men wrapped their gifts, so why do we? Read on for a little insight behind all that fancy paper.

Those crazy (rich) Victorians

If you were a wealthy person living in the Western world in the 1800s, you had the luxury of giving and receiving gifts. In order to make it more fun, these Victorians, who valued ornament and the decorative arts, took to concealing the parcels in paper and tying them with bows. At first, the papers they used to wrap their packages were plain, often manila colored or white. Then printed papers started showing up, and wrapping paper with patterns and pictures was used. The paper, which was heavier in weight and sturdier than typical stationery, was printed with images of birds, flowers, farm scenes, and other intricate patterns. At Christmastime, the papers had holiday themes: Packages were wrapped with images of holly boughs, angels, and Father Christmas. It all seemed unimaginably decadent to the masses, however, who wouldn't dream of spending money on something you were going to immediately throw in the garbage.

Eureka! Hallmark strikes again

By the early 1920s, however, thanks to the mass production of cheap tissue paper, more and more Westerners were wrapping gifts for special occasions. The tissue paper was flimsy and bled whatever color it was dyed, but at least it was something.

Then one day, Joyce C. Hall, one of the Hall brothers that ran the Hall Brothers postcard shop, decided to sell surplus envelope liners as decorative paper. He sold the patterned sheets for 10 cents each, and customers snatched them up. Hall knew he was onto something, and the modern wrapping paper industry was born. The price of the paper increased the following year, and soon the brothers were printing their own papers, the bulk of which were Christmas themed. Before long, wrapping paper sales were trumping their steady business in greeting cards.

But wrapping a present wasn't as easy then as it is today. Since Scotch tape wasn't invented until the 1930s, folks who wanted to wrap their gifts had to get creative. In many packs of paper, manufacturers included small stickers to help fasten corners, but some gift givers used glue or wax in the early present-wrapping process.

Would you like that wrapped?

Over the years, wrapping paper has changed with the times. As the style of art moved from Victorian to Art Deco, from Art Deco to modern, gift wrap adapted. As the symbols of Christmas evolved, the wrapping paper reflected the wishes of the masses, sporting fewer angels and nature images and more Santas, Rudolphs, and nondenominational patterns or designs. Seeing licensing possibilities, companies printed wrapping paper with popular cartoon characters and soon, the wrapping paper industry was worth many millions of dollars every year. Of course, Christmas wrap is sold mostly in the months of November and December, but you can always find holiday wrapping paper at any time of the year on the Internet.

"One of the most glorious messes in the world is the mess created in the living room on Christmas day. Don't clean it up too quickly."

—*Andy Rooney*

Christmas Around the World

POLAND

If you have Polish ancestry, you may be familiar with some of the traditions that surround Christmas in Poland. It's a time of forgiveness and celebration, superstition, good cheer, and great food.

As in many European countries, Christmas in Poland starts well before Christmas Day, during Advent. Church is held each day before dawn, and carolers stroll the streets singing of Christ's birth. Christmas trees are decorated with apples, walnuts, chocolate, and handmade ornaments called *pajaki,* made from eggshells and clay.

The weeks leading up to Christmas are filled with special Polish foods including *oplatek,* a thin wafer pressed into a tin that forms the image of the Nativity or another holy image. The wafers are then shared among families and neighbors as a gesture of glad tidings.

Special treats abound during Advent, but Polish folks pull out all the stops for Christmas Eve supper. The meatless feast consists of 12 dishes representing the 12 months. Fish is served, along with borscht, mushroom soup, sauerkraut, fruit compote, and *kutia,* a sweet grain pudding. Of course, no Polish meal would be complete without pierogi, the classic Polish dumpling. On Christmas Eve, the preferred version is stuffed with sauerkraut and mushrooms.

Very superstitious, writing's on the wall

The Christmas season has long been one full of superstition and fortune-telling, though not as strongly observed today. During Advent and sometimes on Christmas Eve, beeswax is dripped into a bowl of water, and fortunes are told from the shapes that emerge. Some rural residents still claim that on Christmas Eve animals are able to speak in a human tongue; some also claim that maidens can foretell their marriage date by eavesdropping on the neighbors and listening for specific words in their conversation.

Many Polish Christmas superstitions have faded away, but plenty of modern-day Poles still believe that "as goes Christmas Eve, so goes the year." This means that to ensure a good coming year, everyone tries to be extra polite and generous on that day, forgiving each other in the name of the special season.

SANTA WHO?

DED MOROZ

Santa Claus isn't the only game in town when it comes to delivering presents and Christmas cheer. In Poland, Russia, and other areas of Eastern Europe, Ded Moroz, or "Grandfather Frost," is the guy to see about your Christmas list.

Originally an amalgam of various cruel and unflinching Slavic gods, Ded Moroz wasn't a kindly old guy in the beginning. For centuries, he was responsible for harsh winters and death. Then, around the turn of the 20th century, the folklore began to change, and people started believing that Ded could be kindhearted and generous, too. By the time the Bolsheviks led the October Revolution in 1917, Ded Moroz had really started to resemble Saint Nicholas, as people connected him with Christmas, not just winter. The Communists didn't like this much, and Lenin outlawed him, along with the Christmas tree and many other holiday traditions across the land.

Ded Moroz rides again—with a friend
In the mid-1930s, Ded enjoyed a return to popularity, since it occurred to those in charge of the communist government that the figure could inspire good things in children. But Ded Moroz still wasn't be associated with Christmas; he was thus dressed in a blue robe and was relegated to New Year celebrations instead.

He was also given a buddy, which is unique to this part of the world: No other Santa Clauslike figure has a sidekick. Ded's partner in crime is his granddaughter, a young girl named Snegurochka, who helps him dispense presents. Snegurochka was originally a magical sprite also associated with winter, but through the years she came to be associated with the Ded Moroz family.

After communism fell in the Soviet Union, Ded Moroz and Snegurochka fell from popularity as the people embraced Christianity once again and opted for St. Nicholas instead. But Father Frost endures in Russia, where folks still entrust the New Year to him and continue to keep his spirit—Christmasy or not—alive and well during the coldest months of the year.

RUSSIA

Though it was banned for much of a century, many Russians
kept Christmas alive in their hearts. Take that, Lenin!

An American tourist visiting Russia on December 25 might be
shocked at the lack of Christmas festivities
and religious worship and wonder if the
communist ban on the holiday had left a
lasting impression. But the real explanation
is far less sinister: The Russian Orthodox
Church uses the Julian calendar, which most
of the Western world exchanged for the
Gregorian calendar in the late 16th cen-
tury. Christmas in Russia is therefore observed on January 7, which
is 13 days later than it is celebrated in America or Europe. Many
Russians celebrate the holiday with a fervor that could only have been
born of persecution and hardship.

JANUARY 7

The roots of oppression

In 1917, the Bolsheviks gained control of Russia and the Soviet Union
was born. That Christmas was immediately banned in this new country should have come as a surprise to no one. After all, Karl Marx
had famously called religion "the opiate of the masses," and asserted
that "Communism begins where atheism begins." Vladimir Lenin
had gone even further, calling for a program of terror to destroy
Christianity in Russia, even calling for the shooting of "reactionary
clergy." Christmas was banned at the birth of the October Revolution,
but most Russians stubbornly ignored this injunction, leading Lenin to
rage in 1919, "To put up with Nikola [Christmas] would be stupid—the
entire Cheka [secret police organization] must be on alert to see that
those who do not show up for work because of Nikola are shot."

One of the methods that the Soviet Union's totalitarian government
used to get Russians to forget Christmas was secularization. They
figured that if they still allowed their citizens to party during the old
holiday season, fun and festivity would sate their thirst for celebration and eventually religion would be nothing but a dim memory. One

example of this secularization is what was done to the Christmas carol "Nova Radist Stala," or "Joyous News Has Come to Us." Its original lyrics were:

> *The joyous news has come which never was before*
> *Over a cave above a manger a bright star has lit the world,*
> *where Jesus was born from a virgin maiden.*

Lenin's propagandists got hold of it, however, and rewrote it:

> *The joyous news has come which never was before*
> *Long-awaited star of freedom lit the skies in October*
> *Where formerly lived the kings and had the roots their nobles*
> *There today with simple folks, Lenin's glory hovers.*

And St. Nicholas? Well, he was replaced with a guy named "Ded Moroz" (Grandfather Frost) who handed out presents to kids for the "Great Winter Festival," which just coincidentally fell on December 25. These types of changes were made in every area of the culture—in music, in literature, in film, and in the fine arts. After 1,000 years of celebrating Christmas, it was impossible to force Russians to give it up cold turkey.

Religious restoration

In 1917, there were 657 Christian churches operating in Moscow. By 1981, only 46 of those churches were still open for worship, and they were closely monitored by government snitches. All that was about to change, though. After over six decades of communist, totalitarian rule, the counterrevolution happened almost bloodlessly, which was something of a miracle in itself. These days, churches that were nothing more than musty museums open their doors to joyous worshipers. Christmas carols are again sung with their original lyrics. Beautiful religious icons are exhibited without fear. Holiday revelers parade though the streets holding candles and torches. Twelve-course Christmas Eve dinners, with their staples of *kutya* (a porridge made of wheat, poppy seeds, berries, and honey) and *borscht* (cabbage soup with sour cream), often go on until the wee hours of the morning.

Christmas has returned to Russia—if indeed it ever really left.

What Does Xmas Really Mean?

Is the word a commercialized shame, or are its roots in the story of Christ?

The letter X carries negative connotations in our society. In a red circle, we use it to block out symbols of things we don't like. On movie theater marquees and DVD covers, we use it to signify adult entertainment. We even use it to identify the generation of Americans who are supposedly the most cynical and disaffected. So is it any wonder that when we see "Christmas" represented as "Xmas" we instinctively assume it's a bad thing? Digging a little deeper, however, we find that the issue is ancient and complex.

In the early days of the Christian church, many of its first converts were Greek, and the word "Christ" in Greek is *Xristos,* pronounced "Christos." These Greek Christians were hunted and persecuted. Their fellow countrypeople were appalled that they worshipped a Jewish man and were trying to spread his teachings. But the Greek Christians held fast to their beliefs and marked their houses of worship with Xs so they could identify one another.

Tweaking the Greek

For centuries after, Christmas was a strictly religious holiday that was more likely to be celebrated by families and churches rather than large communities. But in the 19th century, that began to change. Businesspeople realized that big bucks could be made from promoting the holiday, and the Industrial Revolution made the mass production of toys and candy far easier than it had been. Advertising was key to this new era of Christmas, and in order to save print space and make their message clear to those who were semi-illiterate, retailers reached back into history and revived "Xmas" as a substitute for "Christmas."

So, yes, the use of "Xmas" today is often a crass and thoughtless tool, but the word itself sprung from the deepest faith and sincerity.

Top Grossing Films Opening on Christmas Day

Christmas can be hectic, and some of us seek the sweet escape only Hollywood can provide.

We've all been there. Everyone arrives at grandma's house on Christmas morning to find a hive of activity. Some family members help in the kitchen, and there's a pack of kids circling the tree as if they were sharks ready for the feeding frenzy. At least one cousin or uncle has found the special eggnog.

When we get tired of the hullabaloo, some of us go to the movies. Some years, like 2000, we even get lucky and the films are brand new on that very day. What follows is a list of the 20 top-grossing films opening Christmas Day and the amount they made in U.S. dollars their first weekend in theaters.

1. *Cast Away* (2000)		$39,852,075
2. *Fun with Dick and Jane* (2005)		21,530,160
3. *Cheaper by the Dozen 2* (2005)		15,340,679
4. *The Family Man* (2000)		15,104,055
5. *Miss Congeniality* (2000)		13,853,686
6. *Dracula 2000* (2000)		8,636,567
7. *The Ringer* (2005)		7,702,439
8. *Rumor Has It . . .* (2005)		7,515,000
9. *Munich* (2005)		6,040,860
10. *Wolf Creek* (2005)		4,908,206
11. *Breakin' 2: Electric Boogaloo* (1984)		2,921,030
12. *All the Pretty Horses* (2000)		1,304,971
13. *Invasion of the Body Snatchers* (1978)		1,298,129
14. *Curse of the Golden Flower* (2006)		711,336
15. *Finding Forrester* (2000)		701,207
16. *State and Main* (2000)		580,163
17. *Awakenings* (1990)		417,076
18. *Heaven & Earth* (1993)		379,807
19. *Casanova* (2005)		231,077
20. *O Brother, Where Art Thou?* (2000)		195,104

Bad Santa!

Yes, it's true. Some people have ended up on Santa's naughty list by committing crimes while impersonating the jolly old elf himself.

Apparently looking like Santa doesn't make one always act like Santa. Over the years, many crimes have been committed by individuals dressed as Santa Claus. Here's a rundown:

- **December 23, 1927** Marshall Ratliff and three accomplices held up the First National Bank in Cisco, Texas, triggering one of the largest manhunts in state history. Ratliff was known in Cisco, so he dressed as Santa Claus to disguise his identity. The robbers were barely out the door when a wild shoot-out and chase ensued. Ratliff and two accomplices were captured; the third accomplice died from his injuries.

- **December 10, 2004** Santa-bedecked Elkin Donnie Clarke, 49, of Atlanta, struck Annie Ruth Nelson in the head with a board outside a shopping mall, knocking her unconscious. When a passerby came to Nelson's aid, police said, Clarke threatened her with the board as well. Clarke was charged with two counts of aggravated assault.

- **December 24, 2008** Bruce Pardo, 45, of Montrose, California, arrived dressed as Santa Claus to a holiday party at his ex in-laws' house. Once inside, Pardo opened fire on the crowd, killing nine and wounding several others. He attempted to set the house on fire, burning himself in the process. Pardo later took his own life.

- **December 22, 2009** A man wearing sunglasses and a Santa suit robbed the SunTrust Bank in Hermitage, Tennessee. According to witnesses, the armed man said he was robbing the bank to "pay his elves."

Christmas Island

*Because Thanksgiving Peninsula and
St. Valentine's Isthmus sound stupid.*

Tucked in a corner of the Indian Ocean near western Australia, Christmas Island was named by William Mynors, captain of the Royal Mary, when the East India Company ship discovered the island on Christmas Day, December 25, 1643. Apparently you don't have to actually land on an island to name it, because it wasn't until 1688 that another English ship would achieve that nontrivial feat.

And now the story has nothing else whatsoever to do with Christmas.

Great Britain annexed the island into its empire in the late 19th century after naturalists found evidence of potentially lucrative lime deposits. Japan attacked and captured the island during World War II. The United Kingdom resumed ownership after the end of the war. During and after WWII, the phosphate mining production declined. The UK transferred the island to Australian rule in 1958.

Because of the island's isolated location, it is home to several species not found anywhere else in the world. A national park now covers 63 percent of the island.

An island so nice they named it twice

Jealous that the Indian Ocean had a Christmas Island, the mighty Pacific got its own island on Christmas Day 1777, when British explorer Captain James Cook discovered it. The United States claimed the island not quite a hundred years later. Prior to British discovery, the island was used by Polynesian traders.

The atoll was ceded to The Republic of Kiribati in 1979. It had been well used by this point: The United Kingdom and United States conducted testing of nuclear weapons there in the '50s and '60s. The inhabitants were not evacuated during these tests. Not very Christmas-y. We can only hope that those weapons testers got coal in their stockings!

Kiribatese (Gilbertese) is the official language of The Republic of Kiribati. The island's name, Kiritimati, is the translation of Christmas.

Getting Carded

Modern holiday well-wishers aren't the only ones crunched for time. Back in 1843, Englishman Sir Henry Cole invented the Christmas card when the demand of writing personal holiday greetings to friends and family on his list threatened to squelch his holiday spirit.

Cole, a renaissance man who wrote and published books on art collections and architecture, ran in social circles where gifts and tokens were synonymous with friendship. Knowing that more than a few of his uppity buddies would be offended if they didn't receive personal greetings from him, he commissioned well-known painter of the time John Callcott Horsley to design a "one-size-fits-all" card that could be sent to everyone on his list.

The lithographed and hand-colored sepia-toned sketch was printed on cardboard and featured a classic Victorian Christmas scene of a family eating and drinking merrily, with the caption, "A Merry Christmas and a Happy New Year to You." On the other side, Cole ingeniously asked for a picture to encourage the care and feeding of the poor, his own personal cause.

Christmas card craze

The idea slowly gained momentum in the Christmases to come, with even Queen Victoria and the British royal family sending specially designed cards focusing on the events of the past year.

Americans joined in the tradition early on by importing cards from England. But in 1875, Louis Prang, a German immigrant who wrote and published architectural books, printed images in color with a series of lithographic zinc plates. The process allowed up to 32 colors to be printed in a single picture, with the finished product resembling an oil painting. His first cards featured flowers and birds, then he moved to snow scenes, fir trees, and glowing fireplaces.

So in demand were these cards that Prang couldn't fulfill all of the orders. Every year following, demand increased, and at one point Prang was printing five million cards a year. His efforts earned him the moniker "The Father of the American Christmas Card."

Glamorous greetings

Well-known illustrators such as children's book author Kate Greenaway and Ellen Clapsaddle designed cards for the public. Early cards could be elaborate. Some were cut into fancy shapes such as bells, candles, and birds. Others made noises. The more elaborate fitted together like puzzles or were embellished with fancy trims and buttons.

The first pop-up card in the United States was designed in the mid-1800s, when New York engraver Richard Pease created a card with a small Santa Claus with his sleigh and reindeer, and drawings of holiday celebrations were placed in each corner. Other popular images included skating rinks with children skating and family scenes around the fireplace.

In 2009, more than 1.8 billion people sent Christmas cards, and anything goes in regard to the style. Clever verses, sports figures, comic strips, celebrities, and animals grace the fronts of cards, and high-tech options with intricate paper cuttings, embedded sounds and songs, and heavily embossed illustrations have become all the rage. Cards have also evolved into other mediums. In 1992, Vodafone sent the first holiday message using a cell phone; today, many people celebrate the holiday by e-mailing Christmas cards to friends and family.

"Happy, happy Christmas, that can win us back to the delusions of our childhood days, recall to the old man the pleasures of his youth, and transport the traveler back to his own fireside and quiet home!"

—Charles Dickens

Fast Facts

EVERYTHING YOU WANTED TO KNOW ABOUT CHRISTMAS CARDS (OR NOT)

- *The most expensive Christmas card is an antique card from 1843, auctioned in 2001 in England for $40,000 USD.*

- *Eighty-five percent of all people will send holiday or greeting cards, letters, or photos in some medium, either by traditional mail, electronically, cell phone, or fax.*

- *This year alone, Hallmark card company will offer 2,000 different Christmas cards.*

- *It is estimated that 500 million e-cards are sent annually.*

- *The busiest day of the year for the U.S. Postal Service is December 17, when 275 million cards and letters—more than three times the average daily volume of 82 million—will be mailed. From Thanksgiving to Christmas, a whopping 20 billion pieces of mail, including packages, will be delivered by the U.S. Postal Service.*

- *Ellen H. Clapsaddle, one of the most prolific holiday card designers in the early 1900s, died penniless and unknown even though her work today is among the most collectible.*

- *In 1941, when the government issued an order to reduce paper by 25 percent, the greeting card industry successfully lobbied for greeting cards to be exempt. They launched the "Defense Stamp Christmas Cards" campaign, which promoted defense stamps and war bonds. Another campaign, "Greeting Cards in Wartime," was created on the premise that Christmas cards boosted soldier morale and helped families keep in touch with each other during the war.*

- *Egyptians used papyrus scrolls to send greetings. The early Chinese also loved to send goodwill messages. However, the oldest known greeting card in existence is actually a Valentine's Day card from the 1400s.*

Smoking Bishop

🕯 🕯 🕯

Don't be dumbfounded over this Dickensian drink.

Most everyone is familiar with Charles Dickens's *A Christmas Carol.* Ebenezer Scrooge bah-humbugs his way through the holiday until a quartet of ghosts appear in his bedroom. Near the end of the story, the now-reformed Scrooge happily cheers Bob Cratchit, "A merrier Christmas, Bob, my good fellow, than I have given you for many a year! I'll raise your salary, and endeavor to assist your struggling family, and we will discuss your affairs this very afternoon over a bowl of Smoking Bishop, Bob!"

According to Dickens's great-grandson Cedric, the Victorians named several drinks after members of the clergy. Some common names include Pope for burgundy, Cardinal for champagne or rye, Archbishop for claret, and Bishop for port.

The recipe (bring your insulin)

The recipe isn't complicated. Bake five oranges and a grapefruit until brown. Push whole cloves into the fruit. Add a quarter pound of sugar and two bottles of red wine. Dickens says to leave this in a warm place for a day, but that's Victorian-era nonsense. You can get a fine result simmering the mixture on a stove on low heat for an hour. Squeeze the juice out of the oranges and grapefruit, then add the port. Again, Dickens says not to boil it, but that's more lack of understanding than anything else. Presumably the fear is that all the alcohol will boil off, but the truth is it takes hours for that to happen. Bring to a boil and then reduce to low heat. Serve warm. By serving warm, the drink is said to be "smoking," hence Smoking Bishop.

Although Dickens makes no mention of it, you can add cinnamon sticks and/or brown sugar (or other seasonal spices such as nutmeg) to taste. If you're accustomed to making mulled wine, you can pick and choose spices and juices to add. Your taste buds will guide you.

And don't forget to raise a glass to Tiny Tim's health!

A Cup of Good Cheer

*For many, Christmas just wouldn't be Christmas without
the many delicious drinks that have been concocted
over the centuries to "make the season bright."*

While moderation is of course recommended in any season, there can be no doubt that a few nips of a holiday potable add a rosy glow to the festivities. So the next time you're planning a Christmas feast, don't just set a few bottles on the table and let your guests fend for themselves. Spend as much time and effort on the liquids as you do the solids for a truly memorable event.

Spiced wine

Also known as mulled wine, spiced wine is almost always a red wine that is served warm. It may seem quite romantic to us these days, but spiced wine was born of practical necessity. Before the bottling process was perfected, wine often spoiled and the result was not a pleasant drinking experience. Our ancestors discovered, however, that by adding spices and honey, a wine gone bad could be revived. It may have been a little iffy healthwise, but hey, it was still safer than the water, right?

Ingredients
1 bottle full-bodied red wine (Burgundy, Pinot Noir, or Merlot)
3 tablespoons honey
2 cinnamon sticks
2 tablespoons cardamom seeds
1 tablespoon black peppercorns
1 sliced orange
1 sliced lemon
½ cup sugar

In a large saucepan, combine all the ingredients. Simmer for 15 minutes. Strain liquid, and pour into mugs. Garnish with a cinnamon stick if you like.

Rum punch

Fruit punch was brought from India to England in the 17th century, and from there it spread like wildfire across the European continent. Naturally, it didn't take long for the English to add liquor to the punch (like, maybe, five seconds), and that liquor was most often rum (preferably from Barbados). The word *punch* has its origin in the Hindi word "panch."

Ingredients
1 cup fresh lime juice
2 cups simple syrup
3 cups amber rum
4 cups orange juice
4 dashes bitters
freshly grated nutmeg to taste

In a pitcher, combine lime juice, simple syrup, rum, and orange juice. Add a few dashes of bitters and some grated nutmeg to taste. Serve chilled over ice.

Eggnog

Eggnog most probably originated in England, and its name may have derived from the word *noggin,* which was used in the Middle Ages to describe a wooden mug made for hot alcoholic drinks. Because it was made with eggs and milk, eggnog was almost exclusively a drink for royals and aristocrats. Lack of refrigeration meant that the urban poor were almost never able to arrange for fresh eggs and fresh milk at the same time. In fact, they rarely saw either in any state. So eggnog was usually consumed by the wealthy on country estates.

Ingredients
6 eggs (use only clean, uncracked eggs)
3 cups milk
8 tablespoons sugar
3 teaspoons vanilla
½ teaspoon nutmeg, ground

In a large bowl, beat the eggs using an electric mixer. By turn, add milk and sugar. Continue beating until mixture thickens slightly. Add vanilla and ground nutmeg. Cover with plastic wrap, and refrigerate until chilled (at least 3 hours).

Hot chocolate...plus

There's nothing that can make one feel like a kid again—while also enjoying one of the delights of adulthood—quite like hot chocolate. The cocoa bean was brought from the North American continent to Europe by the Spanish explorer Cortez in the 16th century, and for about a century after, only the Spanish enjoyed hot chocolate. Luckily, such a delicious secret couldn't be kept forever.

Ingredients
5 ounces hot cocoa
1 ounce coffee liqueur
1 teaspoon sugar
1 tablespoon whipped cream

Combine hot cocoa and coffee liqueur in an Irish coffee cup, and sweeten to taste. Top with cream, sprinkle with grated chocolate, and serve. Pluck a candy cane off the tree, and plop it in to add a peppermint twist.

"Christmas at my house is always at least six or seven times more pleasant than anywhere else. We start drinking early. And while everyone else is seeing only one Santa Claus, we'll be seeing six or seven."
—W. C. Fields

Crunching the Christmas Numbers

- **200:** Number of mincemeat pies eaten by Gus the camel after breaking out of his pen at an Irish school's Christmas party. He also drank several cans of Guinness, which he opened with his teeth.

- **28:** Average number of Christmas cards each U.S. household mails each year

- **1948:** Year the Marine Corps adopted the Toys for Tots program

- **2 million:** Number of visitors expected at *Christkindlesmarkt,* the famous Christmas market in Nuremberg, Germany

- **3:** Number of gifts the magi presented to the baby Jesus, according to the Bible

- **1,300:** Costumes worn during the Radio City Music Hall *Christmas Spectacular*

- **848,600:** Cost (in U.S. dollars) of a Japanese chocolate Christmas cake decorated with 100 diamonds

- **31 million:** Approximate number of real Christmas trees Americans buy during Christmastime

- **5,343:** Number of people who live in Snowflake, Arizona

- **53%:** Americans who prefer "Merry Christmas" on Christmas cards. "Happy Holidays" is the choice for 21 percent, and 12 percent prefer "Season's Greetings."

Every Day Can Be Christmas

If you open up the Christmas store, they will buy!

Christmas in America once meant that the season began a week or two before December 25. Not only was the holiday less commercialized than it is now, but most people just didn't have the kind of leisure time we do to prepare their homes and shop for gifts. To them, a nice dinner, a few presents, a religious service, and a day off work was more than enough.

Leisure time, shopping time!

After the Industrial Revolution, Christmas changed and kept changing, some would say not for the better. Retailers were bound and determined to milk the holiday for all it was worth, and they knew that with every passing year, technology gave more people more time for what were once considered frivolous activities, such as shopping. The "Christmas season" expanded from weeks to months, and though everyone seemed to complain about it, they also went out and spent money, thus ensuring that "Christmas" would only continue to get bigger and longer.

Christmas every day

It was therefore inevitable that year-round Christmas stores would begin popping up. Yes, there are stores in America that sell nothing but Christmas items 365 days of the year. Silly? Tacky? Shallow? The stores have been mocked as all of these things, but their owners are usually laughing all the way to the bank, and most of them would argue that it is their love of the Christmas spirit, not some year-round greediness, that inspires their work. From way up in Skagway, Alaska, to way down in Dallas, Texas, year-round Christmas stores keep chugging along as other retailers struggle.

Stand up Christmas sisters

To understand the popularity of year-round Christmas stores, one must understand the lure of the Christmas season itself, especially among American women. Despite decades of feminism, the celebration of Christmas can still feel like some kind of litmus test for them. No one thinks anything negative about a man who doesn't prepare properly for Christmas. In fact, it only seems to enhance his manliness—witness all the women who think it's "cute" that they have to wrap their boyfriends' presents for them at the last minute. "Oh, it's just easier," they'll tell you. "He wouldn't know how to do it, anyway," they'll add, as though present wrapping was more difficult than, say, building a skyscraper or sending human beings to the moon. The sad truth, ladies? *Dudes just don't like wrapping presents, and they know you'll do it for them rather than be embarrassed in front of the family.* Yes, holiday preparation is still largely women's work, and the guilt they feel over badly wrapped gifts is the same guilt that sends them into a Christmas store in June.

Not that year-round Christmas stores are all about guilt. Plenty of things about Christmas are fun, obviously, and plenty of us wish it came more than once a year. Year-round Christmas store owners want to give patrons that happy holiday glow, and though some also have Web sites on which to sell their wares, for many, the brick-and-mortar store is what it's all about. They don't just want to sell things; they want to create an experience for those who visit them.

Watch that personal touch

Customer service and a "personal touch" are extremely important to them, and often the employees of year-round Christmas stores do far more than just stand behind counters and wait to ring up purchases. They are proactive in their work, advising customers on everything from gift-giving etiquette to interior decoration. Their love of Christmas is infectious and a big part of why year-round Christmas stores are often very successful.

Year-round Christmas stores continue to change and grow. Though some are still "Christmas only," many have expanded to include other holidays as well. A Christmas section is kept all year round, while another area of the store alternates Easter, the Fourth of July, Halloween, and perhaps even some Jewish and/or Muslim holidays.

Mr. Christmas

Life behind the scenes wasn't always so merry!

With his annual Christmas television specials, Andy Williams became the embodiment of family values. Always joined in these specials by his lovely wife and adorable children, Williams seemed to have avoided the Hollywood trap and kept his priorities in order. When everything fell apart, another man might have resigned his title of "Mr. Christmas" forever. But Williams fought through it, and after an eight-year absence, his Christmas specials reappeared.

Midwest test

Andy Williams was born in Wall Lake, Iowa, on December 3, 1927. Raised in a devoutly Christian home, his first musical venue was the local Presbyterian church. At the age of eight, he and his three brothers formed a singing group, the Williams Brothers, and began performing live and on radio around the Midwest. The brothers cut their teeth as backup singers for such popular entertainers as Bing Crosby and Kay Thompson, but Andy was really the only one in the family who had a driving ambition when it came to music. When his siblings quit the act in 1952, Andy continued without them.

Andy struggled on the RCA Victor label, releasing a song that went nowhere in the early 1950s. Talk show host Steve Allen liked what he heard, however, and made Williams a regular on his show in 1955. This provided the leverage Williams needed to switch to Cadence Records, a boutique label in New York that was able to give him more attention. It all paid off when his third single, "Canadian Sunset," shot into the Top Ten in 1956, and it was soon followed up with a No. 1 hit, "Butterfly." Williams was a smart businessman who retained ownership of his Cadence songs and later formed his own label, Barnaby.

Williams had a variety show that began in 1959 and another, *The Andy Williams Show,* in 1962. These shows aired on CBS and NBC, respectively. He was instrumental in building the career of the Osmond family, who would go on to enormous success in the 1970s. His Christmas specials began when he scaled back his variety show in 1971, preferring to do three specials a year rather than continue the weekly grind. The Christmas specials were an immediate hit. Williams's laid-back, mellow style meshed perfectly with the holiday. Something about his soothing, caressing voice made viewers want to curl up by the fire with a cup of hot cocoa.

Spider woman

Williams was a family man, and it was important to him to include his family in his work, the Christmas shows especially. His wife was the beautiful Claudine Longet, a French singer he met in 1960 in Las Vegas; she was dancing with the Folies Bergère at the time. For a time their marriage was very happy, and they had three children: Noelle, Christian, and Robert, who was named after their close friend, Robert F. Kennedy. But cracks began to appear as the '60s changed the face of America. Williams said of their compatibility problems, "Her interests were so different from mine. I was interested in the Establishment. She would be playing tennis with Peter Fonda, and I would be playing golf with Bing Crosby."

When their marriage fell apart, Williams put the Christmas specials on hold because he felt it would be too awkward and revealing to go on without Claudine, who had become famous by singing with him every holiday season. Claudine moved to Aspen, Colorado, and filed for divorce. Williams may have thought that would be the low point in the whole mess, but the worst was actually to come. In 1976, Longet was charged with manslaughter after shooting her lover, skier Spider Sabich. Williams supported her contention that the shooting had been accidental, and he trumpeted her innocence throughout the trial. Longet wound up serving only 30 days in jail.

The scandal took its toll on Williams, but after lying low for eight years, he resumed his Christmas specials in 1982 and continued to bring holiday joy to America well into the 1990s.

How Do You Say That?

MERRY CHRISTMAS!

Columbia: Feliz Navidad

Croatian: Sretan Bozic

Czech: Prejeme Vam Vesele Vanoce

Danish: Glædelig Jul

Duri: Christmas-e-shoma Mobarak

Dutch: Vrolijk Kerstfeest! *or* Zalig Kerstfeast

English: Merry Christmas

Equine: Neigh whinny whinny bfffffff!

Eskimo (Inupik): Jutdlime pivdluarit ukiortame pivdluaritlo!

Esperanto: Gajan Kristnaskon

Estonian: Rõõmsaid Jõulupühi

Ethiopian (Amharic): Melkin Yelidet Beaal

Farsi: Cristmas-e-shoma mobarak bashad

Feline: Meow purrrr meow

Finnish: Hyvaa joulua

Flemish: Zalig Kerstfeest

French: Joyeux Noël

Frisian: Noflike Krystdagen

Galician: Bo Nada

Gaelic: Nollaig chridheil agus Bliadhna mhath ùr!

German: Fröhliche Weihnachten

That's Myrrh-riffic!

You definitely know what gold is. And frankincense has something to do with perfume. But what the heck is myrrh? Here's a little information on one of the first Christmas gifts ever.

Myrrh has been used in religious rituals for thousands of years, but when most people think of myrrh, it's because of the story surrounding Jesus' birth. The wise men went to Bethlehem and brought gifts to the baby. According to the Bible, those gifts included gold, frankincense, and myrrh. Both myrrh and frankincense were highly prized items, on par with gold.

Okay, so what is it?

Myrrh is fragrant, hardened tree sap, or resin. This resin is secreted by the *Commiphora myrrha* tree, which is found largely in Somalia and Ethiopia. Those areas weren't always the famine-stricken, impoverished places they are today; in fact, myrrh sales and trade contributed greatly to the healthy economies of those places for many hundreds of years. The spread of Christianity took down the myrrh trade, since the practice of burning myrrh fell out of favor.

Myrrh was primarily used for incense back then, and in some areas it is still used for that today. The hard, reddish-brown resin is ground and blended into the incense, though small, unground chunks of myrrh resin are sometimes placed on charcoal discs and burned on their own. Its smell is earthy with a hint of sweetness.

Myrrh mouthwash?

Though the incense-friendly properties of myrrh keep it as an ingredient in that industry, there are other applications for myrrh. What makes myrrh good for incense makes it good for perfume, too, so it's sometimes used for that purpose. The sap's deep color makes it a natural colorant for personal care items, such as dyes, lotions, and bath products. Myrrh has a naturally antiseptic nature, which makes it a good ingredient in toothpaste, mouthwash, and wound salves. Chinese medicine practitioners and modern herbalists also find uses for myrrh, as it's largely nonallergenic to most people.

School of Yule

Even Santa has homework!

Department store Santas, Salvation Army Santas, Macy's Thanksgiving Day Parade Santas, they've got to come from somewhere right? You can't just slap on a beard and call yourself Santa, can you? Well, you can, as any corporate holiday party will attest, but the best of the best come from Santa school.

The old guard

What's Santa school without a little competition? The Charles W. Howard Santa Claus School bills itself as the "world's oldest Santa Claus school." Established in 1937 in New York (it's now in Midland, Michigan), the school delivers three days of intensive training. Classes include History and Hygiene 101. Santa school won't get you a Ph.D., but you will know Howard's maxim backward and forward, "He errors who thinks Santa enters through the chimney. Santa enters through the heart." Howard is a Santa lover, not a poet, but he makes his point. Howard was a staple Santa Claus of Macy's Thanksgiving Day Parade and consulted on *Miracle on 34th Street* (1947), so when it comes to the Santa Claus Hall of Fame, he's the Babe Ruth.

Tom Valent, who also plays Santa, took over the school and runs it with his wife, his very own Mrs. Claus. The biggest change since the old days is a discussion of liability insurance. Otherwise, the curriculum is largely the same as Howard's. In addition to mundane necessities of memorizing all the reindeer names and seeing what's for sale at the local Toys "R" Us, Valent also drills fundamentals of Santa behavior: body language, different ho ho hos, and softer greetings so as not to scare the kids.

Santa for dummies

For would-be Santas who can't attend a school setting, there's plenty of take-

---

74

home material in Santa School Inc.'s *All About Being Santa,* a 500-plus page manual of all things jolly. The contents include chapters on costume maintenance, how to take a good picture, and how to deal with nonbelievers.

The late Victor Nevada, a full-time Canadian Santa, established Santa School in Calgary. He learned by trial and error and decided there was a better way to educate future Santas. "Many Santas don't realize they are entertainers and just wing it. It's a recipe for disaster. Nothing on Broadway goes unrehearsed, neither should Santa."

For long-time Claus veterans, Santa schools are a way to keep in touch with others in the profession—to share tips, grooming advice, beard creams, and to bond with people who have the same passion for Christmas.

Elf school
If Santa school sounds like too much pressure, there's always Elf Training Academy in Rovaniemi, Lapland, in Finland. It's the closest city to the North Pole. That fact, coupled with its native reindeer population, has made Rovaniemi the de facto residence of Santa Claus. Lapland Vocational College (the Harvard of Finland) opened the elf training program to take advantage of the city's tourist influx.

Bad Santa
Santa school doesn't guarantee high moral fiber, it only encourages it. While there may be a fair share of drunk, thieving Billy Bob Thornton Santas (2003's *Bad Santa*), there are also many St. Nicks of the world who act a lot more like the Kris Kringle of *Miracle on 34th Street* (1947).

Pro tips
Bleach your beard. Natural beards are rarely, if ever, snow white. A little bleach will turn Grizzly Adams into a jolly old elf. And the bushy eyebrows? Keep 'em; don't trim. The bushier the better. As far as the costume (including a beard and hair for the less well endowed), you get what you pay for. A convincing outfit and hair runs upward of $600 to $700, a fair chunk of change, but mall visits can make that back rather quickly.

"Deck the Halls with Boughs of Holly..."

It's not Christmas until the tree is up and boughs of holly adorn the mantle.

Northern Europe has some of the harshest, coldest, and colorless winters in the world. So when a little plant somehow manages to poke through all that snow, as green in December as it is in July, then it must possess some sort of magical power. At least that's what people believed centuries ago when they spotted holly standing in stark contrast to its wintry surroundings. So taken were they by its color in the dark winter that they began bringing home boughs of holly and draping it over their doors hoping its magical power would drive evil spirits away.

Holy holly?

Early Christians had their own take on the bush. One legend has it that when Jesus walked on the earth, sprigs of holly appeared from his footsteps. Its pointy leaves resemble the crown of thorns he wore on the cross, and the red berries his blood. Even today, wreaths of holly are used at Easter to symbolize the crown of thorns he wore.

Folly holly

Today, holly figures prominently in Christmas decorating. Wreaths, table centerpieces, and garlands are among the items made using branches of its evergreen leaves. The berries, which ripen in autumn and linger through winter to early spring, are a winter food source for birds. In this case, reports about the berries being toxic to humans are true. Ingesting a few can cause severe and prolonged nausea along with drowsiness. It is estimated that 20 berries, if eaten by a human, can be fatal.

Interestingly, holly bushes have evolved into a variety of species that have adapted to all types of climates. This means that whether you live in French Polynesia, France, or Greenland, there's probably a type of holly readily available for holiday decorating.

🎥 CHRISTMAS MOVIE QUIZ

Match the line to the Christmas movie it came from.

1. "What we have here is a failure to accumulate."
   a. *Scrooged*
   b. *The Santa Clause*
   c. *Ernest Saves Christmas*
   d. *The Muppet Christmas Carol*

2. "Our Father, who art in Heaven, hallowed be Thy Name. And forgive my husband. He knows not what he does."
   a. *Christmas with the Kranks*
   b. *National Lampoon's Christmas Vacation*
   c. *How the Grinch Stole Christmas*
   d. *Jingle all the Way*

3. "I'm not a kid, I have pointy SHOES that are older than you."
   a. *Scrooged*
   b. *Ernest Saves Christmas*
   c. *National Lampoon's Christmas Vacation*
   d. *The Santa Clause*

4. "You'll shoot your eye out, kid."
   a. *How the Grinch Stole Christmas*
   b. *The Santa Clause*
   c. *A Christmas Story*
   d. *National Lampoon's Christmas Vacation*

5. "There's no Christmas in the Army!"
   a. *White Christmas*
   b. *Christmas with the Kranks*
   c. *Elf*
   d. *The Santa Clause*

Answers: 1. c; 2. b; 3. d; 4. c; 5. a

Christmas Around the World

CANADA

*Our neighbor to the north shares many traditions with us,
but it also has its own.*

At first glance, it may appear that Christmas in Canada is celebrated no differently than it is in the United States. One must appreciate the history of the country to truly understand its unique customs, especially those related to Christmas and other religious holidays. Among the Anglophones and Francophones who make up the vast majority of Canada's citizenry, there are many similarities—but also many distinctions.

The history's no mystery
Canada and the United States share the world's longest common border, but many Americans are fairly ignorant of Canada's rich history. British and French explorers were roaming the eastern coast of what we now call Canada as early as the late 15th century, and this beautiful territory, populated by indigenous peoples for an estimated 26,500 years, was much desired by both countries. At the end of the Seven Years War, known to most Americans as the French and Indian War, France ceded Canada to the British. But to this day, many of those of French descent in Canada still refer to this war as *La guerre de la Conquête* ("The War of the Conquest").

Canada is now a constitutional monarchy with its own prime minister and parliament. The Queen of England and her viceroys play only a ceremonial role. Still, for many Francophones it is not enough. Most of them live in Quebec, and they would like to see their province separate from Canada and become an independent country. Political parties such as the Bloc Quebecois and the Parti Quebecois cater to these peaceful but vociferous Francophone voters, but they are a minority. An estimated 68.3 percent of all Canadians speak English at home, while only 22.3 percent speak French.

Different strokes
How does this history affect the way Christmas is celebrated in Canada? Well, as you might have guessed, most of the Anglophones

in Canada are Protestants, and most of the Francophones in Canada are Catholic. But whatever their religious, political, or linguistic differences, most Canadians are extremely tolerant of the views and customs of their fellow countrypeople—and never more so than during the holiday season.

Drink that (spiced) wine

Canadians whose roots are in the United Kingdom tend to follow English Christmas traditions, with some variation. Game birds, of course, are the most popular choice in England for Christmas dinner, but while the English often prefer goose, Anglo Canadians feast on roast turkey, often accompanied by fresh or smoked salmon. Plum pudding with brandy sauce and minced pies filled with meat and/or fruit make a most delicious dessert, and like their British cousins, British Canadians quaff plenty of spiced wine, rum punch, and eggnog. While the tradition of mumming has died in the United States (see page 41), it is alive and well in Canada, and after dinner mummers parade through neighborhoods in cities and rural areas, wearing masks, singing Christmas carols, and performing amusing skits.

French Canadians tend to be a bit more religious in their celebrations, and many wait until after midnight mass to serve their Christmas dinner, or *reveillon.* The most important part of this dinner is the *tourtiere,* a meat pie that originated in Quebec and is now served all over the French-speaking area of the country. Every French Canadian family has its own unique recipe for tourtiere. Those who live inland use beef or pork in their meat pie, while those on the east coast of Canada are more likely to use salmon or another type of fish. *Boulettes,* or small meatballs, are another Christmas favorite. French Canadians love to display *crèches,* or nativity scenes, during the holiday season, and they are not confined to houses of

worship. Many take much pride in their family crèches and display them both indoors and out.

Anglo Canadians and French Canadians may never agree on politics, but peaceful, tolerant Christmas revelry and good food are two things they can definitely see eye-to-eye on.

Christmas Carols: A Timeline

*Christmas music before Halloween? That's just wrong.
Yet nowadays, it's the norm for radio stations to blare
holiday tunes well before pumpkins are carved and
trick-or-treat bags are filled. If you're going to be subjected
to thousands of carols before December 25, you might as
well know a little history behind the tradition.*

Christmas carols as we know them are thought to have come about in the 1200s, when churchgoers began composing tunes to accompany Nativity reenactments.

- Chances are, you've been singing the song of angels for years and didn't even realize it. Those Latin words you belt out in church, *"Gloria in excelsis Deo, et in terra pax hominibus bonae voluntatis,"* are the actual words to the first carol sung by angels to announce the birth of Jesus. Their lyrics mean "Glory to God in the highest, and on earth peace to people of good will."

- **1300:** The forerunner of today's Radio City *Christmas Spectacular,* dramatizations of the birth of Jesus were all the rage in the 1300s. Though the actual words to William Sandys's "Noel" were not sung until 1833, the song was no doubt inspired by the subject and melodies of these early dramas.

- **1534:** Never heard of "Coventry Carol?" You're not alone. As what may be the oldest known Christmas carol, it was first sung in "modern times" by sheep shearers and tailors of Coventry, England, on the steps of the city's cathedral from 1534 to 1584. An even older legend has it that mothers in Bethlehem sang the song after King Herod declared that all male sons be killed.

- **1580:** "Greensleeves," the melody to the Christmas song "What Child Is This?" was written by Richard Jones. It wasn't until 1865 that the Christmas story was set to this music.

- **1816:** "Angels from the Realms of Glory," by James Montgomery, tells the story of the angels who sang to shepherds about Jesus' birth.

- **1818:** It is almost certain that "Oberdorf Night" would never have become a Christmas classic. Instead, the hymn that Father Joseph Mohr and organist Franz Gruber hurriedly wrote to play on Christmas when the clock struck midnight went down in history as "Silent Night."

- **1847:** "O Holy Night" by Adolphe Charles Adam was not an instant hit. In fact, the French church was less than pleased with Adam's ballad, citing his "lack of musical taste." In the end, Adam, who also composed the ballet *Giselle,* was vindicated as the song became an all-time favorite that is still sung 160 years later.

- **1855:** "Angels We Have Heard on High" was included in a published collection of holiday carols. It is based on a custom started by French shepherds who would shout "Gloria in excelsis Deo" from hill to hill to celebrate Christmas.

- **1857:** John Henry Hopkins Jr. would likely turn over in his grave to hear the Beach Boys' version of his tune "We Three Kings of Orient Are." Hopkins wrote the song for an elaborate holiday pageant he was organizing for students at the General Theological Seminary in New York City.

- **1857:** If there is one Christmas tune likely to get lodged in your brain, it's "Jingle Bells." James S. Pierpont, a musical director for his brother's Unitarian Church, wrote the song about the rollicking sleigh races he watched as a young man. First published as "One Horse Open Sleigh," the tune became a popular holiday song after being recorded by the Hayden Quartet in 1902.

- **1865:** The little town of Bethlehem isn't so little anymore, but the song by the same name remains a holiday favorite. Philadelphia minister Phillips Brooks wrote it after a moving trip to the Holy Land. His church organist, Lewis Redner, added music so that the Sunday school children's choir could sing the song.

- **1879:** "Go Tell It on the Mountain," an African American spiritual, was popular among slaves because of Jesus' promise of freedom for all. Though it was probably written in the early 1800s, it became well-known after the Jubilee Singers of Fisk University performed it in 1879.

- **1887:** "Away in a Manger" was included in a songbook as "Luther's Cradle Hymn." Confusion with the name credited the song to Martin Luther, but the real author is unknown.

- **1939:** Robert L. May wrote *Rudolph the Red-Nosed Reindeer* as a promotional booklet giveaway for Montgomery Ward department store. In 1949, May's brother-in-law, Johnny Marks, put the story to song. Gene Autry sang the tune the same year, making it one of the best-selling songs of all time.

- **1944:** "The Christmas Song" is a Christmas classic, and nobody croons it better than Nat "King" Cole. Ironically, the carol was written in the middle of summer by Mel Tormé and Bob Wells.

- **1951:** Perry Como made Robert Meredith Willson's "It's Beginning to Look a Lot Like Christmas" a holiday hit. Legend has it that Willson's lyrics, "a tree in the Grand Hotel" refer to the hotel in Yarmouth, Nova Scotia.

- **1960:** Blues singer and pianist Charles Brown released "Please Come Home for Christmas" in 1960, but it took 12 years before taking the No. 1 spot on the Christmas singles chart in 1972. The Eagles covered the song in 1978.

- **1979:** Elmo & Patsy's self-released Randy Brooks song "Grandma Got Run Over by a Reindeer" tells the story of a teetotaler grandma who drinks too much eggnog on Christmas Eve before being run over by Santa's sleigh.

- **1984:** "Do They Know It's Christmas?" was written by Bob Geldof and Midge Ure to raise money for famine relief in Ethiopia. It quickly soared to the No. 1 spot on the UK record charts. In the United States, it never reached that spot due to chart complications, even though it outsold the No. 1 record four to one.

- **1994:** Mariah Carey and Walter Afanasieff wrote "All I Want for Christmas Is You," the holiday pop song that, by 2006, became the best-selling ringtone of all time. Carey wrote the song as a tribute to her high school boyfriend.

A Thanksgiving Tradition

*The Macy's Thanksgiving Day Parade has become
the official kick-off for the Christmas season.
Here's how it all came together.*

For more than 85 years, Macy's in New York City has entertained America with one of the largest, most impressive holiday parades in the world. In fact, the event has become so popular that hundreds of thousands of eager spectators rise before dawn to ensure that they'll get a glimpse of the parade's famous character balloons, lavish floats, and big-name entertainment.

Welcome to America

And to think it all started primarily as a way for the store's immigrant employees to celebrate the American holiday of Thanksgiving.

The first parade, held in 1924, was called the Macy's Christmas Parade. It wound from 145th Street in Harlem to the Macy's store on 34th Street, and it featured colorful floats, marching bands, and live animals on loan from the Central Park Zoo. That year, and every year since except one, the parade concluded with the arrival of Santa Claus.

The procession was renamed the Macy's Thanksgiving Day Parade in 1927, and it quickly grew in both popularity and scope. Today, it takes nearly three hours to complete.

Also in 1927, live animals were replaced with the oversized character balloons that have become one of the parade's most popular attractions. Produced by the Goodyear Tire and Rubber Company in Akron, Ohio, the first balloons included Felix the Cat, a dragon, an elephant, and a toy soldier. The balloons were filled with air, but the following year they were filled with helium and released into the air at the conclusion of the parade. Starting in 1929, a special tag was sewn into each balloon, and whoever found it received a prize from the store. In 1931, aviator Clarence Chamberlain caught the pig balloon in midair so he could claim the $25 reward. As a result, the practice of releasing the balloons was discontinued in 1933.

By the 1930s, the Macy's Thanksgiving Day Parade had achieved national acclaim, and nearly a million spectators lined the streets to enjoy the show, which was broadcast locally via radio. In 1933, the parade was filmed by newsreel crews for the first time and shown in theaters across the country.

Full of hot air

Mickey Mouse joined the parade as a helium-filled balloon in 1934, and he was followed by dozens of other popular characters in the years that followed. Today, character balloons range from Spider-Man to the Pillsbury Doughboy.

The Macy's Thanksgiving Day Parade was halted during World War II. The nation wasn't in much of a celebratory mood, but more importantly, the war effort needed the rubber and helium that went into the manufacture of the parade's trademark balloons.

The celebration resumed in 1945, and two years later the parade achieved unique cultural status when it was featured prominently in the movie *Miracle on 34th Street*, which contained footage filmed during the 1946 parade.

Because it is an outdoor event, the parade has experienced its share of mishaps, including escaped and deflated balloons and even a snowstorm. To avoid potential problems, the balloons, which are inflated the day before the parade, are now carried closer to the ground for greater control during windy conditions.

Of course, celebrities are another important aspect of the Macy's Thanksgiving Day Parade. A veritable who's who of entertainment has taken part over the years, including Bob Hope, Jackie Gleason, Harpo Marx, Shania Twain, Dolly Parton, the Jonas Brothers, and Christina Aguilera, just to name a few.

The big guy

At the end of the day (or end of the parade!), however, it's Santa Claus the crowds come to see, and for good reason. The arrival of the jolly old elf means the arrival of the Christmas season itself. And few things are more exciting to the child in all of us.

Fast Facts

MACY'S THANKSGIVING DAY PARADE

- More than 300,000 Macy's employees have participated in the parade since its inception.

- Horses pulled the floats during the first Macy's Thanksgiving Day Parade in 1924. However, one white horse went AWOL just minutes before the event was supposed to start; it was scheduled to help pull the Ben-Hur float.

- The parade was first televised in New York in 1945.

- In 1971, the wind was so strong that the decision was made not to raise the balloons. Instead, television viewers were treated to clips from the 1970 parade.

- Santa Claus has concluded the parade every year except one. In 1933, he led the parade.

- The Macy's Thanksgiving Day parade is the second-largest consumer of helium in the United States. At number one is the United States government.

- During a helium shortage in 1958, the government asked the parade to cut down on its use of the lighter-than-air gas. To aid the cause, balloons were filled with air and held aloft with cranes.

- At the start of World War II, Macy's donated its rubber balloons to the war effort during a ceremony held on the steps of New York City Hall.

- NBC first broadcast the parade live to a nationwide audience in 1948.

- Dino the Dinosaur—one of the parade's most memorable balloons—was inducted as an honorary member of the Museum of Natural History in 1975.

- The parade has endured its share of cold days, but in 1989 participants marched through the first parade snowstorm.

Deck the Halls:
Christmas Decorations 101

So much of the fun of the holiday season is festooning the house, the office, the shops, and even the streets with festive decorations. From winter-friendly flowers to silvery tinsel, here's some insight into the most popular choices in home dec around Christmastime—but feel free to decorate however you like and start your own traditions!

Tree ornaments

A leftover from a bygone pagan era, the Christmas tree has long been a fixture of the holiday. But from the start, it wasn't enough to just sit a big tree down in the middle of the room—it had to be decorated! The earliest ornaments were placed by central Europeans and included fruit, nuts, and onions, among other items. As time progressed, the ornaments got a lot more fun and included glass-blown balls, candles, and tinsel (see next page.) The figurines, ceramic objects, and countless different types of ornaments we use today truly came into vogue in the 1960s, when pop culture decided that the more colorful and varied the ornaments, the better the Christmas tree.

Christmas tree lights

A Christmas tree wouldn't be the same without lights, now would it? Before electricity, folks lit their trees by placing small candles on the branches, which as you can imagine is pretty dangerous. Lanterns were used around the turn of the 20th century, but a few years before that, in 1882, the first Christmas tree was lit by electricity. The man who did it was named Edward Johnson, and he created the first string of electric lights by hand-wiring red, white, and blue bulbs. Within a matter of years, his invention was being mass-produced and people everywhere were lighting their trees with tiny glowing bulbs. The lights weren't fail-safe, however; in 1917, an inventor named Albert Sadacca developed a safer string of lights and became a millionaire when he developed something else the world loved to see—colored bulbs.

Tinsel

Christmas trees were really catching on in Germany in the 1600s, and people were looking for things with which to decorate them. Since reflective surfaces looked so good in the glowing candle- and firelight, anything shiny was in high demand. Around 1610, machines were created that would shred actual silver into little strips, which were then gathered and tossed around the house and on the tree. Silver tarnishes, however, so before too long different metal alloys were used in the making of tinsel. Eventually, plastics and polymers were implemented in tinsel production. These days, we hang ropes of it everywhere we want to see sparkle and shine.

Garlands and wreaths

When the settlers from England came to America, they brought many Christmas traditions with them, including the garland and the wreath. When the winter months arrived and there was no harvesting to be done, many families would collect the boughs of pine, spruce, and cedar trees and bind them together to make fragrant, festive garlands that they could sell. The same went for wreaths, which folks placed on or above their doors to bring health and happiness. The wreath actually dates back to ancient Greek times, when athletes and important people wore laurel diadems (wreaths, basically) on their heads to announce victory or status.

Lawn ornaments

Way back in 1223, St. Francis of Assisi held the first ever nativity scene in a cave in Italy. He used real, live people to depict the scene of Christ's birth as a way to remind people of the meaning of Christmas. Live nativity scenes caught on, but eventually the scenes were arranged with statues. These could be said to have been the first Christmastime lawn ornaments. Once the Industrial Revolution happened and mass commercialization really fired up, producing lots and lots of holiday statues became easier—and the more variety the manufacturer could offer, the more money he'd make. Thus, your neighbors next door feel compelled to light the block with an inflat- able Rudolph, that twirling Santa, a blinking Frosty, and...

Tamale Time!

♨ ♨ ♨

*In Texas, it just wouldn't be Christmas
without some delicious tamales!*

A variety of different foods have come to be associated with
Christmas, including fruitcake, ham, eggnog, and that proverbial
favorite, figgy pudding. But tamales? Absolutely! Especially if you're
a Texan.

For generations, dining on Christmas tamales has been a popular
tradition in the Lone Star State and its southwestern neighbors.
Some people hand-prepare the zesty Latin American dish, while
others special-order them from neighborhood shops. The meal is
typically eaten on Christmas Eve.

Tamales are made using a starchy, corn-based dough called masa,
which is filled with seasoned meat, vegetables, chilies, or cheese,
then wrapped in cornhusks and steamed. (The cornhusks are dis-
carded before eating.) Tamales are fairly time-consuming to prepare,
which is why some folklorists believe tamales have come to be
associated specifically with Christmas—it's the one special occasion
most people are willing to put in the extra effort.

As a result, Christmas tamales have become a fond family custom
for many. It allows relatives to gather, visit, and catch up while
everyone participates in the creation of the flavorful feast.

An ancient dish

According to historians, tamales can be traced as far back as
8000 B.C. They were a staple among the ancient Aztecs and were as
popular then as peanut butter sandwiches are today. Spanish explorers discovered tamales upon their arrival in Mexico, and they quickly
took to the yummy dish, bringing it with them to all of their colonies.
It was an ideal food because tamales transported well.

So this Christmas, add a spicy bit of ancient history to your
holiday meal by making your own tamales. (You can find a variety of
easy-to-follow recipes on the Internet.) If it sounds like too much
work, any Mexican restaurant will be happy to oblige you.

Lord of Christmas Cheer!

*J. R. R. Tolkien crafted an amusing take on Christmas
in a series of whimsical letters written to his children.*

J. R. R. Tolkien is unquestionably one of the most revered (and best-read) fantasy authors ever to put pen to paper. He is best known, of course, as the literary genius behind *The Hobbit* and the epic *Lord of the Rings* trilogy, but no less fascinating is one of his lesser-known fantasies: *The Father Christmas Letters.*

Never heard of it? You're not alone. The book *The Father Christmas Letters* tends to be overshadowed by Tolkien's more popular fantasy works. But it's definitely worth seeking out, especially during the holiday season.

Children's fantasyland

The letters were actually a personal family endeavor that Tolkien likely never thought would be read by outsiders. Between 1920 and 1943, the acclaimed British writer assumed the identity of Father Christmas in an annual letter written to his children. The letters chronicled the adventures of Father Christmas, and they featured a variety of amusing side characters, including goblins, elves, and the North Polar Bear and his two cubs, Paksu and Valkotukka.

Each holiday, Father Christmas would update the Tolkien children on what had transpired on the North Pole the previous year. The tales were raucous, full of adventure, and intentionally included subjects of interest to the Tolkien children, such as cave paintings and fireworks. Tolkien also wrote portions of some of the letters in a unique elf language that he created, as well as one letter from the North Polar Bear written in goblin. But Tolkien did much more than simply write the letters from Father Christmas. He also painstakingly illustrated each note with color drawings, which only adds to their uniqueness.

Luckily, the Tolkien children kept all the Father Christmas letters written by their father, and much to the delight of fantasy fans everywhere, the stories were published in 1976.

Spice Up Your Christmas...

... and give your mouth and nose the presents they crave.

One of the most wonderful things about Christmas is that it is a taste and olfactory sensation like no other, in large part due to the many spices that are traditionally used during the holiday season. Incorporate the spices on our list into your home and/or cooking for a truly memorable sensory experience.

- **Ginger:** What would Christmas be without ginger? Like the sweet potato, ginger is a root tuber, and it can be used for either culinary or medicinal purposes. Grown all across Asia and in some parts of Africa and the Caribbean, its pungent flavor is familiar in everyday recipes in China and India. Here in the West, however, we are more likely to use powdered dry ginger and to reserve it for the winter months, when we make ginger cookies, gingerbread houses, ginger ale, and ginger beer.

- **Cinnamon:** This very popular spice is derived from the bark of a tree called the *Cinnamomum verum,* an evergreen first cultivated in Sri Lanka. By the time of the writing of the Old Testament, cinnamon had found its way from East Asia all the way to the Middle East, and Moses was commanded to mix the spice into oil used for worship. Today, the smell of cinnamon wafting from a warm kitchen is a wonderful way to greet holiday guests, and its use in Christmas fare such as frosted cinnamon buns, pies, candies, cereals, hot chocolate, teas, and liqueurs is a yearly tradition for many cooks.

- **Cloves:** Cloves are the dried flower buds of an evergreen tree that is native to India and Indonesia. Cloves resemble tiny brown nails, and their smell and taste is refreshingly strong. A fun way to use cloves in your Christmas decorating is to follow the English and European tradition of making pomanders. Stud four or five oranges with whole, dry cloves, attach ribbons at the top of each orange, and hang them around your home or on your Christmas tree. Pomanders are both beautiful to look at and marvelous to smell.

- **Nutmeg:** Nutmeg is a spice made from the seed of a tree in the genus of *Myristica.* It is associated with Christmas because it is often used—sometimes fresh, sometimes dried—in eggnog, mulled cider, and mulled wine. In Europe, nutmeg is often incorporated into both potato dishes and processed meats, and it is especially popular in the Netherlands. But nutmeg is not only useful in cooking; it is also used around the globe as an ingredient in essential oils.

- **Myrrh:** Myrrh is of course best known as one of the three gifts of the magi, the kings who followed a star and traveled far to pay homage to the newborn Jesus Christ. The dried sap of trees found in Yemen, Ethiopia, and Jordan, myrrh is rarely used in private homes in the western world, but is often used in incense and candles in the religious services of Roman Catholics and the Eastern Orthodox here in America, as well as in embalming oil. All over the world, myrrh is considered to be very effective as a medicine and an antiseptic.

- **Frankincense:** Another of the gifts of the magi, frankincense is a resin that is harvested from a genus of trees called *Boswellia* that grow across the Middle East and in parts of Africa. Used now across the globe in both incense and perfume, in ancient times the Egyptians charred it, turning it into kohl, the black eyeliner that was such a distinctive part of their culture. Frankincense and kohl were found in the tomb of their most famous leader, King Tutankhamun.

While some of these spices may at first seem too exotic or foreign for an American Christmas, they can really add interest to any Christmas celebration when mixed with more familiar traditions. And with online sources, they are easier than ever to obtain.

They Died on Christmas Day

Not that there's ever a good time to go, but...

Yes, dying on Christmas Day stinks, but sometimes it stinks more than others—like when you're standing up against a wall and a firing squad is pointing their rifles at you and your spouse. Though a few of our December 25 deceased went peacefully, famous Christmas deaths are just as often quite grisly, and one of our subjects would not even be famous at all if it weren't for her horrific murder.

- **Charlie Chaplin (1977)** Sadly, Chaplin was accused in the 1950s of "un-American activity" and exiled to Europe for his alleged political views. Though he returned briefly to the United States to collect an honorary Oscar in 1972, he died at his home in Vevey, Switzerland. After his corpse was stolen in an attempted extortion plot, it was reburied under six feet of concrete to dissuade further crimes and vandalism.

- **Eartha Kitt (2008)** Eartha Kitt's death positively drips in irony, darlings! You see, Miss Kitt's most famous song in her long, successful career was "Santa Baby," in which she purred and cooed to the man in red about wanting a fur coat, a yacht, and jewelry from Tiffany's. Famously proclaimed by Orson Welles to be "the most exciting woman in the world," she worked almost to the end, starring in an off-Broadway musical as late as 2006.

- **Dean Martin (1995)** For those who love his smooth, hip, Las Vegas style, Dean Martin is an essential part of their Christmas soundtrack. And for a while there, back in the '60s, it seemed as though Martin released a Christmas album every year: *My Christmas Album, My Kind of Christmas, The Dean Martin Christmas Album*, etc. In the '70s, he was still a much-sought-after guest on almost every variety show, especially those around the holidays. Something about Dean Martin and Christmas just seemed to go together—so Martin's "going" on Christmas is apt.

- **Nicolae Ceauşescu (1989)** Ceauşescu and his wife, Elena, were executed by firing squad as the whole world watched, but no one really cared, much less lifted a finger to help them. The communist dictator had driven Romania into economic ruin by exporting much of its agricultural and industrial production to pay off astronomical foreign debts. Citizens suffered greatly in a physical sense; many were so poor they were forced to dump their children in orphanages. They also suffered mentally, so afraid of the secret police that they rarely discussed their troubles even with loved ones. Thus, many Romanians considered Ceauşescu's execution to be a Christmas gift.

- **W. C. Fields (1946)** It is hard to argue that the Christmas death of Fields had much meaning, for his image seemed to be in complete opposition to everything good and right about Christmas. A misanthrope, an alcoholic, and a child-hater, Fields built his very successful comedy career out of being a not-so-nice guy who couldn't care less whether or not there was peace on earth. Fields claimed to despise Christmas, and when a friend caught him reading the Bible on his deathbed, he said he was "checking for loopholes." Strangely, Frank Capra had considered Fields for the role of Uncle Billy in *It's a Wonderful Life,* but he wisely decided to go with Thomas Mitchell.

- **Billy Martin (1989)** Known best as the contentious, five-time manager of the New York Yankees, Martin's career in baseball was a roller coaster of big wins, shocking losses, screaming fits, physical altercations, and alcoholism. His feuds with such luminaries as George Steinbrenner and Reggie Jackson are legendary, and they made him so famous that he was referenced long after his death in such television shows as *Seinfeld* and *Married with Children.* In an ESPN miniseries, he was portrayed by actor John Turturro. Though not the driver, Martin died in a car accident that unsurprisingly followed a long day of heavy drinking.

- **JonBenet Ramsey (1996)** America was shocked when six-year-old Ramsey was murdered in her parents' luxurious home in Boulder, Colorado, on Christmas Day. No one was ever charged with this heinous crime, and authorities were widely criticized for bungling the investigation, but they weren't the only ones who were criticized. Both of JonBenet's parents, but particularly her mother, Patsy, were pilloried in the press for allowing their daughter to participate in child beauty pageants, sometimes in disturbingly skimpy outfits and makeup. (DNA evidence exonerated the parents of the crime.)

- **James Brown (2006)** Known as "The Godfather of Soul" and "The Hardest-Working Man in Show Business," James Brown was widely considered a musical genius who left the world such gems as "Papa's Got a Brand New Bag," "I Got You (I Feel Good)," and "Get Up (I Feel Like Being a) Sex Machine." For a man who was famous for his manic exuberance and electrifying performances, Brown went to the Great Beyond in a most quiet, dignified manner. Suffering from pneumonia and congestive heart failure, he whispered, "I'm going away tonight" and gently passed on.

- **Denver Pyle (1997)** Though Pyle's career in film and television stretched over a few decades, he didn't become famous until he was almost 60 years old. That was when he landed the role of Uncle Jesse Duke in the CBS television show *The Dukes of Hazzard*, which ran from 1979 to 1985. An action show that often blended in sitcom-type humor, it seemed perfectly tailored for Pyle's grizzled looks and down-home acting style. Pyle died of lung cancer at the age of 77 and was buried in Forreston, Texas.

- **Hiroaki Hidaka (2006)** This revolting serial killer was hanged along with three other prisoners by the Japanese government on Christmas Day. Hidaka's execution came after he was convicted of killing four women, one only 16 years old. Before his bloody rampage, which lasted from April to September of 1996, he had led a debauched life of drinking and carousing. He did not appeal his death sentence.

Toys That Caused a Christmas Riot

There are toys, there are popular toys, and then there are the toys that caused riots when stores ran out of them as the long line of anxious parents reached the door. Some of these toys have remained popular long after their first Christmas rush, while others are gathering dust in boxes marked "What were we thinking?" Here are some of the most popular Christmas toys ever.

Slinky

The idea for the Slinky was born when naval engineer Richard James knocked over a spring he was working with and watched it "slink" down from shelf to table to floor before recoiling to a stop. He started a company to make the toys and convinced Gimbels department store in Philadelphia to let him demonstrate them during the 1945 Christmas season. Within 90 minutes of setting up his display, all 400 Slinkies he had made were sold for a dollar each.

Pet Rock

California advertising executive Gary Dahl decided that a rock would make a perfect no-fuss, no-mess, no-walk pet. He packaged polished stones on piles of straw inside boxes with holes, wrote a book called the "Pet Rock Training Manual" and started selling them in August 1975 at a gift show in San Francisco for $3.95. Dahl announced his toy with a press release sent to major media outlets. *Newsweek* magazine carried an article about it, newspapers ran stories, and Johnny Carson featured it on *The Tonight Show*. The fad ended after Christmas 1975, but the phrase "pet rock" lives on.

Twister

The hottest game of Christmas 1966, in more ways than one, was Twister. The first game to use humans as board pieces, Twister players tie themselves in knots by putting their hands and feet on colored dots until someone can't reach or the players fall over.

Invented by Charles F. Foley and Neil Rabens, Twister was produced by Milton Bradley and was unofficially introduced to the United States in May 1966 when Johnny Carson and actress Eva Gabor, wearing a low-cut dress, demonstrated it on *The Tonight Show*. Over three million Twister games were sold in its first year.

Cabbage Patch Kids

Cabbage Patch Kids are cloth dolls invented by Debbie Morehead and Xavier Roberts and first sold at craft shows in Kissimmee, Florida. Roberts eventually sold them at an old medical clinic he renamed the Babyland General Hospital, and adoption papers were provided for each doll. Coleco bought the line in 1982, gave the dolls plastic faces, and changed the name to Cabbage Patch Kids. They were introduced at the International Toy Fair in New York City in 1983, and by October they were sold out in most stores, causing massive crowds whenever a few were spotted for sale. The Cabbage Patch Kids brand is on many products from cereal to clothing, and the dolls are still popular today.

Care Bears

The Care Bears started out as cuddly cartoon characters on greeting cards from American Greetings. In 1983, stuffed Care Bears toys were marketed by Parker Brothers and Kenner in conjunction with their first TV special, *The Land Without Feelings*. Care Bears were a popular toy that Christmas and over 40 million were sold between 1983 and 1987. More TV shows, movies, and the greeting cards have helped the Care Bears remain on the market.

Teddy Ruxpin

Kids who loved the talking animatronic animals at amusement parks and restaurants got their wish for a home version when the Teddy Ruxpin doll was released by Worlds of Wonder in 1985. Teddy's mouth moved as an audio cassette recorder in his back supplied the sound. Voice actor Phil Baron supplied the voice of Teddy Ruxpin for the toy and *The Adventures of Teddy Ruxpin* TV show, which ran from 1987 to 1988. Worlds of Wonder folded in 1991, but Teddy has been resurrected three times by other companies and now has a digital voice player.

Tickle Me Elmo

A furry red Muppet monster on the children's show *Sesame Street*, Elmo became the hot Christmas gift in 1996 when Tyco released Tickle Me Elmo. It is a plush toy that giggles when squeezed once and shakes and laughs hysterically when squeezed three times. The toys were in short supply because of unexpected demand, causing stores to raise prices and parents to fight over them. Injuries were common, and newspapers ran ads offering one doll for as much as $1,500. Elmo spawned other Muppet Tickle Me characters, and in 2006, Elmo became popular again as TMX (Tickle Me Extreme), with more actions such as rolling on the floor and pounding his fist.

Furbies

Talking Furby robots that had their own language and appeared to communicate with each other were the hit of the 1998 Christmas season. Invented by Dave Hampton and Caleb Chung, they debuted at the International Toy Fair in 1998 and quickly became the season's must-have toy, with 1.8 million Furbies sold in 1998 and a total of over 40 million in three years. Priced at $35, shortages caused some to be resold for over $300.

Nintendo Game Boy

Christmas 1989 was the first time many kids found a handheld video game player under the tree. The Nintendo Game Boy was released in North America on July 31, 1989, and it became an immediate hit. The Game Boy was priced at $109, powered by four AA batteries, and included Tetris, a puzzle game. Other games could be loaded using miniature cartridges. The monochrome Game Boy was replaced by the Game Boy Color in 1998.

Xbox 360

Microsoft unveiled the Xbox 360 videogame console on May 12, 2005, to replace the original Xbox. It was not released to the American public until November 22, 2005, causing a huge rush of Christmas purchases that Microsoft underestimated. At one point, an estimated 10 percent of all Xbox 360s available were on sale through online auction sites. By the end of the year, over 900,000 had been sold in the United States.

Finding Hope in Sorrow

Composer George Frideric Handel hit rock bottom,
but he got by with a little help from his friends.

Beethoven once said of George Frideric Handel, "Handel is the greatest composer who ever lived. I would bare my head and kneel at his grave." But in 1741, Handel sure didn't feel "great." He felt like a pathetic wretch and a complete failure. At the age of 56, he was all washed up professionally, which led to severe financial problems and a deep depression. His health, too, just kept getting worse. He could hardly sleep at night. Desperate, he prayed for a way out of his misery.

Laying down the law

Handel had never had it easy. Though he was born in 1685 with a magnificent musical gift, his stern father wanted him to study law. Luckily, his mother encouraged his musical talent, and the patriarch relented, allowing young George to first study music in his hometown of Halle, then to move on to Hamburg, where he continued to learn more about the pipe organ and the harpsichord. When his father died in 1697, Handel's guilt prodded him into studying law for several years at the University of Halle. But his true passion could not be denied; he yearned to return to music.

The future (and last) Grand Duke of Tuscany, Gian Gastone de Medici, invited Handel to Italy in 1706. Medici had mental and substance abuse issues, but he knew good music when he heard it. He, along with his brother, Ferdinando, and the court librettist, Antonio Salvi, became important mentors to Handel. The Pope had temporarily banned opera, so Handel turned to sacred music, writing *Dixit Dominus*, a piece inspired by Psalm 110. When the opera ban was lifted, Handel's operas *Rodrigo* and *Agrippina* made him a star composer in Italy.

In 1710, Handel's life took another unexpected turn at the hands of a powerful mentor. George, the Elector of Hanover, Germany, took a great interest in his talent and called him back to his homeland. Handel became George's *Kapellmeister,* or director of music. And when, soon after, George became King George I of Great Britain, he brought Handel along with him when he moved to England. Handel became a huge star in Britain, and he loved his life there, becoming a naturalized citizen in 1727. Unfortunately, Handel was not as skilled a businessman as he was an artist. He had become involved in operatic management, investing everything he had into it, and he lost a small fortune.

His eyesight was giving him trouble, and primitive surgery only made the condition worse. Then, in 1736, he suffered some kind of strokelike attack and lost the use of his right arm. Desperate to regain its function, Handel traveled to Aachen, Germany, a spa town famous for its healing hot springs that were channeled into bathhouses. The treatment worked, but by the time he returned to England, his life was in shambles. His fame was waning fast, and he couldn't pay his debts.

Friends with benefits

Handel prayed for relief, and amazingly, his prayers seemed to be answered. His old friend the Duke of Devonshire wrote him a letter inviting him to come to Dublin and perform some benefit concerts for various hospitals and prisons. But what would Handel play? He was depressed and just couldn't get inspired. Luckily, another letter came soon after from an eccentric acquaintance named Charles Jennens. Many considered Jennens to be a kook with crazy pipe dreams, but this time his idea—an oratorio about the story of Christ—struck Handel as one worth pursuing. He locked himself away in his study, and 24 days later emerged with *Messiah,* now considered a masterpiece of classical music.

Messiah was first performed in Dublin on April 13, 1742. Its success allowed Handel to live the rest of his life in comfort. Despite it being about the complete life of Christ, it has become a Christmas staple, and choirs around the world will no doubt be singing his Hallelujah chorus for centuries to come.

Christmas Around the World

AUSTRALIA

...where December the 25th is never white and activities are more likely to include surfing than sledding.

Australia is different from any other country on earth—just ask an Australian. A mix of indigenous peoples and Caucasians descended from Britain's infamous penal colony, Aussies do things their way—Christmas included. Anyone tired of the same-old, same-old around the holidays would do well to book a flight to this warm, welcoming continent, where Christmas is a bright, sunny blast of fun.

Feelin' hot, hot, hot

In some ways, an Australian Christmas looks familiar to Americans and Europeans. Homes are decorated with lights, Christmas trees are festooned, and gifts are exchanged. It is not surprising that we share many holiday traditions, considering that the vast majority of Australia's 22 million people are the ancestors of citizens of England, Ireland, or Scotland. But Australia's population has quadrupled since the end of World War I, with Germans, Italians, Greeks, Chinese, and Vietnamese adding to the country's multicultural mix. The blending of backgrounds has created a unique culture in which many traditions—Christmas included—have taken on new features.

Australia's climate, too, ensures that in other respects an Australian Christmas will be very different from the one we know. The 25th of December falls during Australia's early summer, and whether one is in the tropical north, the temperate southeast, or the desert of the Outback, it's almost always hot. In fact, the temperature can soar to as high as 30 degrees Celsius (that's 86 degrees Fahrenheit to you and me). This heat, of course, plays a big role in how the holidays are celebrated down under.

Australians have a well-deserved reputation as an active, physical, fun-loving people, and never does this stereotype seem more apt than during the Christmas season. Unlike their long-left-behind cousins in the United Kingdom, who huddle indoors with roast goose and plum pudding, Australians love to spend the holidays outdoors. Young people, especially, flock to the beaches or campgrounds to enjoy their scheduled breaks from school or university. In Sydney, Bondi Beach alone welcomes over 40,000 Christmas sun worshippers a year, many of them international tourists.

They do it their way

Australians follow their own charming customs and traditions during the Christmas season, and perhaps in no other area are they more unique than in music. While they do sing many of the same Christmas carols and songs as Americans and Europeans, they also have their own tunes, which add a distinctive flavor to the holidays. John Wheeler's beloved "The Three Drovers" is a carol written just for Australians, and it has special meaning to them, as it ties the common Australian occupation of cattle- or sheepherding to those shepherds who kept watch near Bethlehem on the very first Christmas. In a more lighthearted vein are Rolf Harris's "The Six White Boomers" (about a lost joey who finds his kangaroo mummy with a little help from Santa) and Colin Buchanan's "Aussie Jingle Bells" and "Australian Twelve Days of Christmas."

While we in America immediately think of the poinsettia when we hear the phrase "Christmas plant," the Australian Christmas plant is Christmas bells, or *Blandfordia nobilis.* Smaller and more delicate-looking than the poinsettia, Christmas bells have downward-drooping, bell-like blossoms that are red with yellow tips. There is also an Australian Christmas bush and an Australian Christmas orchid. Which plant or flower one chooses to decorate with often depends on the part of the continent in which one resides.

Of course, like everywhere else in the world, food is a huge part of Christmas in Australia, but again because of the heat, many Australians forgo the traditional hot roast dinner of their ancestors. Instead, they feast on cold turkey, ham, seafood, and salads. Even their plum pudding is served cold, which would be unthinkable back in the United Kingdom! But in Christmas, as in everything else, the Aussies do it their way.

Christmas at the Crawfords

🕯 🕯 🕯

No ... artificial ... Christmas ... trees ... EVER!!!

Joan Crawford is now so strongly identified with bad mothering that it is almost impossible for most people to associate her with anything else. But before she was "Mommie Dearest," Crawford was a true superstar—a liberating countercultural agent, an Academy Award–winning actress, a chameleonlike fashion icon, and a proto-feminist role model for working, single women.

Like most "old school" stars, Crawford kept her fans at arm's length while giving the illusion of complete transparency and openness. She did let them into her private life, but it was the private life *she* wanted to reveal, one of strict-but-loving childrearing, charity toward the less fortunate, and well-informed concern for global issues. What better time for Joan to get her message across than Christmas Eve, and what better way to communicate it than on the radio?

Work it, girl!

A lot of awful things have been said about Joan Crawford, but even her biggest critics acknowledge she worked her butt off for everything she achieved. Born into a poverty-stricken family in San Antonio, Texas, as Lucille Faye LaSueur, Crawford slaved at menial cleaning and laundry jobs from the time she was just a small child. Her father abandoned the family, and her mother was too busy with backbreaking work to pay much attention to Joan and her brother, Hal. But when Joan was still a little girl, her mother remarried to a man named Henry Cassin, a vaudeville showman who gave Lucille the nickname "Billie." Young Lucille/Billie fell in love with performing, and with a goal in mind, she was able to overcome the hardships of her very rough childhood and become one of the biggest stars in Hollywood, known as "Joan Crawford."

After several failed marriages and several disappointing miscarriages, Crawford decided to adopt children. She welcomed baby Christina in 1940 and baby Christopher a few years later, and she immediately began using the children in her publicity photos and interviews. To be fair, most stars at that time did the same, and many stars still do today; look how many include their children in their reality shows. The radio show Crawford taped from her home on Christmas Eve 1949, however, was about anything but "reality." The tape, which can be found on content-sharing sites, including YouTube, has become a camp classic and a holiday tradition for her fans.

Fishing expedition

By this time, Crawford had added three-year-old twins Cynthia and Cathy to her family, and all four children joined her on *The George Fisher Show.* Fisher began by giving listeners some details about Crawford's "tastefully decorated home," such as the fact that her "colorful Christmas tree" was "almost snowed under with packages" and that her "stately Colonial fireplace" was "prepared for the flames that will be warming the room before long." In rehearsed dialogue so wooden and stilted that it's almost embarrassing to listen to, Fisher asked the two eldest children about the Crawford family Christmas traditions. Ten-year-old Christina tells him, "We insist that Mother hang her stocking right beside ours" and expresses the hope that she'll get a "collie dog, just like Lassie."

Though Crawford seems perfectly calm and reasonable throughout the interview, a touch of *Mommie Dearest* comes through when she tells Fisher, "I don't let them have all their presents at one time. They'll get to play with them all day tomorrow, and then we'll put a large group of them aside. From tomorrow on, they *earn* their gifts."

Christina complained in her book that Joan actually only let them keep a few presents and gave the rest to orphanages, but this was recently refuted by daughter Cathy in Charlotte Chandler's biography about Crawford, *Not the Girl Next Door.* In any case, it seems that even after reaching an incredible level of success, Joan Crawford's impoverished childhood still affected her and her family.

The Cola Claus

*Although the Coca-Cola Company helped popularize
Santa Claus, it cannot take credit for creating
the ubiquitous Christmas image.*

Nothing says "Christmas" like the image of a white-whiskered fat man in a red suit squeezing down a chimney with a sack full of toys. But Santa Claus hasn't always looked that way. When the Coca-Cola Company used the red-robed figure in the 1930s to promote its soft drinks, the classic image of Santa was cemented in the public consciousness.

Sorting out the Santas

Santa Claus evolved from two religious figures, St. Nicholas and Christkindlein. St. Nicholas was a real person, a monk who became a bishop in the early fourth century and was renowned as a generous gift-giver. Christkindlein (meaning "Christ child") was assisted by elfin helpers and would leave gifts for children while they slept.

Santa Claus originated from the Dutch poem "Sinterklaas," and the legend was added to by different writers. Until the early 20th century, though, Santa Claus was portrayed in many different ways. He could be tall and clad in long robes like St. Nicholas, or small with whiskers like the elves who helped Christkindlein.

Have yourself a corporate Christmas

In 1881, Thomas Nast, a caricaturist for *Harper's Weekly,* first drew Santa as a merry figure in red with flowing whiskers, an image close to the one we know today. Printer Louis Prang used a similar image in 1885 when he introduced Christmas cards to America. In 1931, the Coca-Cola Company first employed Haddon Sundblom to illustrate its annual advertisements, choosing a Santa dressed in red and white to match the corporate colors. By then, however, this was already the most popular image of Santa Claus, one that was described in detail in a *New York Times* article in 1927. If Coca-Cola had really invented Santa Claus, children would likely be saving the milk and leaving him Coke and cookies on Christmas Eve.

The Holiday Season?

Every year the debate begins as to whether or not to call it "Christmastime" or the "Holiday Season."

As much as many of us love Christmas, the fact remains that there are a number of holidays on the calendar right around the same time. Some are old, some are new, and some aren't really celebrated by anyone anymore.

Ashura	Varies; mid-December–January	Islam
Boxing Day	December 26	British Commonwealth
Dongzhi Festival	December 22	Various Asian cultures
Festivus	December 23	Consumers, *Seinfeld* fans
Hanukkah	Varies; typically December	Judaism
Humanlight	December 23	International Humanists
Kwanzaa	December 26–January 1	African Americans
Natalis Invicti	December 25	Pagan Rome—Sol Invicti
Pancha Ganapati	December 21–25	Hinduism
St. Nicholas Day	December 5/6	Christianity
St. Stephen's Day	December 26/27	Christianity
Saturnalia	December 17–23	Pagan Rome—Saturn
Yalda	December 20	Zoroastrianism
Yule	December 25	Pagan Northern Europe

When Christmas Was Canceled

♟ ♟ ♟

*Numerous children's stories and movie plots concern
themselves with the terrifying question, "What if Christmas
never came?" Well, in England in the mid-17th century,
it didn't. Under the rule of Oliver Cromwell and
the Long Parliament, Christmas was officially banned.*

England's Christmas past

In England in the 1600s, under the rule of King Charles I, Christmas
was a big deal. December 25 marked not just the birth of Christ but
the beginning of an extended period of celebration. "The Twelve
Days of Christmas" comes from this time, as Christmas Day was just
the first day of the party. The next 12 days were full of feasting,
carnivals, and celebration, all to mark the highest holy day of the
year. Though the English calendar wouldn't be synched up with the
Continental calendar for another hundred years or so, most folks
recognized January 1 as the start of the new year, so the winter
holidays for English people at that time looked a lot like ours do
now.

Some people didn't see all the merrymaking as positive, however.
Along with the happy gift-giving, garland decorations, mincemeat
pies, and days off of work came a fair amount of drunkenness and
gambling. For some—many of whom were soon to come into
power—Christmas was a gross display of sin and debauchery and
had to be stopped.

The Puritans take over

After the execution of King Charles (he had made more than a few
enemies during his tumultuous time as king and was beheaded in
1649), a soldier and politician named Oliver Cromwell helped
dissolve England's monarchy and turn it into a commonwealth. The
Long Parliament ran things until Cromwell, one of the most contro-
versial figures in world history, conquered Ireland and Scotland and
ruled as Lord Protector from 1653 until his death in 1658.

Cromwell and the members of the parliament were Puritans, which meant that for them, the English Reformation hadn't gone far enough when it split from the Roman Catholic Church. Puritans advocated for more purity and piety in worship and doctrine—they were evangelical and liked it that way. For Cromwell and his parliament, the Christmas ways of the time were detestable holdovers from Catholicism and had no place in their new England. So they decided to cancel it.

Christmas is canceled

In the early 1640s, the dampening of Christmas began. Parliament started by calling December 25 "Christ-tide," doing away with the "mass" part of the word, which to them sounded way too Catholic. They decreed that the day should be recognized, if at all, as a day of fasting and seeking the Lord. They also set in motion a fasting schedule for the people that requested they fast every last Wednesday of the month. They hoped that "Christ-tide" would get absorbed into these typical fasting days and be no big deal.

By 1644, parliament was firm in its forbidding of the holiday-formerly-known-as-Christmas. They decreed that the day was to be observed with fasting and humiliation only, not with gifts or demon drink. In fact, they recommended that much of the day be spent in remembering those sinners in the past who had used the holy day as a reason for all play and no work. By 1645, it was actually illegal to celebrate Christmas. By 1647, people were also banned from celebrating Easter. Cromwell and his parliament were firm: Only Sundays were considered holy days for worship and prayer. All the old holidays were "vulgar" and "had no warrant in the Word of God."

Yeah, no thanks

Just because the new, bold government had made its decree didn't mean everyone followed it. In fact, open defiance toward the law was commonplace among those who refused to allow the government to interfere with their religious beliefs. Semi-clandestine religious services marking Christ's Nativity were held all over England and Wales, and though the police were instructed to punish those who held them, they could hardly get to everyone. People also refused to work on Christmas, boldly closing up shops that Cromwell had told them must be kept open. This didn't happen without incident, of course; there were countless altercations between the police and the people and also between those who conformed to the new rules and those who didn't.

Christmas: back and better than ever

But the Puritans didn't last long. Cromwell died of malaria in 1658 and his son Richard took over for a year, but he was inept and lost control almost immediately. The Protectorate was dissolved, and the monarchy was restored with the crowning of King Charles II in 1660.

After the Restoration, all legislation from the period of 1642 to 1660 was declared null and void, including the Directory of Public Worship, which had abolished Christmas. Both the religious and the secular elements of the full 12 days of Christmas could once again be celebrated openly. People rejoiced far and wide, and the Christmas holiday came back with a bang.

Once again, the goodwill of Christmas returned to England and Wales. William Winstanley, a poet—and one of those people who never stopped celebrating Christmas in the first place—wrote that roaring log fires should be lit in every room and an "especially jolly blaze" should be tended in the hall. He suggested that "Good, nappy [nut-brown] ale" was to flow freely, and that tables should groan with beef, turkeys, geese, ducks, and capons, as well as mince pies and plum puddings. Winstanley, like most of his peers, believed that Christmas was a time to show goodwill toward one's fellow human and to enjoy the many blessings of the day. He and his compatriots were among those who brought Christmas back from the dead and helped make the holiday the massive event it is today.

Postscript: take that, Cromwell!

Speaking of dead, what about Cromwell's legacy? You'd think people would be pretty angry with the guy. You're more right than you know. In 1661, Cromwell's body was exhumed from his grave at Westminster Abbey and was subjected to a posthumous execution—that's how angry people were. They hung his corpse in chains in the village of Tyburn, the primary location of the execution of London criminals. After that, they stuck his head on a stake outside Westminster Hall for over 20 years until it was eventually buried at Cambridge.

Merry Christmas, Cromwell!

Spin Mobsters

*In times past, the Mafia's PR machine went
into overdrive during the holidays.*

Members of the Mafia always claimed to outsiders that "the Mafia" didn't even exist, but they weren't dumb enough to believe that anyone was buying that line. They knew that the general public was aware that La Cosa Nostra controlled everything from gambling to prostitution to garbage pickup in some cities across America. Throughout the 20th century, New York, Chicago, Las Vegas, and every major metropolitan area in the United States had an active mob presence, and the leaders of these criminal gangs were eager to pacify the "little people" in the communities they controlled. What better time to present a kinder, gentler face of the Mafia than Christmas?

A turkey you can't refuse

New York gangster Joe Colombo tried denying the Mafia's existence by founding such groups as the Italian-American Civil Rights League (first called the Italian American Defamation League), which fought the stereotyping of Italians as mobsters and even sent members to picket the offices of the FBI. But Chicago mob boss Al Capone took a more practical approach to community relations. When the holidays rolled around, he'd roll his troops into the poor Italian, Irish, and Jewish neighborhoods he controlled. Their trucks were piled high with booze, turkeys, and toys. Compared to the money they were making on their nefarious dealings, what they spent on these Christmas handouts was just a drop in the bucket, but to the poverty-stricken residents of the ghettos, it looked like a fortune.

Why wasn't the mob prevented from manipulating the poor in this deceitful manner? The truth is, many in law enforcement turned a blind eye because they, too, were being paid off. It would be many years before the Mafia was pressured to end such public displays during the Christmas season.

Christmas Windows: A Glimpse of Heaven (and Presents!)

If you've ever been downtown in a large city around the holidays, you've likely gone to check out the window displays created by the big department stores. Those fantasyland scenes that inspire thousands of Christmas lists every year were born not so very long ago.

Right this way, Mr. Field

In Chicago in the mid-1800s, there was a shopping revolution afoot. A dry-goods store owned by a merchant named Marshall Field was expanding. Opened in 1852, the store traded hands a few times before becoming the domain of the savvy entrepreneur. Field made dozens of advances in the shopping experience that turned the typical dry-goods store into what was deemed a "department store." Field's flagship location on Chicago's bustling State Street boasted, over the years, the first escalator, the first bridal registry, the first personal shoppers (a free service), and was even the first store to offer revolving credit.

In 1897, the popular store pioneered window display design, too. Up until then, window displays were heavy on product and light on art; in 1897, Field hired a full-time window designer named Arthur Fraser to focus on making the windows of the State Street store works of art, not just product displays. He figured it would draw more business, and it did; but it also became a destination spot for Chicagoans and visitors from around the world.

Christmas blitz

The window display extravaganzas continued through World War II. Fraser was a bit of a dictator, giving strict orders to his staff in order to make the windows look just so. The State Street store had 65 huge windows for Fraser to play with, and he implemented the design flavors of the years, sometimes working up funky Art Deco scenes, sometimes playing with minimalism—but he always delivered serious Christmas bling.

During wartime, a plan was hatched that would take the store's Christmas window design to the next level. Fraser's team designed theme windows that spanned the *entire* length of State Street. As shoppers and passersby walked from one end of the block to the other, the windows told an intricate, tricked-out Christmas story.

Before long, the windows were a Chicago institution and department stores across the country began to follow suit, including Macy's in New York. Children (and adults) delighted in the scenes, which often involved moving parts, such as toy trains and automated figurines, snow scenes, reindeer, and of course, lots of mouth-watering products that could be found inside the department store.

To window dressing, and beyond!

High-style window dressing has always been about the sale, even if it seems like art for art's sake. The reason Field's started the trend was to get people who were looking at the windows outside to come *inside* and make purchases. It's certainly no different now—and with more stores doing window decorations, plus the added threat of online shopping, the stakes are even higher. This competition translates to ever more opulent window dressings at Christmastime.

Product and movie tie-ins are common, reflecting the tastes and the trends of the year. Harry Potter–themed windows were big in the early part of the 2000s, and in 2009, the friendly characters from *The Fantastic Mr. Fox* film were incorporated into the Bergdorf Goodman holiday display windows. Visitors to New York's Macy's will find that there are two sets of Christmas window displays at that particular store; one along 34th Street that is always a *Miracle on 34th Street*–themed window display (part of the movie takes place at Macy's, after all) and the other display on Broadway that changes every year.

Though it was Chicago's Marshall Field who pioneered Christmas window dressing, windows into the wonder of Christmas and a child's imagination can be found today at many stores, including Saks Fifth Avenue, Bloomingdale's, Lord & Taylor, Bergdorf Goodman, and others.

Happy window shopping!

This Verse Is Worse

*Here are some later verses of well-known Christmas carols.
See if you can guess the song.*

1. **Bring me flesh and bring me wine/Bring me pine logs hither/Thou and I will see him dine/When we bear him thither.**
   a. "Here We Come A-Wassailing"
   b. "It Came upon the Midnight Clear"
   c. "Good King Wenceslas"
   d. "We Three Kings of Orient Are"

2. **Myrrh is mine, its bitter perfume/Breathes of life of gathering gloom/Sorrowing, sighing, bleeding, dying/Sealed in the stone-cold tomb.**
   a. "While Shepherds Watched Their Flocks"
   b. "It Came upon the Midnight Clear"
   c. "Good King Wenceslas"
   d. "We Three Kings of Orient Are"

3. **No more let sins and sorrows grow,/Nor thorns infest the ground;/He comes to make His blessings flow/Far as the curse is found.**
   a. "Good King Wenceslas"
   b. "Joy to the World"
   c. "It Came upon the Midnight Clear"
   d. "O Come, O Come, Emmanuel"

4. **Next year I'll be going straight;/Next year I'll be good, just wait/I'd start now, but it's too late.**
   a. "The Chipmunk Song"
   b. "Santa Baby"
   c. "Jingle Bell Rock"
   d. "Nuttin' for Christmas"

Answers: 1. c; 2. d; 3. b; 4. d

Dead as a Doornail?
Perish the Thought!

Shakespeare scripted it and Dickens popularized it, but people have been using the phrase "dead as a doornail" as a description for demise for as long as words have been printed on paper.

Although the origin of the phrase "dead as a doornail" is not entirely known, its meaning is certain. To be "dead as a doornail" is to be truly and without question expired, passed on, totally bereft of life, and pushing up daises. The phrase was used in the poem "The Vision of Piers Plowman," which was written by William Langland sometime in the late 1300s. And in Act IV, Scene X of his epic play *Henry VI, Part 2*, William Shakespeare also scripted the slogan. The character John Cade utters this threat, "if I do not leave you all as dead/as a door-nail, I pray God I may never eat grass more."

Nailing down the truth

Okay, so the dead part is clear enough; it's the doornail part that leaves most scholars scratching their heads. Charles Dickens popularized the parlance in the opening lines of his iconic novel *A Christmas Carol* when the narrator states emphatically that Old Marley is dead as a door-nail, but just a few lines later, the narrator continues: "Mind! I don't mean to say that I know, of my own knowledge, what there is particularly dead about a door-nail."

Some astute authorities in the diction of demise have decided the most logical conclusion relates to carpentry. If you hammer a nail through a piece of timber, such as a door, and bend the end over on the other side so it cannot be removed—a technique called *clinching*—the nail is said to be *dead*, because it can't be used again.

MEXICO

In Mexico, a day-long party is a good excuse to skip work or school, but a week-long festival is even better. Las Posadas, the cherished Mexican Christmas holiday, is no exception.

Mexicans need little reason to throw a party. Indeed, a quick glance at the calendar and you'll find a festival or holiday to celebrate in every month. This is especially true in December, when Christmas festivities kick into high gear mid-month with *Las Posadas*. As colorful as carnival, this beloved nine-day event began eons ago as a way to help children learn the Nativity story. So loved is the Las Posadas holiday that in many places pre-Posadas parties are held before the real event begins. And as these fiestas get closer to Christmas, they become more elaborate.

No room at the inn
Starting at dusk on December 16, *los niños* (children) dress in bright costumes and parade throughout their neighborhood from one house to another. Little girls vie for the role of the Virgin Mary, who gets to lead the parade through the streets riding a burro led by a boy playing Joseph. A host of heavenly angels carrying candles and Wise Men bearing gifts follow close behind. Moving down the street, the procession stops at houses along the route to request shelter at the inn—the *posada*—for the night. Like the Holy Family, they are turned away several times. At the last stop, which is often unannounced, the doors fling open to welcome the group inside. A party with refreshments or dinner usually follows, with children each getting a turn to break open a piñata.

Inn style
Many of the traditions celebrated south of the border are the same as those kept in the United States, and Mexicans go all out with holiday decorating. It's not enough to deck the halls with red and green—purple, gold, silver, and bright

yellow are also used lavishly to signal the holidays. Lights, Christmas trees, and poinsettias both inside and out are popular for decorating, but it's the Nativity that takes center stage.

In many homes, nativities, or *crèches,* are displayed prominently—at times taking up the entire room. While the Holy Family remains the focal point, entire flocks of sheep and livestock accompanied by shepherds, a host of angels, and other villagers join them in the midst of a true-to-life landscape. Small stables and workshops are tucked between waterfalls, cacti, and palm trees. Only on Christmas Eve, when baby Jesus is tucked into the manger, is the scene complete.

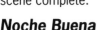

Noche Buena

The good night (Noche Buena) in Mexico is Christmas Eve, and what a night it is. The revelry begins in early afternoon when family and friends get together for the last posada. After a late-night *Misa de Gallo,* or rooster's mass, everyone heads home to eat. Forget the usual fare of tacos and queso—platters of roast pig or turkey accompanied by tamales, rice, and a traditional Christmas Eve fruit salad made of beets, mandarin oranges, pineapple, jicama, and lettuce are customary dishes. Glasses of *rompope,* the Mexican version of eggnog, are passed around the table to wash it all down.

The party stretches into the wee hours, ending with a visit from *el Niño Dios,* the Christ child, who brings presents on Christmas Eve night. Santa, who began visiting Mexico only in the last 50 years, leaves his gifts Christmas morning for the children. After almost a month of merrymaking, Christmas Day itself is low-key, with most folks staying home and resting.

Of course, the siestas don't last long; just around the corner on January 6 is Epiphany, or Three Kings' Day, one of the first big festivals of the new year.

A Real American Hero

Ever wonder how G.I. Joe invaded the holiday toy aisle?

In the 1960s, Mattel's Barbie was the "it" toy for girls. Larry Reiner, who designed toys at Ideal Toy Company, envisioned a Barbie-type doll for boys. Instead of a fashion doll, it would be a military soldier with articulated limbs. Reiner took the idea to Stan Weston, a licensing agent, who took it to Hasbro.

G.I. Joe was born in 1964. As Mattel did with Barbie, Hasbro gave the 11½-inch-tall character different outfits and accessories. Instead of dresses and handbags, though, Joe donned military uniforms and weapons. Instead of being called a doll, he was marketed as an "action figure." Antiwar sentiment about Vietnam changed Joe from military man to the G.I. Joe Adventure Team. The famous kung-fu grip was added in 1974.

Since petroleum is an important part of the plastic-making process, the oil crisis of the '70s had a drastic effect on 11½-inch action figures. They shrunk. G.I. Joe became an 8-inch figure, matching the Marvel and DC Comics superheroes from Mego.

A galaxy far, far away

The release of *Star Wars* in 1977 changed everything about action figures. George Lucas wanted scale toys of the spaceships in the movie, but it was too expensive to make one for an 8-inch figure. Instead, Kenner made 3¾-inch figures that could fit into reasonably priced X-wing fighters. When Hasbro relaunched G.I. Joe in 1982, they followed suit. They also introduced a new villain. Gone were the Adventure Team's outer-space foes from the '70s, the Intruders. G.I. Joe was back in the military. He fought Cobra Command, a secret, international terrorist organization. An animated TV series followed. The figures were more articulated than their *Star Wars* counterparts, and in 1983, they got "swivel arm battle grip," which allowed the Joes (and Cobras) to fold their arms across their bodies.

G.I. Joe continues to storm the holidays thanks to the success of the first live-action film in 2009. Sequels promise to keep the toys under the tree for many Christmases to come.

A Different Kind of Yule Log

In Catalonia, they celebrate Christmas in a truly unique way—with a defecating log.

The people of Catalonia, one of Spain's 17 autonomous communities, celebrate Christmas pretty much like the rest of the world. But they have one special holiday custom found almost nowhere else: the *Caga Tio,* or pooping log.

Feed me!

The specially designed logs, which often come with tiny legs, cute painted faces, and a beret, are offered for sale at the beginning of each holiday season. Beginning on December 8, at the start of the Feast of the Immaculate Conception, the children give the log a little "snack" each day and cover it with a blanket to keep it warm.

As Christmas approaches, parents secretly substitute larger and larger logs to give the impression that the Caga Tio is growing. Then, on Christmas Eve or Christmas Day, as the family sings, the covered log is placed midway in an unlit fireplace (if the household has one) and ordered to "defecate" while being struck with sticks. Hidden under the blanket is a selection of small treats, such as candy, nuts, coins, and dried fruit, which are shared by all family members. The fun is over when the Caga Tio "poops" a salted herring, which signifies that it is empty. (Don't tell, but the parents place it there!)

Another pooper?

A similarly themed Catalonian Christmas custom is the *caganer,* or "pooper." Traditionally, this is a small wood or porcelain figurine of a person squatting, which is discreetly hidden in a dark corner of a nativity scene so as not to be disrespectful. In some parts of Catalonia, children make a holiday game of searching for the caganer in their family's nativity arrangement.

The origins of the caganer tradition are vague, but some believe it started among peasant farmers who believed the figure's fecal offerings would help ensure that their fields remained fertile and productive in the coming year.

Poinsettias

It wouldn't be Christmas without bright red poinsettias. Known as the "Christmas flower" in America, these leafy botanicals have a storied history.

The story of the poinsettia actually begins in Mexico—not America. In 1828, Joel Roberts Poinsett, the first United States Ambassador to Mexico and a novice botanist, scoured the Mexican countryside in his free time in search of interesting, new plant species. He found a brilliant shrub with large red flowers growing wild next to a roadside. With cuttings he brought back to his greenhouse in South Carolina, Poinsett cultivated plants to give as gifts. In doing so, his famed reputation as a statesman was eventually overshadowed by his Christmas gift to future generations: the poinsettia.

A humble gift

Mexicans have long credited Pepita, a poor Mexican girl, with the origin of the poinsettia. When she was to approach the Christ child and present a gift one Christmas Eve, she was wrought with sadness by the fact that she had no gift to offer. "Even the most humble gift, if given in love, will be acceptable in his eyes," consoled her cousin, Pedro. She considered his advice, then gathered a handful of common weeds. Still, she grew embarrassed by her scraggly offering and cried, but she remembered her cousin's thoughtful words as she knelt at the manger in the nativity scene. Suddenly, the bouquet of weeds bloomed a brilliant red, and it was proclaimed by all who saw it a Christmas miracle. Since that fabled Christmas Eve night, the red flowers have been known as *Flores de Noche Buena,* or Flowers of the Holy Night, since they bloom yearly during the Christmas season.

Getting the facts

As with many Christmas traditions, the poinsettia has a colorful history. Some of the tales are true; others completely false. Consider these points to set the record straight:

- Over 70 million poinsettia plants are sold throughout the United States each year, making the poinsettia the number one flowering potted plant sold.

- Poinsettias are NOT poisonous but they do have an acrid, bitter taste. Some believe that the myth of their toxicity started in 1919, when a two-year-old child in Hawaii was found dead under a full-grown poinsettia tree, grasping a poinsettia leaf in her hand. However, the POISINDEX Information Service estimates that a 50-pound child would need to ingest about 500 to 600 poinsettia bracts, or leaves, for a potentially toxic dose. The plant is not harmful to pets, either, though it can cause a tummy ache.

- A German botanist by the name of Wilenow assigned the plant its botanical name, *Euphorbia pulcherrima;* the second word means "very beautiful." It is estimated that there are 700 to 1,000 species found throughout the world.

- Poinsettias are warm weather tropical plants. In their native Central America and Mexico, they grow as shrubs and can reach up to 10 feet tall. Though they are best known as Christmas plants, they cannot withstand cold temperatures but thrive best inside at room temperature.

- The most popular color for poinsettias is the traditional red, but they are also available in white, cream, pink, and yellow and can be striped, spotted, or marbled (or even spraypainted other colors).

- Poinsettias don't have flowers. Instead, their leaves, called bracts, give the plant its colorful appearance. About eight weeks before Christmas, nurseries place the plants in complete darkness for at least 14 hours a day to force the bracts to change color. Because the ratio of sunlight hours to darkness triggers the coloration, the longer the plants are left in darkness, the brighter their leaves.

Christmas Hits
Not Christmasy?

*You'd think the No. 1 Billboard hit on Christmas Day
would make you feel all warm and cozy, but I don't think
Snoop Dogg's "Drop It Like It's Hot" is what we're going for!*

Over the last 50 years, the No. 1 hit on Christmas Day in America,
according to *Billboard Magazine,* has not been a Christmas song.
Though a few have had religious overtones (see 1998 or 1970), none
has mentioned our favorite holiday by name. We have to go back
over 50 years for the last time that happened! There are a few other
interesting facts to note about this list as well. The Beatles have two
No. 1 spots on the list, and Ringo Starr is the only Beatle to not have
a solo hit on the Christmas list. Americans have favored almost every
genre of popular music on Christmas Day, and the only Belgian song
to ever reach No. 1 in the United States is on the list for 1963.

2009	"Empire State of Mind," Jay-Z and Alicia Keys
2008	"Single Ladies (Put a Ring on It)," Beyoncé
2007	"No One," Alicia Keys
2006	"Irreplaceable," Beyoncé
2005	"Don't Forget About Us," Mariah Carey
2004	"Drop It Like It's Hot," Snoop Dogg, featuring Pharrell
2003	"Hey Ya!," OutKast
2002	"Lose Yourself," Eminem
2001	"How You Remind Me," Nickelback
2000	"Independent Women Part I," Destiny's Child
1999	"Smooth," Santana, featuring Rob Thomas
1998	"I'm Your Angel," R. Kelly and Celine Dion
1997	"Candle in the Wind 1997," Elton John
1996	"Un-Break My Heart," Toni Braxton
1995	"One Sweet Day," Mariah Carey & Boyz II Men
1994	"On Bended Knee," Boyz II Men
1993	"Hero," Mariah Carey
1992	"I Will Always Love You," Whitney Houston

1991 "Black or White," Michael Jackson
1990 "Because I Love You (The Postman Song)," Stevie B
1989 "Another Day in Paradise," Phil Collins
1988 "Every Rose Has Its Thorn," Poison
1987 "Faith," George Michael
1986 "Walk Like an Egyptian," The Bangles
1985 "Say You, Say Me," Lionel Richie
1984 "Like a Virgin," Madonna
1983 "Say, Say, Say," Paul McCartney and Michael Jackson
1982 "Maneater," Daryl Hall & John Oates
1981 "Physical," Olivia Newton-John
1980 "(Just Like) Starting Over," John Lennon
1979 "Escape (The Piña Colada Song)," Rupert Holmes
1978 "Le Freak," Chic
1977 "How Deep Is Your Love," The Bee Gees
1976 "Tonight's the Night (Gonna Be Alright)," Rod Stewart
1975 "Let's Do It Again," The Staple Singers
1974 "Angie Baby," Helen Reddy
1973 "Time in a Bottle," Jim Croce
1972 "Me and Mrs. Jones," Billy Paul
1971 "Brand New Key," Melanie
1970 "My Sweet Lord/Isn't It a Pity," George Harrison
1969 "Someday We'll Be Together," Diana Ross and the Supremes
1968 "I Heard It Through the Grapevine," Marvin Gaye
1967 "Hello Goodbye," The Beatles
1966 "I'm a Believer," The Monkees
1965 "Over and Over," The Dave Clark Five
1964 "I Feel Fine," The Beatles
1963 "Dominique," The Singing Nun
1962 "Telstar," The Tornadoes
1961 "The Lion Sleeps Tonight," The Tokens
1960 "Are You Lonesome Tonight," Elvis Presley
1959 "Why," Frankie Avalon
1958 "The Chipmunk Song" ("Christmas Time Is Near"), David Seville & the Chipmunks

We Three (?) Kings

Tradition tells us that three kings came from the East to honor Jesus at his birth. But they weren't kings, and there may have been more than three of them.

According to the Gospel of Matthew, "After Jesus was born in Bethlehem in Judea, during the time of King Herod, magi from the east came to Jerusalem." The word *after* is important: Countless Christmas pageants notwithstanding, the magi ("wise men") were not present at the manger scene with the sheep, goats, and shepherds. Although it's not known exactly what country the wise men came from—it could have been Persia or Babylon—the journey must have taken weeks or even months. By the time the men arrived, Joseph and Mary had been able to find more comfortable lodging. (Matthew indicates this when he says, "On coming to the house, they saw the child with his mother, Mary.")

So who were the magi? They appear to have been religious or governmental officials who were well versed in astrology. They may have been followers of the Persian prophet Zoroaster.

The wise men interpreted the mysterious star of Bethlehem as the birth announcement of an extremely important king, and they headed off to pay their respects. They took along valuable gifts—gold, frankincense, and myrrh—just as diplomatic visitors today might bear gifts representing the best of their country's offerings.

Because Matthew mentions three gifts, early readers assumed that there were just three magi. People also began to think of them as kings, probably seeing the visit as a fulfillment of this verse in the Bible (Psalm 72:11): "All kings will bow down to him and all nations will serve him." But Matthew is unclear about their job titles and doesn't say anything about their numbers. So the song "We Three Kings," written by John H. Hopkins Jr. in 1857, is more poetic than accurate.

Santa, Baby

*The best Christmas gift Babe Ruth
gave to kids was himself.*

There is a famous photograph that shows Babe Ruth surrounded
by what seems like a hundred clamoring children, yet that moon face
and huge grin under the straw boater are unmistakable for their goofy brightness. Ruth was in his
element, surrounded by his biggest fans and
most starstruck admirers, and he was loving
every minute of it.

Throughout his career, after ball games
and at special appearances, Ruth spent up
to several hours at a time signing autographs. He couldn't bear the thought of any
tyke going home disappointed. In New York
and on the road as well, the Babe frequently
visited hospitals to help cheer up sick children.
In 1931 alone, he played Santa Claus for hundreds of kids at city
hospitals. He also spent a lot of time visiting orphanages—probably
because he basically grew up at Saint Mary's Industrial School for
Boys, an orphanage in Baltimore.

By 1947, when Ruth could no longer deliver joy to fans with his
majestic home runs and, in fact, could barely walk, one thing he still
could do was make children happy. That December, the cancer-stricken Ruth painfully pulled on a Santa Claus suit, beard and all,
and handed out presents to young victims of polio at the Hotel Astor
in New York. As their faces lit up, it was clear their delight gave
Babe much joy. Afterward, he pulled down his beard and addressed
the cameras and microphones. Though his voice was subdued and
raspy, he spoke with the utmost sincerity. "I want to take this opportunity," he said, "to wish all the children—not only in America, but
all over the world—a very merry Christmas." Throughout his life,
Babe Ruth had played Saint Nick to a lot of kids in a lot of ways, and
his last Christmas was no different.

The Cost of Being Santa

Santa has an expensive job. It's no wonder he has an army of cheap laborers making toys for him year-round.

With all the other costs associated with being the big man, there's no way that Santa could afford to purchase all those toys and goodies for everyone—so those elves come in handy! Even with some of the great deals on the Internet these days, there's just no way Kris Kringle could come up with the money for gifts and operating expenses without a government bailout.

In the red ... suit

At the very least, Santa needs to stay bundled up. If not for the signature red and white fur suit, he'd look like any other attendee at a Grizzly Adams convention, so it's important that he dress the part. That said, Santa's threads are pricey. A good Santa suit can run upward of $500, and that's assuming he hasn't shaved his signature whiskers. A quality replacement beard will run him at least another $100!

Studying more than the naughty & nice list

Of course, it takes more than white hair and a red outfit to fill the boots of the world's jolliest bringer of joy. There are a number of schools, seminars really, for those who would don the mantle of Santa. For a day or two of time, and often more than $400, Santa can keep up on the best tricks of his trade! Luckily, with as busy as he gets, Kris Kringle can also order a correspondence course for only $200 if he wants to brush up without leaving the North Pole. After all, a man who travels the entire globe can never be too prepared!

The Christmas blessing of anonymity

For a busy man like Santa, known and adored the world over, getting away for a vacation might seem next to impossible. After all, with such a well-known face, he has to expect that autograph seekers and paparazzi will hound him wherever he goes. The safest way to plan a vacation then would probably be to crash the Santa convention in Gatlinburg, Tennessee, and try to blend in. If he decided to attend as just another impersonator, he could expect to pay over $300 ($420 if he registered late). Alternatively, he could always attend as a vendor and teach some of his secrets for a fee. Setting up a booth for that would run him between $350 and $2,000 for the three-day event. Unfortunately, he would also have to factor in other costs, such as meals, the Jingle Bell Ball, and parking for his sleigh and eight tiny reindeer.

Not just giving at the office

Finally, we would do well to remember that Santa is the master of charitable contributions. In 2009, the Make-A-Wish foundation received up to a $1 million contribution from Macy's, the home of the real Santa, so add that to his tab. We also should not forget Santa's militia: the Salvation Army. The bell ringers donning his visage help bring in more than $800 million in charitable contributions to the organization every year. Then there's the work he does with the U.S. Marine Corps, bringing in over $80 million in cash and gifts for needy kids across America. All charitable donations aside, Santa also does a road tour, visiting 25 cities around the United States in the month leading up to Christmas Day. Factor in the cost of the tour bus, roadies, and carting a team of elves from city to city to visit various children's hospitals, and Mr. Kringle's bills must be astronomical!

So remember folks, when the holidays draw near, and belts get tighter, at least the rest of us don't have to worry about the extra costs of the season that Saint Nick incurs without complaint each and every year.

"Christmas is not as much about opening our presents as opening our hearts."
—Janice Maeditere

Christmas Around the World

SWEDEN

*When the Swedes say it's cold outside, you'd better believe it:
It's cold outside. What better way, then, to ward off the winter
drearies than with a party that lasts almost two months?*

With the North Pole as a nearby neighbor, it's no wonder Scandinavians are crazy about Christmas. After all, making merry for the holidays is a welcome distraction, dangling as they are in the frigid cold above all the other European countries. Most welcome the snowy weather and the outdoor activities it affords: Skiing, snowshoeing—even reindeer-sledding—are popular pastimes. Between sports, everyone finds time to celebrate the holidays.

Seeing red

The dawn of December signals Advent, a month-long holiday honoring the birth of Jesus celebrated by Christians worldwide. Each Sunday leading up to Christmas, families light a candle, with the last candle being lit on Christmas Day in honor of Jesus' birth. The difference in Sweden, however, is that the Advent season also kicks off a series of parties and feast days.

December is filled with several "red days," so named by the Swedes since holidays are generally printed in red on calendars. A favorite is St. Lucia Day, or the Festival of Lights, which is not an official holiday but kept nonetheless by most people throughout Sweden. Celebrated December 13, the day honors St. Lucia, a young girl martyred for her Christian faith in the fourth century. Hers is a grotesque story: Legend has it that she was stabbed, her eyeballs were gouged out, and she was thrown into a fire to burn. As such, she is remembered as the patron saint of light. The Festival of Lights coincides with St. Lucia Day and marks the promise of the sun's return—an all-important promise since there is little sunlight in the winter in many parts of Scandinavia.

In the past, St. Lucia Day was marked by a young girl dressing in a white gown with a red sash. A wreath of lit candles was placed on her head in honor of the martyred St. Lucia, blinded for her Christian beliefs. Today, however, the tradition lives on with girls wearing the gowns and wreaths of (battery-powered) candles on their heads. The oldest daughter awakens her family on the morning of December 13 with songs, saffron buns, and coffee.

Elf watch

The biggest celebration of the year, however, is Christmas Eve—*Julafton*—when families feast on a traditional Swedish smorgasbord. Christmas ham, pickled pigs' feet, *lutefisk* (fish soaked in lye), boiled wheat (*cuccidata*), cabbage pudding, baby potatoes, sweet carrots, deviled eggs, saffron buns with raisins, lingonberry pie, *pepparkakor* (sweet ginger cookies), and rice pudding are part of a typical holiday meal. Of course, no party would be complete without *glögg*, a strong but sweet hot mulled wine that instantly warms the body.

Just after dinner, children look for *tomte* to arrive. These mischievous elves live underneath the floorboards but come out once a year to deliver presents on Christmas Eve to everyone. In the past, they were thought to protect the livestock and children of farmers. One in particular, *Jultomte,* dresses much like Santa Claus in a red and white suit (see page 128). In the late evening and early morning, families head to church.

The Twelve Days of Christmas and Epiphany follow in January, but the season doesn't end until St. Knut's Day on January 13. On this day, the 20th day after Christmas, with *knut* being the word for 20, families take down the Christmas tree and polish off any edible ornaments left over from the holiday.

"And that, of course, is the message of Christmas, we are never alone."

—*Taylor Caldwell*

SANTA WHO?

JULTOMTE

"Finns det några snälla barn här?" asks Jultomte.
Well, are there any nice children here?

Scandanavian boys and girls can tell you about *Jultomte,* their version of Father Christmas. If your Swedish Jultomte (Norwegian *Julenisse,* Danish *Julemand,* or Finnish *Joulupukki*) knowledge is lacking, read on for more about the version of Santa for the folks near the North Pole.

Farmer's little helper

In the beginning, Jultomte was a shape-shifting, often one-eyed creature that kept an eye on the family farm. Sometimes called "Robin Goodfellow," *Tuftekall,* or *Tomtegubbe,* the legend of this sprite goes back for centuries. Sometimes he has a beard, sometimes not; sometimes he wears woolen underwear. Whatever the incarnation, the *tomte* wasn't purely benevolent. In the beginning, this *nisse,* or "brownie," was said to have a hot temper and little patience for farmers who showed the land or their animals disrespect.

As the region was Christianized in the 14th century, the tomte became an issue. Christian believers decried pagan characters and belief in them was met with scorn or even punishment. That didn't keep many Scandinavians from believing in the tomte, but they didn't talk about it. In the 19th century, the tomte came back into fashion.

With the help of popular fairy tale authors, including Hans Christian Andersen, the nisse would find their day in the sun again, but not without a facelift. In Denmark in the mid-1800s, various articles, poems, and paintings began to emerge that connected the character with the spirit of Christmas. The trend caught on, perhaps since the Jultomte was more fun than the celebrated *Julbock,* or Yule Goat.

Jultomte has begun to resemble the European and American Father Christmas, but there are differences. Jultomte isn't fat and doesn't come down chimneys—he comes in the door on Christmas Eve—and he forgoes reindeer for a goat. He appreciates porridge left out for him, but he doesn't live at the North Pole, opting to relax in a forest nearby until it's Christmas again.

Mrs. Claus:
First Lady of Christmas

Behind every great man is a great woman—and Santa Claus is no different. Mrs. Claus has been around for less than 200 years, but she is definitely a fixture on the Christmas scene today. You go, girl!

References to the unexamined wife of Santa Claus popped up around the mid-1800s, several in pretty highbrow places. *Yale Literary Magazine* made a reference to her in 1851, and *Harper's* mentioned a Mrs. Claus in an 1862 piece. *Lill's Travels in Santa Claus Land and Other Short Stories* hit stores in 1878 and told how Mrs. Claus helped Santa record names of the good (and bad) children.

But it wasn't till 1889, with the publication of Katharine Lee Bates's poem "Goody Santa Claus on a Sleigh Ride," that Mrs. Claus got significant press and jumped full-time into the Christmas season. The poem was published in a collection of Bates's children's stories, and it featured the "goodwife" or "goody" of Santa. Bates, who wrote the lyrics to "America the Beautiful," was a gifted storyteller and used the poem to tell of Mrs. Claus's first ride with her husband and how she mended the stocking of a poor child so that he could receive gifts on Christmas. From then on, fans of Christmas had a new character to enjoy during the holiday season.

Will the real Mrs. Claus please stand up?

Because Mrs. Claus is a fairly new figure on the scene, her image and personality are still up for interpretation. Most of the time, this white-haired, bespectacled, plump older lady is simply the devoted wife of Santa, helping him manage the elves and keeping the register of children both naughty and nice. She's often seen in the kitchen, baking cookies and sweets for Santa, who loves and appreciates her.

Mrs. Claus has taken on various different guises in books, movies, and advertisements. She's been seen as a feminist, a woman bored with her marriage, and a rather amorous woman (to put it nicely). However she's seen, she's a fixture in the cast of modern-day North American Christmas and is sure to stick around for a long time.

The Poetry of Christmas

*The beauty of the season lent itself well to
some of the greatest poets who ever lived.*

Sure, everyone remembers Clement Clarke Moore's poem "A Visit
from St. Nicolas," which is better known these days as "'Twas the
Night Before Christmas." But sadly, the same can't be said for a few
of these other Christmas poems that were written by some of the
brightest minds of the 17th, 18th, 19th, and 20th centuries. Which
ones do you recall?

- **"Christmas Bells," Henry Wadsworth Longfellow:** This poem
  is well known because it was later set to music by John Baptiste
  Calkin in a carol: "I heard the bells on Christmas Day/Their old
  familiar carols play/And wild and sweet/The words repeat/Of
  peace on earth, good will to men!" Many people do not know,
  however, that Longfellow wrote those words in 1864, as the Civil
  War raged. He included the lines, "God is not dead, nor does he
  sleep/The Wrong shall fail/the Right prevail..." Longfellow's hope
  was remarkable in light of his wife Fanny's death in a freak sealing-
  wax accident a few years before.

- **"A Christmas Carol," G. K. Chesterton:** Though Chesterton
  did not convert to Roman Catholicism until 1922, this poem—
  published at the turn of the 20th century—hints that he was
  headed that way. It is almost as much about the Virgin Mary as it is
  about the infant Jesus. Mary's name is invoked in the first line of
  each of the four stanzas, as it is here in the first: "The Christ-child
  lay on Mary's lap/His hair was like a light/O weary, weary were the
  world/But here is all alright."

- **"A Christmas Carol," Samuel Taylor Coleridge:** Yeah, this
  one is called *A Christmas Carol* too, but it was written a whole
  century before Chesterton's. Coleridge was part of the English
  Romantic movement and is better known for such epic poems as
  The Rime of the Ancient Mariner and *Kubla Khan*. Idealistic and
  progressive, he used "A Christmas Carol" to decry and personify

war: "A murderous fiend, by fiends adored/He kills the sire and starves the son...Plunders God's world of beauty; rends away/All safety from the night, all comfort from the day."

- **"Nativity: A Christmas Poem," John Donne:** Raised in an English Catholic family at a time when being a Catholic in England could get one killed, and later denied degrees from both Oxford and Cambridge because of his religion, Donne finally converted to the Church of England in the early 1600s. His devout Christianity is apparent in many of his poems, including "Nativity": "Seest thou, my soul, with thy faith's eyes, how He/Which fills all place, yet none holds Him, doth lie?/Was not His pity towards thee wondrous high?"

- **"The Oxen, A Christmas Poem," Thomas Hardy:** So famous for late-19th century novels, including *Tess of the d'Urbervilles* and *Jude the Obscure,* that his poetry is often forgotten, Hardy employed his trademark realism in this rather dark and dreary Christmas poem: "If someone said on Christmas Eve/'Come see the oxen kneel/In the lonely barton by yonder coomb/Our childhood used to know'/I should go with him in the gloom/Hoping it might be so." Honestly, we don't know what a "barton" or a "coomb" is either, but...depressing, huh?

- **"Ring Out, Wild Bells," Alfred, Lord Tennyson:** Tennyson's 1850 Christmas poem is a lot more upbeat than Hardy's. "Ring Out, Wild Bells" looks forward to the future as a time when Christ's teachings will make the earth a more peaceful, merciful, just place to be: "Ring in the love of truth and right/Ring in the common love of good." It is part of a longer elegy called "In Memoriam," which a grief-stricken Tennyson wrote when his best friend, Arthur Henry Hallam, died suddenly of a brain hemorrhage.

Yes, Virginia, There Is a Santa Claus

A child's question elicited an adult answer.

Every year, kids write letters to Santa Claus. It's a right of passage for many. In 1897, one 8-year-old girl decided not to write a letter to Ol' Saint Nick. Instead, she wrote to *The New York Sun,* on the prompting of her father. The newspaper's response has been reprinted in newspapers around the country as a holiday tradition.

Fat man, small chimney

Virginia O'Hanlon asked her father whether Santa Claus existed. Her friends no longer believed, and she began to have her doubts, too. Her father told her to write to the newspaper and explained, "If you see it in *The Sun* it's so." Francis Pharcellus Church wrote the reply to Virginia's letter.

Church famously wrote, "Yes, Virginia, there is a Santa Claus.... How dreary would be the world if there were no Santa Claus. It would be as dreary as if there were no Virginias."

Most children who grow up celebrating Christmas have these doubts about Santa at Virginia's age. What starts as a funny story about a fat man stuffing himself down narrow chimneys and dashing around the world with a sack of gifts eventually suffers the gaze of incredulity. "How can he travel that distance in so short a time?" kids ask. "How can reindeer possibly fly?"

Kid stuff or existential angst?

On one hand, Church's editorial is charming and quaint. But is it too quaint? On quick glance, it almost seems facile—the kind of answer any parent gives to a child when they don't want to answer the question: "Of course there's a Santa Claus!" That doesn't wash for two reasons. Virginia is asking for the truth, not platitudes. In her letter, she writes, "Please tell me the truth; is there a Santa Claus?" Her dad dodged the question, and now she wants a real answer. Secondly, if we take Church's answer at face value, it's a poor one: "Nobody sees Santa Claus, but that is no sign that there is no Santa Claus." This is a very common logical fallacy. The fancy Latin name is *argumentum ad ignoratum.* Simply, it's an argument from ignorance or argument from negative evidence. It's saying that something is true because there's no evidence that it's false.

We all want to believe

Would the letter have resonated so deeply with people if it were merely a weak, off-handed piece by a bored *Sun* editor? Unlikely, and a deeper reading rewards the diligent. Church is after something much more sincere. He begins, "Virginia, your little friends are wrong. They have been affected by the skepticism of a skeptical age." This is not a response to a child. This is a response to *adults.* It is a response to the zeitgeist of a skeptical age, a century that saw factories replace the landscape during the Industrial Revolution and the country ripped in two during the Civil War. Santa Claus "exists as certainly as love and generosity and devotion exist, and you know that they abound and give to your life its highest beauty and joy," Church wrote. He knew adults need Santa Claus as much as children do, for without him, "there would be no childlike faith then, no poetry, no romance to make tolerable this existence."

There's a rather brilliant line of dialogue in *Miracle on 34th Street.* Though the film debuted 50 years after the letter, it has the same message. Maureen O'Hara's boyfriend has just quit his law firm to try to prove Kris Kringle is Santa Claus. She admonishes him for his idealism and "lovely intangibles," to which he replies, "Don't overlook those lovely intangibles. You'll discover those are the only things that are worthwhile."

Santa's Doppelganger?

*In certain parts of Europe, Santa has a twin—
and he's not a nice guy.*

Throughout most of the world, Christmas is all about gift-giving and other seasonal pleasantries. But in Germany, Austria, and other parts of Europe, there's a dark side to the holiday, and his name is Krampus.

The legend of Krampus (which is derived from the German word "krampen," which means claw) originated in the alpine regions of Germany, and it spread throughout Austria, Hungary, Bavaria, and Slovenia. Simply speaking, Krampus—who is believed to be based in part on the Norse god Loki—is an evil spirit with thick fur and large, menacing horns who delights in punishing bad children as much as Santa Claus enjoys giving gifts to those who are good. In some regions, Krampus is considered Santa's evil twin, accompanying St. Nick on his rounds.

Watch those hands!

Interestingly, in his earliest incarnations, Krampus was frequently viewed from a much more adult perspective. A product of ancient European pagan practices, he was very sexual by nature, and early depictions of the naughty spirit often showed him advancing on women the way drunken frat boys advance on coeds during spring break. His leering expression and wagging tongue clearly gave away his lascivious intent.

Krampus remains especially popular in Austria, where Krampus Night celebrations are held every December 5, the eve of St. Nicholas Day. Traditionally, young men dress up as the evil spirit and roam the streets frightening children and young women, sometimes gently (or not so gently) smacking them with a whip.

In Hungary, Krampus isn't quite as nasty. Over the years, his image has softened a bit, and he is more commonly considered a sly trickster rather than an outright evil spirit. But his mission is the same: to encourage children to be good.

How Do You Say That?

MERRY CHRISTMAS!

Haiti (Creole): Jwaye Nowel

Hausa: Barka da Kirsimatikuma Barka da Sabuwar Shekara!

Hawaiian: Mele Kalikimaka

Hebrew: Mo'adim Lesimkha. Chena tova

Hindi: Shub Naya Baras (good New Year not Merry Christmas)

Hungarian: Kellemes Karacsonyi unnepeket

Icelandic: Gledileg Jol

Indonesian: Selamat Hari Natal

Iraqi: Idah Saidan Wa Sanah Jadidah

Irish: Nollaig Shona Dhuit *or* Nodlaig mhaith chugnat

Iroquois: Ojenyunyat Sungwiyadeson honungradon nagwutut. Ojenyunyat osrasay.

Italian: Buone Feste Natalizie *or* Buon Natale

Japanese: Shinnen omedeto. Kurisumasu Omedeto

Korean: Sung Tan Chuk Ha

Lao: souksan van Christmas

Latin: Natale Hilare

Latvian: Prieci'gus Ziemsve'tkus

Legalese: Whereas the Party of the First Part, aka "Bill," wishes to extend a heartfelt Merry Christmas to the Party of the Second Part, aka "Harry," as authorized under Provision 12, Paragraph 3, Subsection 22.

Lithuanian: Linksmu Kaledu

Low Saxon: Heughliche Winachten

No Room at the Inn?

*In the traditional Christmas story, an innkeeper turns
Mary and Joseph away from his at-capacity establishment
but offers them the use of his stable. It's a nice tale,
but there are problems with the details.*

No vacancy

In describing the event, the gospel writer Luke says, "And she
brought forth her firstborn son, and wrapped him in swaddling
clothes, and laid him in a manger; because there was no room for
them in the inn" (2:7, King James Version).

To modern readers, the word *inn* conjures up images of a cozy
bed-and-breakfast. But in Luke's original Greek, the word for inn is
kataluma, which can also be translated as "lodging place." He uses
the same word later, when referring to the guest room in which Jesus
ate the Passover meal with his disciples just before his death. At the
time, most houses had such rooms, usually on an upper level and
often with a separate entrance, which could be used by visiting
guests. It may be that Mary and Joseph were headed to such a guest
room at the house in Bethlehem, but they arrived too late and the
room was already occupied.

Away in a what?

The word *kataluma* can also refer to a large, covered shelter with
open cooking fires where travelers gathered with all their family
members and animals—a hot, crowded, noisy place that Mary and
Joseph might have wanted to avoid at the time. In any event, there
was no room, so they went to a stable, correct? Sorry—the gospels
don't mention a stable, either. After Jesus was born, Mary laid him in
a manger, or feeding trough. If the *kataluma* was in a private house,
the manger may have been in the lower level where the family's
animals were kept. Or the manger may have been in a nearby cave
where animals could stay out of the elements—not exactly the three-
sided wooden shelter of nativity scenes, but at least a more private
place in which to give birth.

Liquid Christmas Dinner

No, we're not talking about alcohol. We all know that can be disastrous at a family dinner. But Seattle-based Jones Soda Co.—which seems to have decided that if it isn't innovative it's not worth drinking—has made some interesting flavors (see bullets) through the years. Take a gander, and a drink, if you dare!

Getting the kids to sleep on Christmas Eve is always a headache and a chore. Check out this flavor to get those dreams flowing:

• Sugar plum

What sweeter way to start off Christmas morning? And you'll need to give your house a lovely Christmas feel for the family gathering:

• Jelly doughnut
• Christmas tree

The family has gathered, and it's time for appetizers:

• Salmon pâté

Everyone's stomach is growling, and it's time to sit down for dinner. Here is the menu:

• Turkey and gravy, Christmas ham
• Mashed potatoes and butter, Wild herb stuffing
• Broccoli casserole, Brussels sprouts with prosciutto, Green bean casserole

We all know that the best part of Christmas dinner is dessert:

• Fruit cake, Lemon meringue pie, Pecan pie, Pumpkin pie

After that scrumptious repast, it's time for the couch and the football games. But we all know there is usually another component to most holiday feasts:

• Antacid

Urp! Merry Christmas!

Crunching the Christmas Numbers

- In 2008, Americans spent $1.03 billion on real Christmas trees. They spent $709 million on fake ones.

- Three out of four Americans plan to pay off their holiday credit card debt within three months, but a third of consumers are still paying off debt from holiday purchases made three years ago.

- Credit counselors see approximately 40 percent more customers in January than in any other month.

- On average, 20 to 25 percent of shoppers wait until the last minute to do their shopping.

- According to the Greeting Card Association, the U.S. Postal Service delivers around 2 billion cards each Christmas. The cost of the cards comes to about $30 per family, not including postage.

- According to the Society of American Florists, poinsettias make up 83% of the holiday season's floral purchases, and the average flower customer spends about $20 a year on flowers.

- Shoppers plunk down approximately $90 apiece on groceries every Christmas.

- Close to two billion candy canes are made each season, according to the National Confectioners Association.

- Holiday sales in 2006 reached $457.4 billion; the number fluctuates slightly but that's an approximate average year to year.

- The average consumer spends about $750 each year on gifts for family members and loved ones.

- Consumers end up gifting themselves too: An average of $99 is spent on oneself while out Christmas shopping.

Christmas in Alaska

. . . where the North Pole is a reality, not a fantasy.

A luxury Christmas cruise to Alaska has become one of the most popular cruises for Americans to take, and it's not hard to figure out why. It is a myth that there is no sunlight in southern Alaska during the winter months (though the days are quite short), and nothing could possibly convey the spirit of the season better than the rugged, subarctic beauty of the 49th state. Alaska offers American travelers the adventure and exoticism they crave while still maintaining the safety and comfort of home, and this combo makes it a wonderful place to enjoy the winter holidays.

Apart, yet a part of us

Alaska may be as American as apple pie, but you won't find apple pie at most Alaskans' Christmas celebrations. Maple-frosted doughnuts are the traditional sweet served on Christmas Eve, but they come after the main course, which includes such Native Alaskan delights as maktak (raw whale), walrus, caribou, and owl. Too far out of your comfort zone? Try the nigiglik (duck), piruk (fish pie), or smoked salmon.

Though Alaska is the least religious state in the Union, with only 22 percent of its citizens identifying themselves as church-goers, the Christian faith was well-established by Catholic, Protestant, and Eastern Orthodox missionaries. Many Native Alaskans as well as other residents consider themselves to be Christian, and the Aleut phrase *Gristuusaaq suu'uq,* or "Christ is born" is seen and heard often during the Christmas season.

Christmas in North Pole

Of course, nowhere in Alaska is Christmas more popular than in the North Pole, where the "Christmas in Ice" festival features beautiful ice sculptures by artists who come from as far as China to share their talent. Music, food, and special events for the kids make this a truly memorable Christmas event.

Christmas Myths!

♪ ♪ ♪

*Be careful what you believe—the Christmas holidays are
rife with urban legends, very few of which are true.*

Christmas has spawned a variety of urban legends over the years,
myths and incredible stories that, upon closer examination, almost
always prove to be false. Here is a sampling of the most popular:

1. **Myth:** The number of suicides jumps dramatically over the
   Christmas holidays.
   Fact: Proponents of this urban legend believe that the joy of the
   Christmas season exacerbates the hopelessness felt by many,
   causing them to take their own lives. However, numerous studies
   have found this not to be true. One of the most compelling was a
   Mayo Clinic survey of suicides over a 35-year period that failed to
   find even a small spike in self-inflicted deaths before, during, or
   after the Christmas holidays.

2. **Myth:** *The Twelve Days of Christmas* was written as a coded
   reference to Catholicism during a period in British history when
   the religion was illegal.
   Fact: According to this myth, *The Twelve Days of Christmas* is a
   "catechism song" chock full of hidden meaning. "Two turtle
   doves," for example, refers to the Old and New Testaments of the
   Bible, and "three French hens" means the theological virtues of
   faith, hope, and charity. However, there is absolutely no historical
   evidence that this claim, which dates back only to the 1990s, is
   true. At best, it's mere speculation.

3. **Myth:** Salvation Army bell ringers get to keep a portion of the money placed in their kettles.
Fact: This is absolutely untrue, Salvation Army officials state. Most bell-ringers are volunteers, though some are paid seasonal employees, often recruited from homeless shelters and the Salvation Army's own retirement homes when volunteers are in short supply. Those hired receive a straight salary, while all of the money dropped into their kettles goes toward a variety of charitable endeavors.

4. **Myth:** A dad who was supposed to miss Christmas because he was on a business trip decided to cancel the trip at the last minute and surprise his kids by dressing up as St. Nick and sliding down the chimney. Unfortunately, the man became stuck and died of asphyxiation. His family knew nothing about his plans . . . until they lit a fire in the fireplace.
Fact: This is one of the oldest and most oft-repeated holiday urban legends to make the rounds. It's certainly a great story, but a single real-life case has yet to be verified. You can find a variation on this urban legend in the movie *Gremlins* (1984); it's how Phoebe Cates's character lost her dad.

5. **Myth:** The common abbreviation for Christmas—Xmas—is a disrespectful attempt to remove Christ from the holiday.
Fact: Everyone needs to calm down. The use of "Xmas" as an abbreviation for Christmas is eons old and based on the fact that the Greek word for Christ begins with the letter *chi,* which is represented in the modern Roman alphabet by a symbol that closely resembles an "X."

6. **Myth:** The candy cane was invented as a tribute to Jesus. The shape represents the letter "J" and the red and white stripes symbolize purity and the blood of Christ.
Fact: A variation on this urban legend also suggests that candy canes were created as a form of secret identification among Christians during a period of persecution; both stories are false. The truth is that this popular Christmas candy has been around at least since the late 17th century (when there was little persecution of Christians in Europe), but the color striping is strictly a 20th century invention developed for decoration and flavor.

Favorite Christmas Traditions

*Some traditions are special, some are silly,
but we do all of them in December.*

- **Presents:** This one's obvious. Who doesn't like getting presents? Well, maybe fathers. There are only so many ties and black socks a man can use.

- **Tree:** Plastic trees are a lot less messy, but nothing compares to a lush, fresh tree . . . and the family arguments that ensue over who gets to put the star on top.

- **Advent calendar:** The little panels help us tick down the days to Christmas Day. The horrid, stale chocolates make us wish the holiday turkey would arrive sooner.

- **Eggnog:** When it's not socially acceptable to swig a flask of whiskey, eggnog comes to the rescue. Even Christmas needs a social lubricant sometimes.

- **Milk and cookies:** The true cause of bulging holiday waistlines is the sugary snack kids leave out for Santa (and which moms and dads greedily devour).

- **Nativity scene:** It looks like a toy. The three wise men action figures. The farm animals. Christianity's original Barbie and Ken hanging out in the Deluxe Manger Playset. Yet moms don't like it when kids play with baby Jesus.

- **Hanging Christmas cards:** This is the true test of one's social worth. Whoever has the most friends wins.

- **Stockings:** Few children grew up without the threat of coal in their stocking if they misbehaved. What's Christmas without a little bribery?

- **Yule log:** The way to warm Santa's heart is through his bottom, as he slides down the chimney and into the fire. Poor guy can't catch a break. This old European tradition has evolved to include the Yule log cake, because at the end of the day the true meaning of Christmas is food.

- **Fruitcake:** This is the most popular gift from estranged aunts. Interestingly, even the people who *like* it never want to take it home with them, leaving it with you to become a stale paperweight.

- **Mistletoe:** Whoever invented this tradition deserves a medal. Adding kisses to the festivities gives new meaning to the phrase "holiday joy." On the downside, are we supposed to ease off a second helping of dessert so our bellies don't ruin a potential mistletoe moment?

- **Caroling:** The only thing better than opening the door to yuletide carolers is closing the door for some yuletide quiet.

- **Letter to Santa:** Dear Santa, Please bring me a new Nintendo game. Peace on earth would be great too, but mostly I'm looking for a new video game.

- *It's a Wonderful Life:* Sometime during the holiday season, it's always nice to pour glass of eggnog, toss another fruitcake on the yule log, and hunker back on the couch for the best holiday movie ever made.

- **Visiting granny:** Sure, these days granny may just as well be out playing tennis as in the kitchen making cookies, but she still loves to spoil us, right?!

The Warm Glow (and History) of the Advent Wreath

Don't mistake this Christmastime object as just another decoration—it's got plenty of symbolism and history behind it.

Not all wreaths are hung on doors at Christmas. The Advent wreath is placed on a table or other flat surface and holds lit candles in its greenery. Advent is the beginning of the church year for most churches in the Western tradition.

Way back when

The origin of the Advent wreath is probably best traced to the Scandinavians, who would light candles around a wheel and pray that the god of light would turn the wheel of the earth back toward the sun. (Wintertime in Scandinavia is pretty rough.)

The Christians picked up the practice around the Middle Ages, but for them, Christ was the bringer of light, so they adapted the practice accordingly, switching out the wheel for a wreath. By about 1600, both Lutherans and Catholics had formal Advent wreath practices.

The wreath part

The actual wreath itself is chock full of meaning. Not only does it symbolize the crown of thorns that Christ wore at his crucifixion, its never-ending, no-beginning-no-end nature of a circle reminds followers that God's love is infinite. Traditional Advent wreaths are made from fresh evergreen, and the various elements have symbolism, too: Laurel signifies victory over persecution and suffering, pine and holly represent immortality, and cedar signifies strength.

The candle part(s)

But what's an Advent wreath without its candles? The four lit candles in an Advent wreath are what make it special for Christmas. The candles represent a thousand years each, summing up the 4,000 years that passed from Adam and Eve to Christ's birth.

For those wanting to honor the "old school" Advent wreath, only colored candles will do: three purple and one pink or rose colored. The atypical Christmas colors are there for a reason. The purple candles, lit the first, second, and fourth weeks of Advent, represent prayer, penance, and the charitable work and good deeds people do during the time leading up to Christmas. The pink or rose-colored candle is lit on the third week, called Gaudete Sunday (that's the midpoint of Advent). The priest who lights it wears matching rose vestments at Mass, and the rose candle symbolizes rejoicing.

Minor alterations

Some modern-day adaptations include lighting a white candle in the middle of the wreath, which represents Christ and is lit on Christmas Eve. Other folks replace the three colored candles with four white candles and light them throughout the Christmas season. In any case, the Advent wreath is a reminder to Christians of the real excitement and joy behind the season.

"A Christmas candle is a lovely thing; It makes no noise at all, but softly gives itself away; while quite unselfish, it grows small."

—*Eva K. Logue*

Sporting Santas

*Charitable giving at Christmas is one area in which
pro athletes are perfect angels.*

All too often it seems, the news we hear about the private behavior
of professional athletes is anything but admirable. From gambling on
games to taking steroids to flagrant womanizing, many seem to have
a knack for getting in trouble and generating gossip. But there is no
denying that many pro athletes have given a lot of time and energy
to charity, and never is their charitable giving more enthusiastic than
during the holiday season. A cynic might smirk and call it nothing
but photo ops and public relations fluff, but surely many of these
jocks have a heart for the less fortunate—especially children.

The TLC of three

For LaDainian Tomlinson, a running back for the
New York Jets, the Christmas season is the
most important time to show needy kids that
they're not forgotten. In fact, the holidays
are so important to him that he named his
philanthropic program the Touching Lives
Holiday Program. Through Touching Lives,
Tomlinson is able to distribute over
2,000 gifts to children who are hospitalized.

Jeff Suppan, the pitcher for the Milwaukee Brewers, hosted a
holiday party in which hundreds of local kids were given Christmas
gifts and signed backpacks. Suppan also gave generously from his
own bank account to help dozens of military families ship holiday
packages to relatives serving in Afghanistan.

Tamika Catchings, a WNBA star who plays for the Indiana Fever,
hosts a yearly Christmas party for 100 disadvantaged children.

One could cite hundreds (okay, maybe dozens) more examples
of professional athletes giving back to their communities at
Christmastime, but perhaps former San Diego Charger and current
pastor Miles McPherson sums it up best: "It is about people helping
other people to make a difference."

Christmas Around the World

FRANCE

The French have plenty of reasons for their year-round joie de vivre, reasons that are especially potent at Christmas.

The art. The architecture. The food. The wine. It's enough to garner an *ooh-la-la* from the most seasoned of travelers. Indeed, any time is the right time for a sabbatical in France, but if you really want to experience the country like a Frenchie, visit during the winter holidays. In December, most cities have experienced at least a sprinkling of snow; others are blanketed almost the entire winter. Regardless, the powdery white stuff does wonders in transforming the landscape into a winter wonderland. Holiday displays, already glittery with the twinkling of lights and sheen of tinsel and ornaments, grow even brighter when reflected against such a dazzling backdrop.

Beware the spanker

It's no surprise that official records indicate that the country's first Christmas occurred in Reims as far back as 496. Such a storied history gives France more than 1,500 years of experience in celebrating the season with the style and verve expected of this epicenter of fine art and culture. In some areas, the holiday begins as early as December 6 with the Feast of St. Nicholas. Small gifts and candies are exchanged, and if *le Pere Fouettard* (see page 149), the French-centric Father Spanker, accompanies St. Nick, naughty children can expect a spanking as their reward for bad behavior.

The big night for celebrating, however, is the same as that in many European countries—Christmas Eve. Families dress up to attend church then return home for *le reveillon,* a late-night dinner celebration. Food plays a huge part in Christmas festivities, and the menu varies depending on the region of France. There are traditional dishes, such as turkey and chestnuts, that are also served in other countries, as well as the more traditional French dishes of oysters, foie gras, goose, and buckwheat cakes with sour cream. A *buche de noel,* a spongy cake rolled in the form of a Yule log and slathered with frosting, is the highlight of the dinner.

Because the meal is served after church, young children typically stay home and go to bed early, but not before placing their shoes in front of the fireplace. During the night, *le Pere Noel,* the French equivalent to Santa Claus, stops by to hang small toys, candies, and fruits on the branches of the Christmas tree and place gifts in each child's shoes.

They said it first

France has made several contributions to the legacy of Christmas. A notable first is that it was the first country to proclaim "Noel!" during the holidays, a custom that began when Queen Isabeau of Bavaria visited in 1389. Likewise, France was the first to declare the fir tree as the official holy tree of Christmas, thanks to a 1605 Strasbourg celebration that included a tree decorated with roses, apples, and angels to symbolize the tree of life in the garden of Eden.

And France was also the first country to introduce the manger, or crèche, to Christmas traditions. As early as the 12th century, the French began reenacting the story of the Nativity, and many ancient churches still standing today feature mangers outside next to the church or inside the sanctuary. It was another four centuries, however, before families began including small nativities in their homes. Today, these vignettes, which are displayed prominently with rocks, moss, and branches used to create lifelike backdrops, can take up substantial space. The figurines, known as *santons,* or "little saints," include the Holy Family, shepherds, angels, and wise men, but also villagers: a butcher, baker, farmer, mayor, and priest.

Joyeux Noël!

SANTA WHO?

PERE FOUETTARD

Unsurprisingly, there's a bit more emphasis on the "naughty" in France. That's where the French "Correction" comes in.

We Americans have been known to make fun of the French as wimps, but when it comes to Christmas and kids, they're actually a lot more hardcore than we are. Sure, we *say* our Santa keeps an eye on who's naughty and nice, but it's obvious we've had enforcement issues for centuries. The naughty American kids aren't worried about not getting presents. They aren't losing any sleep about finding coal in their stockings on Christmas morning. Well, not so in France, my friend. Those French kids are shaking in their footie pajamas.

J'accuse!...of being a brat
You know those action movies that feature a "good cop" and a "bad cop"? That's how it goes down in France during the Christmas season. I'm sure we can all guess who the good cop is: Pere Noel, of course. (Pere Noel is pretty much just Santa Claus, except way classier.) And the bad cop? Oh, that would be a fellow named Pere Fouettard. Pere Fouettard's name may sound all French and highfalutin', but trust me—this is not a guy you want to meet in a dark Parisian alley at three in the morning. Dude has a thing for whips and dressing all in black—know what I'm sayin'?

Tattletale
Pere Fouettard ain't all that, though. Sure, he can be tough, but he'll snitch when he has to. Heck, snitching is his job. He keeps a list of all the naughty *enfants* in France and then runs and tattles to Pere Noel. Pere Noel is the boss, the captain, and he don't want to get his hands dirty, see? But with Pere Fouettard around, his rep stays as clean as whistle, and all the kids keep giving him *beaucoup d'amour*. Nice, huh?

Fast Facts

ALL ABOUT *RANGIFER TARDANDUS*, OTHERWISE KNOWN AS *REINDEER*

- *Santa's actual reindeer were probably not reindeer at all, but a compilation of traits from several members of the deer family. In some pictures, the reindeer have white tails—not a trait of the Lapland reindeer—as well as the facial structure of an antelope.*

- *So much for those wild reindeer games—at least in Lapland. It seems that the last of the wild herds were hunted out around 1900. Around the same time, the U.S. government imported 1,300 reindeer from Siberia to Alaska to provide food for Eskimo peoples. Herds grew to a million over the next 30 years but were also decimated by white hunters. In 1972, Alaska wildlife officials set quotas to protect the remaining herds of reindeer.*

- *Reindeer are generally herbivores, which means they prefer vegetation over other forms of food. In the summer, they eat leaves and herbs. In the winter, they eat lichen and moss. During dry spells when vegetation is sparse, however, they have been known to eat bird eggs and small birds. Well-endowed male reindeer use their imposing antlers like a shovel to break through the upper crust of snow to reach the vegetation underneath.*

- *Contrary to belief, reindeer don't run very fast. In fact, a normal-size deer could outrun a reindeer. And not only can reindeer swim, but their soft, hollow hair is buoyant.*

- *Talk about getting special perks from the guy in the red suit.... Before a poem entitled "The Children's Friend" and then Clement Clarke Moore's "'Twas the Night Before Christmas," Santa had to hoof it from house to house. (Moore apparently drew inspiration from the previous poem.) Moore was the first to outfit Santa with a sleigh and eight, albeit "tiny," reindeer.*

Sing a Song of Winter!

*In Wales, the midwinter blues are cast aside
with merry songs and clever verse.*

Music and song have long been an integral part of the winter holiday season. But no one does it like the Welsh, where the ancient custom of Mari Lwyd is still practiced in certain regions.

Sing me a *pwnco*!

Traditionally performed around New Year's Eve, *Mari Lwyd* ("the grey mare") was a celebration unlike any other. It involved dressing up in costume, often as a horse with a real horse skull, and arriving at someone's doorstep, where the visiting merrymakers challenged the homeowners to an often bawdy singing contest—in Welsh verse.

The goal was to be granted entrance so everyone could eat, drink, and have a good time. But to simply say, "hey, come on in!" was too easy. After all, where's the fun in that? So in the spirit of the seasonal contest, the homeowners would engage in a spirited musical give-and-take with their wannabe guests, responding with rhyming verses of their own (called *pwnco* in Welsh). When both parties were especially skilled, the challenge could go on for some time, ending only when one side gave up or simply couldn't think of an appropriate musical response.

The custom of Mari Lwyd is centuries old and is believed to have influenced other holiday traditions, specifically trick-or-treating on Halloween. Sadly, its popularity gradually started to fade in the 1800s, thanks in part to fiery sermons from preachers who took moral issue with the custom's emphasis on alcohol and rowdiness as the caroling troupes worked their way through the village.

By the 1920s, Mari Lwyd had also become a victim of the growing popularity of other forms of entertainment, such as motion pictures. However, the custom has refused to disappear completely, and is still practiced each year in many towns around Wales where the old traditions remain strong.

Why Is That on Your Tree?

Everyone who's sung "O Tannenbaum" and realized it sounds suspiciously like "O Christmas Tree" has probably figured out that the tradition of the holiday tree comes from Germany. While most of the decorations we place on our trees have German beginnings, a few come from all over the world and all have interesting traditions.

Fruits, nuts, and gingerbread

The early Christmas trees in Germany were decorated with things normally found on trees, namely fruits and nuts. Smaller fruits such as cranberries were strung with string and draped around the tree, a custom still seen today with popcorn. When those became boring, gingerbread cookies were baked in the shapes of fruits, stars, hearts, angels, bells, and people and hung from the branches. Plastic ornaments in the shape of gingerbread figures are still popular today, especially in homes with pets.

Tinsel

Like the Christmas tree, tinsel traces its shiny roots to Germany. Sometime in the 1600s, real silver was rolled flat and pressed into thin strips. Although durable, silver tinsel was tarnished by the candles burning on trees. Later versions were made from pewter and aluminum, but most tinsel used today is shiny plastic.

Lights

Candles have long been a part of religious celebrations, but also a fire hazard around dry evergreen trees. One popular legend explaining the origin of Christmas tree lighting starts with Martin Luther in Germany in the 1500s. Luther is said to have placed candles on his tree to symbolize the stars in heaven. As a result, for a long time tree lights were more popular in Protestant homes than in those of Catholics. Edward H. Johnson is called the Father of Electric Christmas Tree Lights. In 1882, while vice president of the Edison Electric Light Company, the associate of Thomas Edison had red, white, and blue Christmas tree lightbulbs hand-wired for his tree at his home on New York City's Fifth Avenue. Electric tree lights didn't become popular until the 1930s when they became more affordable.

Ornaments

As decorating trees became more popular in Germany, people who were not handy at baking, cutting tin, or other do-it-yourself decorations looked for an easier option. The city of Lauscha, Germany, was a center of the glass-blowing trade in the 19th century, and the skills used to make bottles, goblets, and barometers were perfect for creating colored glass ornaments. They started making glass copies of fruits and nuts but quickly expanded to hearts, stars, saints, religious icons, and other shapes. F. W. Woolworth began importing German glass ornaments to the United States for his stores in the 1880s. Artists in Dresden, Germany, used pressed and embossed paper to create ornaments in shapes that couldn't be easily made from blown glass, including birds and animals.

After World War I, a German backlash caused Americans to look to other sources for ornaments. The Corning Company used its lightbulb-making equipment to move into the ornament business. Eventually, the costs and dangers of glass gave way to the plastic ornaments we use today.

In 1973, the Hallmark Company created the first Keepsake Christmas ornaments, starting a tradition of collecting ornaments that are dated with the year of release (see page 274).

Candy canes

A popular legend about the origin of the red-striped candy cane is that in 1670, a choirmaster at Cologne Cathedral in Germany bent straight candy sticks into canes to represent a shepherd's crook and used them to keep children quiet during services. The first mention of candy canes in the United States was in 1847 when a German-Swedish immigrant named August Imgard put candy canes on his Christmas tree in Wooster, Ohio. Both of these types of canes were probably white. Christmas cards prior to the year 1900 showed only all-white candy canes. There's no real evidence that the red stripes originated as religious symbolism, and the hook in the cane may have just been a convenient way to hang the candy on a tree.

🎥 CHRISTMAS MOVIE QUIZ

Match the line to the Christmas movie it came from.

1. "A fine night for spirits—of one form or another, sir!"
   a. *The Nightmare Before Christmas*
   b. *A Christmas Carol*
   c. *Jingle All the Way*
   d. *How the Grinch Stole Christmas*

2. "One man's toxic sludge is another man's potpourri."
   a. *Holiday Inn*
   b. *Christmas with the Kranks*
   c. *How the Grinch Stole Christmas*
   d. *Fred Claus*

3. "You're skipping Christmas! Isn't that against the law?"
   a. *Elf*
   b. *Christmas with the Kranks*
   c. *Mixed Nuts*
   d. *We're No Angels*

4. "You could melt her heart right down to butter, if you'd only turn on the heat!"
   a. *Holiday Inn*
   b. *It's a Wonderful Life*
   c. *A Christmas Story*
   d. *I Saw Mommy Kissing Santa Claus*

5. "You call this a happy family? Why do we have to have all these kids?"
   a. *Christmas with the Kranks*
   b. *National Lampoon's Christmas Vacation*
   c. *Fred Claus*
   d. *It's a Wonderful Life*

Answers: 1. b; 2. c; 3. b; 4. a; 5. d

154

Santa, Is that You?

America's Santa Claus owes a big thank-you to a German artist.

Thomas Nast is famous in American history as the cartoonist whose drawings brought down Boss Tweed. Less well known is that jolly ol' Santa Claus might look very different today if it wasn't for Nast.

Ho, ho, er, *who* are you?

Initially Santa's image followed his origins as St. Nicholas, and he was often depicted as a stern, lean, patriarchal figure in flowing religious robes. Around 1300, however, St. Nicholas adopted the flowing white beard of the Northern European god Odin. Years passed, and once across the Atlantic Ocean (and in America), Nicholas began to look more like a gnome. He shrunk in size, often smoked a Dutch-style pipe, and dressed in various styles of clothing that made him seem like anything from a secondhand-store fugitive to a character from *1001 Arabian Nights*. One eerie 1837 picture shows him with baleful, beady black eyes and an evil smirk.

Santa savior

Into this muddled situation stepped Nast. As a cartoonist for the national newspaper *Harper's Weekly,* the Bavarian-born Nast often depicted grim subjects such as war and death. When given the option to draw St. Nicholas, he jumped at the opportunity to do something joyful. His first Santa Claus cartoon appeared in January 1863, and he continued to produce them for more than two decades.

Nast put a twinkle in Santa's eye, increased his stature to full-size and round-bellied, and gave him a jolly temperament. Nast's Santa ran a workshop at the North Pole, wore a red suit trimmed in white, and carried around a list of good and bad children.

Nast surrounded Santa Claus with symbols of Christmas: toys, holly, mistletoe, wishful children, a reindeer-drawn sleigh on a snowy roof, and stockings hung by the fireplace. Nast tied all these previously disparate images together to form a complete picture of Santa and Christmas. Other artists later refined Santa Claus, but it was Thomas Nast who first made Santa into a Christmas story.

The Snowflake Man

In photographing snow,
Wilson A. Bentley was decidedly not a flake.

You've heard the phrase "no two snowflakes are alike," but have you ever pondered its origins? The discovery can be credited to Wilson A. Bentley (1865–1931), a self-educated farmer-turned-scientist whose lifelong interest in snow crystals earned him the nickname "The Snowflake Man." In 1885, in a sleepy little town called Jericho, Vermont, Bentley—then 19 years old—became the first person to take a photograph of a snowflake. He did so using a special process called *photomicrography* and went on to take more than 5,000 snowflake images over the course of his lifetime.

In both these snow photos and in articles he wrote on the subject (for publications such as *National Geographic, Scientific American, The New York Times Magazine,* etc.), the shy, self-taught photographer elegantly merged art and science. In an article titled "Snow Beauties," he wrote poetically of snowfall: "Here is a gem-bestrewn realm of nature possessing the charm of mystery, of the unknown, sure richly to reward the investigator."

Bentley's painstaking process

In order to capture an image of such "gems," Bentley couldn't simply catch one in his glove and snap a quick pic. Such a method would be impossible because snowflakes are tricky subjects; they melt almost instantaneously after being caught, and cameras in the late 19th century could not come close to enabling a person to snap a quick picture.

Instead, Bentley affixed a heavy bellows camera to a compound microscope and, catching a snow crystal on a piece of black velvet, hurried to an unheated shed where he transferred the snowflake to a glass slide. He then used the camera/microscope combo to take a photomicrograph, which involved leaving the shutter open for quite a few seconds to capture the crystal before it changed shape.

After more than a year of painstaking experimentation, he finally achieved his first image on January 15, 1885. Overjoyed, he wrote of the experience, "The day that I developed the first negative made by this method, and found it good, I felt almost like falling on my knees beside that apparatus and worshipping it! It was the greatest moment of my life."

A flurry of discovery

Bentley's snowflakes indeed look like gems—sparkling, intricate, and entirely unique. After taking his first image, he continued to obtain more and more photomicrographs, writing notes on the curious differences in shape and size among the snowflakes, which seemed to depend on what type of storm had blown through Jericho. Thirteen years passed before Bentley showed any of his findings to the outside world. At the prompting of a professor from the University of Vermont, he published his first article in *Popular Science Monthly,* referring to the structure of an ice crystal as "dainty hieroglyphics."

Eager to share more of his discoveries, as well as to find more, Bentley began writing widely on the subject of snowflakes, even authoring the "snow" entry in the 14th edition of the *Encyclopedia Britannica.* He also explored other water formations in nature, including fog, clouds, and rain, and he became the first person to record the sizes of raindrops. In addition, he kept a daily log of weather observations—all while maintaining his farm.

Ahead of his time

In the 1920s, Bentley's photomicrographs were collected by jewelers and textile companies, and in 1931, McGraw-Hill published 2,500 of the images in a large volume entitled *Snow Crystals* (now out of print). Shortly thereafter, Bentley contracted pneumonia, after walking home in a blizzard, and died. Had he not devoted years to photographing what he described as "exquisite crystals from cloud-land," it might've been some time before people grasped the true complexity and uniqueness of snowflakes. Indeed, Bentley was ahead of his time, both in his scientific observations and mastery of photomicrography.

The next time you see an image of a snowflake adorning holiday decorations or stationery or sweaters, be sure to remember "The Snowflake Man."

THE NETHERLANDS

*In Holland, the holiday is as comfortable
as an old shoe.*

In The Netherlands, the most celebrated day of the Christmas season is December 5—the day before the birthday of *Sinterklass.* The reason that major celebrations occur on the *eve* of Saint Nicholas Day is that this is traditionally when children are given presents. On this holiday, children put out clogs or shoes for Saint Nick to fill with gifts. Kids also leave out carrots or hay for his horse, which are replaced with sweets.

Saint Nick arrives in a town in The Netherlands in November, with Zwarte Piet (see page 159) in tow. (According to Dutch tradition, the town varies from year to year, and if he lands in Amsterdam, he goes to the palace to meet the Queen.) He arrives by boat—supposedly having sailed from his home in Madrid, Spain—and church bells chime to announce his arrival. The bearded gift-bearer then rides through town on a white horse, passing out candy to eager kids. He is assisted by "hulp-Sinterklazen," other adults who dress up like Sinterklass.

You're sacked!
Besides filling shoes with gifts on December 5, Saint Nick also delivers sacks of presents. Often there will be a knock on the door, and the sack will be mysteriously waiting outside! Sinterklass parties, typically held on the 5th, include treasure hunts, marzipan biscuits shaped into letters (representing the first letter of each party goer's name), and *pepernoten*—a cookielike candy made with cinnamon and spice. A traditional Dutch ring cake may also be served. Adults often exchange presents that are wrapped in deceiving packaging and accompanied by a poem to provide clues as to the gift-giver (intended to be a mystery).

Christmas Day in Holland is considerably more subdued. The emphasis is on religious traditions: Families often attend a church service, sing carols, and share a special meal.

SANTA WHO?

ZWARTE PIET

You better watch out, you better not cry....
Black Pete is coming to town!

We know that Santa supposedly keeps tabs on whether children are naughty or nice, but in some cultures, he calls on a sinister sidekick to keep the kids in line. In The Netherlands, Saint Nick's assistant has historically been known as *Zwarte Piet* or Black Pete—a tall, slender fellow with a dark beard and hair who dresses in the colorful garb of an Italian chimney sweep or Renaissance page. While Saint Nicholas passes out presents and sweets, Black Pete doles out coal and (occasionally) knocks naughty children on the head and chases them with sticks.

The character emerged in 15th century Holland, when Spain occupied the country (hence Black Pete's traditionally dark, Spanish appearance). He was supposed to be representative of a pirate or devil, and the bag he carried was said to be for kidnapping children. To get their children to shape up, Dutch parents used to say that unless the kids behaved, Black Pete would come to capture them and take them back to Spain with him.

Later, Black Pete was portrayed as Indian or African. He was depicted as less of a devil and more of a slave. This politically incorrect symbolism was sometimes taken to extremes, with Black Pete shown in shackles and torn clothing and wearing black makeup. Understandably, this caused quite a bit of controversy, much of which continues to this day.

Nowadays, Black Pete can often be spotted wearing short pants, a Renaissance-style shirt with puffy sleeves, and a cap with a garish feather. He acts as a kind of elf, arriving with Saint Nicholas by boat (allegedly from Spain), and helping with the annual feast on December 5. Children still want to be on their best behavior, however, lest Black Pete drop a lump of coal in their shoe!

Holiday Hope from Home

*Grateful Americans send greetings of
peace and joy to our troops for the holidays.*

Christmas is a tough time to be an active-duty U.S. soldier stationed far from home. It's even tougher, though, when fighting in a war that may not be too popular with many of your fellow citizens. The troops in Afghanistan and Iraq know this all too well. Luckily, Americans of all political stripes seem able to separate the conflict from the people serving in it, and they are extremely generous to the troops during the holidays. Whether famous or anonymous, rich or poor, conservative or liberal, U.S. citizens sympathize with their soldiers and want to ease the heartache and homesickness they often suffer around the Christmas season.

Stars of Christmas

The United Service Organizations, Inc. (USO), has worked since before World War II with the Department of Defense to provide comfort and entertainment to troops stationed abroad. While its most popular spokesperson for decades was comedian Bob Hope, the USO goes on without him and has been a great relief recently to our troops in Afghanistan, Iraq, Kuwait, and Qatar. While the USO's Christmas shows are perhaps the most important work they do for U.S. soldiers, they are not without controversy. Celebrities who performed in Vietnam were accused of being government shills, and female stars have been banned from performing in certain Muslim countries where women are expected to remain veiled in public.

The USO's work in our two current wars is just as appreciated as ever. World Wrestling Entertainment (WWE) films its *RAW* "Tribute to the Troops" every year in Afghanistan and Iraq, much to the delight of the many wrestling fans in the military. In recent years, stars including Robin Williams, Lance Armstrong, and Kid Rock have given selflessly of their time on Christmas tours in these dangerous areas. And USO programs such as Operation Phone Home, in which 2.2 million phone cards have been distributed to our men and women in uniform, ensure that troops will be able to stay in touch with loved ones throughout the holiday season.

Everyday heroes

One certainly doesn't have to be rich or famous to support our troops in Afghanistan and Iraq. All over the United States, people quietly help our troops during the holidays without expecting any attention or reimbursement. One of the most easy and inexpensive Christmas gifts that can be given is a simple letter of thanks. Many schoolchildren write to our troops this time of year, and their letters can provide not only comfort but unintentional humor as well. The kids at Hayesville Elementary School in the Willamette Valley of Oregon, for example, came up with a few doozies in their 2009 Christmas greetings to the troops. "I have a kitty. It looks like a cow," one second-grader informed his pen pal, while another thought she was being polite when she wrote, "Merry Christmas, and rest in peace." Thank goodness that nowhere is dark humor more appreciated than in Afghanistan.

Many involved in private charities in the United States work tirelessly to make the holiday season just a little less lonely for the overseas troops. Operation Give's Operation Christmas Stocking program encourages generous Americans to donate Christmas stockings stuffed with everything from toys to personal care items, which the group then sends on to Afghanistan and Iraq. These stockings are distributed to the children of the area by soldiers. It's a way to boost the morale of the troops while also giving them a way to bond with the local population. Of course, the soldiers themselves are not forgotten, as volunteers work through charities such as WarmthForWarriors.com (knitting and sending hats and other comfort items) and TellThemThanks.com (sending letters and care packages) to make the season bright.

Sadly, as in other altruistic areas, giving to military charities dropped in 2009 due to the recession, but many Americans continue to do as much as they can for our troops.

Rudolph's Roots

*Santa just wouldn't be complete without one cheery,
four-legged sidekick. What might surprise you is that
Rudolph the Red-Nosed Reindeer is a very modern
creation with no ties whatsoever to ancient yuletide traditions.
Of course, that doesn't make him any less popular...*

Just a gimmick in their eyes

In 1939, heads of the Chicago-based department store Montgomery Ward were looking for a promotion, something to put into the hands of shoppers to remind them to shop at their store. The store had long given out holiday coloring books, but that was getting too expensive. The managers decided a nice short story would be a welcome change of pace and would cost less to produce.

The managers took their idea to in-house copywriter Robert L. May, who had experience writing children's books. May began brainstorming and decided upon a classic underdog story, possibly pulling from his own experiences in school—he was a short kid who got picked on a lot. Some have suggested May got the reindeer thing from Norse mythology depicting goats pulling Thor, the god of thunder, across the sky, but this is speculation. May decided to write about a reindeer who wasn't part of the "in" crowd but whose uniqueness would be celebrated by the story's end.

On the drawing board

Rudolph wasn't always Rudolph. At first, May called his lovable reindeer Rollo, but he decided that was too frivolous. He also tried out Reginald but abandoned that idea because it sounded too British. May liked the red nose from the beginning, but he feared his bosses would nix it, since red noses were associated with drunkards and bums. As he wrote the story (which was in rhyming verse) he tested it out on his four-year-old daughter, who loved it.

May took his creation to the store managers, who—with some hesitancy—okayed the story for print. What followed was a phenomenon. People *loved* Rudolph. They loved him so much that by the end of 1939, 2.4 million copies of *Rudolph the Red-Nosed Reindeer* had been distributed. By the end of 1946, that number climbed to six million.

Rudolph's legacy

Because May had created Rudolph for Montgomery Ward, he didn't own the copyright and so at first couldn't get rich from his work. After much back and forth, May was able to get the rights to his creation and proceeded to make licensing Rudolph his full-time job. His character's popularity grew in 1949, however, when Gene Autry made a recording of a song May's brother-in-law had written, called "Rudolph the Red-Nosed Reindeer." It sold an astounding two million copies that year alone and went on to become one of the best-selling songs of all time (only "White Christmas" has sold more). The mega-popular animated feature, starring Burl Ives as the voice of the snowman-narrator, was made in 1964, further fixing the little reindeer in the hearts and Christmas traditions of people everywhere.

"The joy of brightening other lives, bearing each others' burdens, easing others' loads and supplanting empty hearts and lives with generous gifts becomes for us the magic of Christmas."

—W. C. Jones

The Last Act of Christmas

*The last act of Christmas, for many, isn't just tossing
the tree on the curb and vacuuming up the leftover needles
the cat hasn't tried to eat, it's the New Year's Eve celebration.
Scotland, though, has a unique and noisy celebration.*

For some, New Year's Eve celebrations are a quiet night at home shared with loved ones; others gather in large groups to watch balls drop down a pole while they count down the seconds left in the year. In Scotland, however, the season goes out with a real bang in a celebration they call Hogmanay, where the only balls they deal with are the ones they've lit on fire.

Wee, not so wee, and friggin' huge!

While many of us are used to lighting off fireworks to celebrate the New Year, the Scots take Hogmanay to a whole other level. The exuberance exhibited in Scotland for Hogmanay might be matched in the United States, but only when a sports team wins a major championship. Instead of just the Lakers, Red Sox, or Saints winning though, imagine if they all won their respective championships at the same time, and everyone in the country was rooting for them. Now that's a party! In fact, in major Scottish cities such as Edinburgh and Glasgow, they have to sell tickets to the celebration in an attempt to control the massive turnout every year.

Ancient roots of the party tree

A party of this size isn't just part of the modern Scottish culture, it's practically in their blood. Hogmanay dates back further than most modern celebrations, including Christmas itself. Many of the traditional elements of the holiday were established when Scotland was still worshipping Roman and Viking gods. First Footing, for example, is an ancient tradition wherein a dark-haired stranger bearing coal at your door at midnight is a sign that the coming year will bring you luck. In our time, many families gather to tour one another's homes on the day, taking turns each year at the end to make a festive meal for all involved. Other people dress up like ancient sun gods for the various street festivals, while in many communities, lighting bonfires and swinging fireballs through the streets on a chain all lead up to the ringing of the bells at midnight.

"Should auld acquaintance be forgot, and auld lang syne?"—Robert Burns

Still, not all Hogmanay traditions are ancient. Some only date back a few hundred years, and others, like the recent public concerts, are little more than a generation old. The singing of "Auld Lang Syne" at the stroke of midnight, probably the most famous Scottish party export, only dates back to the 18th century, and though the swinging of fireballs through the streets in towns such as Stonehaven may have roots in ancient purification or sun worship, the modern tradition can only be traced to the 20th century. The largest cities in Scotland—Glasgow and the capital city of Edinburgh—host large outdoor street festivals that started in 1992, when Edinburgh hosted a European Union summit that ran over New Year's. These large festivals often feature major musical acts, including the Red Hot Chilli Pipers. That highlights one of the more interesting mixes of new and old tradition over the course of Hogmanay: the inclusion of traditional ceilidhs music alongside modern pop and rock acts. After all, music in Scotland goes hand in hand with pipers piping.

The Scots make New Year's in Times Square look like a quiet night on the town. It should be noted that Hogmanay isn't just a one-day celebration, it is a multiday festival spanning up to a full week, depending on the calendar. In Edinburgh in 2009, for instance, festivities lasted five days, beginning December 29 and ending January 2. Both opening and closing days were marked with a music and dance extravaganza called Off Kilter, which featured a spectrum of dance and music from Scotland's history. The end of Hogmanay is traditionally January 2, but because Hogmanay and New Year's Day are public holidays, if the latter falls on a weekend, the following Monday is also deemed a public holiday. Thus, if January 1 falls on a Friday, the Hogmanay celebrations could potentially extend from December 29 all the way through January 4.

Other places may put on a great New Year's party, but the Scots have built for themselves a holiday to rival Christmas itself, steeped in fire, music, and hundreds of years of tradition!

Christmas in the Third Reich

*Life under Hitler was at its most
bizarre during the holidays.*

In Nazi Germany and its occupied territories, citizens struggled to
retain some sense of normalcy, and celebrating Christmas and other
holidays was an important part of that endeavor. While the Nazis did
not ban Christmas, they did try to mold it into something new—or
perhaps old. To understand their twisted use of the tradition, one
must understand not only the pagan origins of Christmas but also
the anti-Christian and anti-Semitic mind-set of Hitler himself.

Seeds of hatred and persecution

Hitler had been brought up Catholic by a devout mother and a
skeptical father, but he rejected Catholicism and indeed all methods
of Christianity at a very young age (it is doubtful that, once he left
his parents' home, he ever attended mass again). In school, the
young boy was influenced by teachers who embraced Pan-
Germanism, a political movement that called for the unity of all
ethnic-German peoples ("Volksdeutsche") and a revival of Germanic
culture. At this point, however, Hitler was not an anti-Semite. There
were few Jews in the nearest large town, Linz, and those he knew
seemed exactly like other Germans in every way, aside from their
religious practices.

All this changed with Hitler's experiences as a young man. In
order to further his fledgling career as a painter, he moved to
Vienna, a city with a Jewish population of about 200,000 (out of
2 million). Some of these Jews looked different than the Jews he had
observed in Linz: They wore black caftans and ear-locks, and they
seemed to live their religion every moment, not just on one day of
the week. Hitler's life in the big city was interrupted when he served
in the Kaiser's army during World War I, and like many Germans, he
felt humiliated and full of rage in the face of Germany's total defeat.
The argument that international Jewish bankers were behind his
homeland's degradation resonated with him, and he became a
confirmed anti-Semite.

The state as God

While still a young radical, Hitler used inflammatory, antireligious language to fire up his base: "We do not want any other god than Germany itself. It is essential to have fanatical faith and hope and love in and for Germany." As time went on and his popularity grew, however, he knew he had to either give lip-service to Christianity or content himself with a small place in German history. Anti-Christian rhetoric made the average German too uneasy, and the

powerful Catholic Church had to be placated—at least until he had completely secured his power. And so Hitler changed his tune a bit and began to issue statements such as the one he made in 1933: "The National Government regards the two Christian confessions (i.e., Catholicism and Protestantism) as factors essential to the soul of the German people . . . . We hold the spiritual forces of Christianity to be indispensable elements in the moral uplift of most of the German people."

Still, throughout his entire career, Hitler mixed paganism and pan-Germanism into his public statements. This is because these two ideas had deep roots in the German culture that had never really been eradicated by Christianity. Before Christianity, until about the 7th or 8th century, the Germanic peoples practiced a polytheistic tradition, the head of which was a deity known as Woden. Much of the worship centered on nature and the harvest. That paganism was never really stamped out in Germany is obvious in examples as varied as Richard Wagner's Teutonic operas (which Hitler loved) and the nudist movement that sprang up in the 1920s (which Hitler banned, aside from its portrayals in "tasteful" sculptures).

Christmas without Christ

These seemingly incompatible ideas were combined by the Nazis to form a new religion—the religion of Germany—and never was their amalgamation more evident or bizarre than during the Christmas holidays. Since Christmaslike celebrations had been practiced as a pagan holiday before being co-opted by Christians, the Nazis were able to use the holiday for their own propaganda purposes while completely ignoring the fact that it was celebrated by most German citizens as the birth of a Jewish messiah. The Christian cross was extended into a Nazi swastika, and the stars that topped Christmas trees—so like the stars that German Jews were made to wear on their clothing—were quietly done away with.

Fascinating artifacts of the Nazis' version of Christmas have been left behind: Christmas cards that celebrated "Winter Solstice" rather than Christmas; Santa-size Luftwaffe commander Hermann Goering posing with children on his lap on the winter edition of a magazine; red Christmas tree ornaments stamped with black swastikas; even swastika-shaped cookie cutters. The lyrics of Christmas carols and hymns were purged of references to the Jewish Jesus Christ and rewritten as odes to the struggle of the German people. As the war wound down and Germans realized that defeat was inevitable, the Nazis even tried to use Christmas as a celebration of the glorious German war dead, touting their heroism on everything from posters to postcards.

A sick, twisted balancing act

Just because the Nazis offered up this new religion of pan-Germanism, however, does not mean they ever took any practical steps to end either Catholicism or Protestantism in Germany. While individual Christians who spoke out against the Third Reich or helped Jews in their desperate plight were often dealt with very harshly, most clergy and practicing Christians were left alone, as long as they worshipped discreetly. The last thing Hitler wanted was to fire up some kind of sectarian battle that would distract him from his mission of world domination: "We are a people of different faiths, but we are one. Which faith conquers the other is not the question; rather, the question is whether Christianity stands or falls." Hitler did not want Christianity to fall—yet. And so Christmas was practiced throughout Germany and the occupied territories for the duration of Nazi rule.

Holiday Pet Dangers!

The Christmas holidays can pose a variety of hazards to our pets. Don't let this joyous time be ruined by a tragedy that could have been easily prevented.

With the hustle and bustle that typically takes place over the Christmas holidays, it's easy to overlook the various dangers this special time of year can pose to our four-legged family members.

- Tinsel can cause potentially fatal intestinal blockage if ingested by a dog or cat. If you must use tinsel, place it out of your pet's reach.

- Glass ornaments are another often-overlooked concern. If your pet sees all ornaments as toys, use only unbreakable plastic decorations.

- Never place lit candles where a dog or cat can reach them. Animals are often attracted to flickering flames, and it takes only one accidentally overturned candle to cause a disastrous fire.

- Don't let your pet drink from the Christmas tree stand, especially if you add chemicals to extend the tree's life. If your pet is insistent, place a piece of mesh screen over the stand to keep out thirsty tongues.

- Don't feed holiday "people food" to your pet, no matter how much it begs. A lot of holiday dishes are rich in fat and other ingredients that can cause an animal intestinal distress, especially when consumed in large quantities. Bones, especially from poultry, are another no-no; they can splinter in your pet's mouth.

- Avoid giving your pet holiday candy—especially chocolate, which can be lethal to dogs.

- Tack down all electrical cords so your pet can't chew on them. Even a gentle gnaw can result in a trip to the veterinarian—and really curly hair for your cat!

- Place all decorative holiday plants where your pet can't reach them. Many plants, such as mistletoe, can be toxic if ingested.

SOUTH AFRICA

The sunny holiday here is a celebration
of togetherness, not materialism.

South Africa's history may be war-torn and oppression-filled, but when it comes to Christmas there is, perhaps, something to be learned from its citizens. Their warm, summertime celebration is about love, generosity, and fellowship rather than shopping, stressing, and greed. Furthermore, on Christmas Day, one is just as likely to find a South African exercising his spirituality on a beach as in a church. South Africans—black and white—see God in nature, in friends and family, and in the gift of life itself.

A violent introduction

There is no way to pretend that Christmas was introduced peacefully to South Africa, or indeed to the entire continent. This is not to say that there weren't Christian missionaries who had the best of intentions, for many of them were good-hearted and compassionate. But no peoples have ever given over their lands and culture without a fight, and native South Africans were no exception. Upon first contact with Europeans, which happened in 1487 when Portuguese explorer Bartolomeu Dias reached the southernmost tip of Africa, the two major ethnic groups living in what is now South Africa were the Xhosa and Zulu peoples. Though they fought bravely for their land over the next four centuries, these indigenous inhabitants, with their spears and shields, could not match the firepower of the British and the Boers (Dutch, Flemish, German, and French settlers).

The British finally came out on top at the end of the Second Boer War in 1902, making the Union of South Africa a British dominion. The *Afrikaans* culture of the Boers, however, was not only tolerated but allowed to flourish. This meant that there were two major strains of Christianity in the area in the early 20th century: Anglicanism and Dutch Reformed. Both the Anglicans with their "high church" grandiosity and the Dutch Reformed with their simple, Calvinistic form of worship tried to convert the native South Africans, but they had limited success. Today, though almost 80 percent of South Africans claim Christianity; just 6.7 percent of those identify as Dutch Reformed and even fewer—3.8 percent—identify as Anglicans (the most famous Anglican is Bishop Desmond Tutu).

A precarious present peace
For most of the 20th century, South Africa was ruled by apartheid, that system of legal separation that categorized humans into four groups: white, black, colored (mixed race), or Indian. Under this system, the white minority ruled over the black majority for decades. This came to an end in 1994, when the first elections with universal suffrage were held and Nelson Mandela was sworn in as South Africa's first black president. This total upheaval of the political landscape meant changes that affected everything—even holidays such as Christmas. For while the Caucasian-run government had been very conservative in all aspects, including cultural, Mandela and his African National Congress sought to loosen the government's grip on people's lives, both public and private.

In today's South Africa, Christmas is celebrated in both religious and secular fashions, by both Christians and non-Christians. December 25 falls in the middle of the South African summer, when kids are on a break from school and adults are often on vacation from their jobs. The temperature can reach a high of 90 degrees, and many families head to the beach. Joyous shouts of *Geseënde Kersfees*—"Merry Christmas" in Afrikaans—can be heard as music plays and bar-beques, or *braais,* are fired up on the sand. Of course, there are some South Africans who celebrate in a more traditional, English/European manner, attending church and feasting on mince pies and plum pudding, but the revelry of most South Africans on Christmas may seem almost shockingly casual to us. It is doubtful that our opinions would matter to them, however. South Africans have no desire to trade their holiday of togetherness and relaxation for one of commercialism and stress.

"The best of all gifts around any Christmas tree: the presence of a happy family all wrapped up in each other."
—*Burton Hillis*

What Carol Is This?

Check out these lines, and see if you can pick out which popular carols and songs they come from.

1. We won't go until we get some, so bring it right here
   a. "Blue Christmas"
   b. "Here We Come A-Wassailing"
   c. "We Wish You a Merry Christmas"
   d. "I Only Want You for Christmas"

2. We'll take a cup of kindness yet
   a. "Here We Come A-Wassailing"
   b. "Auld Lang Syne"
   c. "Mistletoe and Wine"
   d. "God Rest Ye Merry Gentlemen"

3. Please, Please, Please, Please
   a. "Please Come Home for Christmas"
   b. "Nuttin' for Christmas"
   c. "Santa Baby"
   d. "Baby Please Come Home"

4. I'm filling my stocking with a duplex
   a. "Deck the Halls"
   b. "Santa Baby"
   c. "Let It Snow"
   d. "The Magic of Christmas Day"

5. Snowing and blowing up bushels of fun
   a. "Frosty the Snowman"
   b. "White Christmas"
   c. "Boogie Woogie Santa Claus"
   d. "Jingle Bell Rock"

6. Is the pudding done?
   a. "Baby Please Come Home"
   b. "Over the River"
   c. "It Feels Like Christmas"
   d. "Sugar Plum Fairies"

Answers: 1. c; 2. b; 3. d; 4. b; 5. d; 6. b

Ugly but Delicious:
The Chocolate Truffle

*Chocolate truffles, a favorite Christmas treat,
may look like grubby little mushrooms, but that's
where the resemblance ends.*

Named for their physical resemblance to the fungus so treasured by chefs around the world, chocolate truffles have their origin in France, where chocolatiers originally set them out as Christmastime goodies. Because of the high cream and butter content of the treats, and because refrigeration wasn't always de rigueur, truffles were only offered for a short time—typically during the winter months, when it'd be easier to keep them from spoiling.

Traditional truffles are made of chocolate paste (chocolate, cream, eggs, and butter) and then rolled in cocoa powder. They may be flavored with brandy, rum, vanilla, cinnamon, or coffee. Americans do it a little differently: We like ours in a hard chocolate shell and flavored with everything from ginger to jalapeño.

Sweet imports

No one really knows where or how the truffle came into being, but we do know that pastry chef Alice Medrich, who first sampled a chocolate truffle when she was living in Paris in the '60s, is largely credited with bringing this little treasure to the United States via her San Francisco store Cocolat. Now, *haut-chocolat* houses from coast to coast offer them: Vosges Haut-Chocolat, which offers retail locations in Chicago, New York, and Las Vegas, showcases savory flavors, while you can still find traditionally flavored truffles at Jacques Torres's Brooklyn, New York–based chocolate factory. Even middle-of-the-road chocolate companies offer their version of the truffle, although you won't find varities such as "gold leaf" among their offerings.

A Christmas Carol: TV and Film Adaptations

When it comes to Charles Dickens's classic,
there are many versions—past, present,
and inevitably many more yet to come.

A *Christmas Carol* has remained a holiday classic since its publication in 1843. The story has been adapted numerous times for the stage and screen: There has been an opera version, a Broadway musical, a ballet, and even a mime show starring Marcel Marceau.

You're probably most familiar with the television and film adaptations of *A Christmas Carol,* which vary widely in format and storyline. Here's an overview of some of the adaptations.

A Christmas Carol (1910)

This 11-minute silent movie version is a quick romp through the classic tale. Only Marley and one other ghost visit Scrooge, and there's no Tiny Tim, but those interested in watching all the adaptations might enjoy seeking out this early retelling.

Scrooge (1951)

Hailed by many to be the best adaptation of Dickens's tale, *Scrooge* (as it was titled for its UK release; in the United States, it was released as *A Christmas Carol*) is a thoughtful character study of the miserly businessman, featuring British actor Alastair Sim in the title role. The black-and-white film (colorized in 1989) is also perhaps the best-known version. As Scrooge, Sim takes the viewer through a colorful range of emotions—from anger to fear to exuberance.

Scrooge (1970)

This musical film adaptation features such numbers as the cynical tune "I Hate People," the rousing ditty "December the 25th," the Academy Award–nominated song "Thank You Very Much," and a medley of reprises. English actor Albert Finney stars as Scrooge, and his performance earned him a Golden Globe for Best Actor in a Musical/Comedy in 1971.

Mickey's Christmas Carol (1983)

Starring Disney characters (Scrooge McDuck as Ebenezer Scrooge, Donald Duck as Fred, Mickey Mouse as Bob Cratchit, and Jiminy Cricket as one of the ghosts), this animated version is only 25 minutes long, but it's undeniably a classic.

A Christmas Carol (1984)

A British made-for-TV movie starring George C. Scott (who was nominated for an Emmy for his portrayal of Scrooge), this version stays relatively true to the book and casts the old miser in a sympathetic light. Although this popular adaptation ran on television for years, it wasn't released on VHS or DVD until 1995 and 1999, respectively, because Scott himself owned the rights to the film. In 2007, it returned to TV again, appearing on AMC.

Scrooged (1988)

A contemporary retelling of the classic tale, *Scrooged* features Bill Murray as a greedy TV exec visited by three ghosts after he begins work on a live Christmas broadcast of *A Christmas Carol.* His life begins to mirror the story in some surprising and predictable ways.

The Muppet Christmas Carol (1992)

Michael Caine and the Muppets star in this live-action musical feature film. Caine is Scrooge, Kermit is Bob Cratchit, and Miss Piggy is Emily Cratchit. The three Christmas ghosts are portrayed by Muppets specially created for the film.

Barbie in A Christmas Carol (2008)

Barbie, taking on perhaps her most challenging role to date, stars as a female version of Ebenezer Scrooge in this CGI direct-to-video retelling. It's *A Christmas Carol* for the under-ten set!

Disney's A Christmas Carol (2009)

This eye-popping 3-D version, made using cutting-edge performance-capture animation, was both celebrated and criticized for its dark depiction of Ebenezer Scrooge. Jim Carrey voices many of the characters, and whatever your opinion, his is a raw, in-your-face depiction of Ebenezer Scrooge.

Christmas Time Is Here

In the last half-century, the folks at Billboard charted only one No. 1 song on Christmas Day that was specifically about Christmas. That unusual honor belongs not to a single artist or musical group, but to a trio of cartoon characters. In 1958, The Chipmunks' debut song, eponymously known as "The Chipmunk Song," made history, launched a franchise, and saved a record company in the process.

In the beginning...

It all began a year earlier when Ross Bagdasarian Sr. bought a variable-speed tape recorder and used it to create the novelty hit "The Witch Doctor" for Liberty Records. Liberty was just as surprised as anyone else that the high-pitched tune performed as well as it did, and months later, when the company was almost broke, it came back to Bagdasarian to see if he had any more voodoo magic that might save their company. While brainstorming, Ross's four-year-old son started bugging him about Christmas... in the middle of the summer of 1958. That excitement for toys and other gifts was soon translated into the squeaky catchiness of The Chipmunks' first single.

Why not roadrunners or squirrels?

According to Ross Bagdasarian Jr., his father was driving through Yosemite one afternoon trying to come up with a character to attach to the voice when he was challenged for the right of way by a defiant and bold creature: a chipmunk. Though Walt Disney had used chipmunks with high-pitched voices in shorts from 1943–1956, Chip 'n' Dale were no Alvin, Simon, and Theodore. For one, Bagdasarian had used a different technique to create his voices, one whereby the voices were played at a normal speed but retained the squeak factor. Disney's tree-dwelling duo, no matter how cute, had always spoken with such alacrity that it was sometimes difficult to understand what they were saying. Bagadasarian's trio didn't have that problem, and instead of a dog, they had a human foil to play off.

Using the stage name David Seville, Ross Bagdasarian recorded all the parts of "The Chipmunk Song" on a $200 tape recorder and put it all together for his three kids to hear before handing it off to the executives at Liberty Records. We don't know how Alvin Bennett, Simon Waronker, and Theodore Keep felt about having singing rodents named for them, but one can be sure that they were pleased with the resulting success of the song.

A legacy begins

When the song was released toward the end of 1958, it quickly became a success, selling more than 4.5 million copies in only seven weeks. After January 1959 passed, so too did the popularity of "The Chipmunks Christmas" song, but not that of the Chipmunks themselves. Soon, Alvin, Simon, and Theodore would see life in the first of their many TV incarnations, win several Grammys, and become one of the most successfully licensed properties in America.

After Ross Bagdasarian Sr. passed away in 1972, his son, Ross Bagdasarian Jr., picked up the torch. He has carried his father's beloved rodents into the 21st century. Continuing the traditional connection between The Chipmunks and Christmastime, the trio have starred in two successful live-action films, both released to American theaters just before Christmas in 2007 and 2009.

"Christmas isn't just a day, it's a frame of mind."

—*Kris Kringle*, Miracle on 34th Street

CHRISTMAS TREES!

- *The first Christmas tree was decorated in Riga, Latvia, in 1510.*

- *The first printed reference to Christmas trees occurred in Germany in 1531.*

- *In the United States, commercial Christmas trees have been around since 1850. The first commercial Christmas tree lot was established in New York in 1851 by entrepreneur Mark Carr.*

- *An estimated 25 to 30 million real trees are sold in the United States each year.*

- *There are an estimated 15,000 Christmas tree growers in the United States. The industry employs approximately 100,000 people.*

- *Christmas trees are commercially grown in every state, including Hawaii.*

- *Oregon is the leading grower of Christmas trees, producing more than six million trees each year. Other top tree-producing states include North Carolina, Pennsylvania, Michigan, and Virginia.*

- *Several different types of trees are sold commercially as Christmas trees. The most popular are Scotch pine, Douglas fir, Noble fir, and Fraser fir.*

- *On a typical Christmas tree farm, approximately 2,000 trees are planted per acre. Of that number, only 1,000 to 1,500 will survive.*

- *Every day, an acre of Christmas trees provides enough oxygen to support 18 people.*

- *It can take up to ten years for a Christmas tree to grow large enough for harvesting. However, the average is seven years. For every tree harvested, two to three saplings are planted the following season.*

All About Elfdom

Santa is nothing without his elves.
Have you seen how much an Xbox 360 costs?

Santa can't afford to shop retail, so he relies on his toyshop workers to make everything he needs to carry with him the night before Christmas. These are Santa's elves. They can build anything in a year's time, and they have an endless supply of "Made in Taiwan" stickers. But they have a history older than Santa Claus.

The short and tall of it all

The two most common images we have of elves are Santa's workshop helpers and J. R. R. Tolkien's aloof immortals. The two couldn't be more different. Santa's elves are short, diminutive creatures. They work in his toyshop to make all the toys Santa needs to deliver on Christmas. Typically, they have pointed ears and shoes that curl upward at the toe. They're very close to what we associate with mythical dwarves: hearty and hard-working, but not all have beards.

Tolkien's elves, on the other hand, are tall, thin, and majestic. They are magical creatures and looked up to by humans as demi-gods. Tolkien divided his elves (Eldar) into three groups: Noldor, Sindar, and Silvan. At this point it gets complicated; suffice it to say that this division roughly led to the common view of fantasy elves as either high elves, regular elves, or wood elves. They are all immortal but can die in war or through violence.

Norse mythology: light and dark

Tolkien's elves have their roots in Norse mythology. Odin and the other Aesir (gods) created elves to inhabit their new world. The Aesir turned worms into dark elves (sometimes called gnomes or dwarves, depending on the text and translation). These creatures lived underground in Svartalfheim mining gold and other metals.

It is in Norse mythology that elves are divided into light and dark. Elves of the Light are handsome and beautiful. They enjoy life and music. If humans were to stumble upon an elven festival, they might become enchanted by the music and let themselves be carried off to

Alfheim (Elfland in English tales). These elves are symbols of fertility and celebration.

Elves of the Dark are shriveled and warped creatures. They live underground where light cannot reach them. In some stories, light turns them to stone. They like to frighten humans by echoing their voices. The dark elves created Thor's hammer and Freyr's warship, which could hold all the gods yet still be folded into one's pocket.

Tolkien, too, divided elves into the light and dark, in a fashion. Morgoth, a fallen god, created Orcs as a corruption of elves. Like the Norse mythos, Orcs preferred the dark. They were bred for one purpose: war. Just as Norse mythology ends in war (Ragnarok, the apocalypse) and a fading away of the old gods, Tolkien's elves also sail away from Middle Earth.

This leitmotif of steady, inevitable decline is in sharp contrast to the productivity of Santa's elves. In some ways, they have more in common with the industrious, subterranean dwarves. They're a strange hybrid between the dark elves' hearty craftsmanship (toys) and the light elves' celebrations (Christmas).

What's in a name?

Although we know them as elves, these creatures were known as Alfar or Alvor in Sweden, Denmark, and Norway. In Germany, an elf was often called an Alb. It is only when their stories reached England, Scotland, and Ireland that the name changed to Aelf (later elf).

In the Anglo-Saxon world, elves were sometimes conflated with mischievous fairies. No longer exclusively human-size, they began to be portrayed as smaller, spritely creatures until Lord Dunsany's *The King of Elfland's Daughter*, which predated Tolkien's *The Hobbit*.

Elves on film

Santa Claus Is Coming to Town (1970) sheds light on Santa's origin while providing a good look at the toyshop amidst a ban by the evil mayor. *Rudolph the Red-Nosed Reindeer* (1964) has a couple of good early scenes in Santa's workshop. One elf, however, would rather be a dentist than a toymaker and runs off with Rudolph.

In 1934's *Babes in Toyland (March of the Wooden Soldiers)*, Laurel and Hardy work for the Toymaker. Santa's toys aren't made by elves at all, and Laurel and Hardy mix up an order of 600 soldiers at one foot high as 100 six-foot soldiers.

In Will Ferrell's *Elf* (2003), a human baby crawls into Santa's sack and is raised in the workshop until, oversized and out of place, he leaves to find his parents.

Elves in otherworlds

Tolkien's re-imagining of elves has had a profound effect on elves in subsequent fictional settings. Many are Tolkien derivatives. Elves are slender, regal, and sport pointy ears. Elves in Dungeons & Dragons (a fantasy role-playing game invented in 1974) are largely derived from the Middle Earth setting. The popular MMORPG (massively multiplayer online role-playing game) *World of Warcraft* keeps the Norse light and dark elf distinction while retaining many elements of Tolkien's work. It's more of a hybrid between the two. In a small twist, WoW's version of dark elves, Night Elves, aren't strictly evil.

Perhaps the most well known and developed Tolkien derivative is the Warhammer universe. Warhammer is a fantasy setting where the High Elves and Dark Elves fought a civil war, sending both into decline. In Warhammer 40,000, a space fantasy setting, the traditional Tolkien races are thrust into space across millions of worlds. The Eldar (space elves) were masters of the universe but succumbed to decadence. Their race gave birth to a god of Chaos, and the Eldar who embraced Chaos became Dark Eldar, while the rest fled into exodus and decline.

Made in the North Pole

Despite Tolkien's massive influence, despite the images of space elves prancing around the galaxy, and despite the Vikings' success throughout Europe and North America, we still have our beloved workshop elves cranking out toys for Santa. They are small and have terrible fashion sense, but we love them . . . as long as they're still cranking out Xboxes and Barbie dolls. After all, what *else* is there to do at the North Pole?

More Than Just Children's Toys

*Part of Christmas for many children is sifting through
the weekly and even daily advertisements and catalogs
that come in the mail. Though they know they won't
get every toy, it's still fun to see the possibilities.
For adults, however, comparable ignition of the imagination
is as close as the annual Neiman Marcus catalog.*

A lot of bull

It all began back in the 1950s with advertising pioneer and Neiman Marcus president, Stanley Marcus. He put his company on the map with several successful national advertising campaigns, including the now famous Neiman Marcus Christmas Book. Press inquiries from the likes of Edward R. Murrow started coming in about their unusual gifts when Marcus offered a Black Angus steer, deliverable either butchered or still mooing, and accompanied by a silver-plated outdoor cooker for only $1,925.

If a live bull was news in 1959, then what Marcus had planned for the next year was the stuff of headlines. Starting in 1960, the Christmas Book began offering his-and-hers gifts that would break the bank for most holiday shoppers. The first was a pair of Beechcraft airplanes for the low, low price of $176,000. Later years would see matched hot air balloons, robots, and even a couple's luxury light sport aircraft in 2009 for only $250,000!

Something for everyone

While most of the catalog is filled with normal items, shoppers every Christmas peruse its pages for the extravagant. Be it a submarine for $20 million or designer iPhone cases for $175, the Neiman Marcus Christmas Book seems to have a little something for all of us. In 2009, they even offered an exclusive dinner with some of the pre-eminent literary minds of the day for the price tag of $200,000, with all proceeds going to charity. You see, no matter how outrageous the gifts, it's still about the spirit of giving.

Crunching the Christmas Numbers

- **1958:** Year Brenda Lee recorded "Rockin' Around the Christmas Tree"

- **493.3 million:** Amount of sales by U.S. Christmas tree farmers in 2007

- **40:** Width in feet across the base of America's official national Christmas tree in Kings Canyon National Park near Sanger, California

- **50,000:** Number of letters the post office at Nuuk, Greenland, receives annually addressed to Santa Claus

- **88:** Percentage of plant sales attributed to poinsettias during Christmastime

- **23 billion:** Amount spent on catalog and online shopping in December 2007

- **8:** Number of reindeer assigned to pull Santa's sleigh in the original 1823 poem

- **90:** Percent of electricity saved by using LED lights instead of traditional lights

- **20 billion:** Pieces of mail the U.S. Postal Service delivers between Thanksgiving and Christmas

- **$47.14:** The amount the average household spends on Christmas decorations each year

- **$1.2 billion:** Value of Christmas ornaments imported from China

- **175,000:** Number of real Christmas trees that are ordered online or by catalog and shipped via mail each year

Christmas Pantomime

Panto? What's that?

In America, we know that pantomime is only about that last part: the mime. We know better than to entertain that solely British tradition of mixing fairytales with modern song and dance, especially around Christmas. These holiday plays are somber, solemn events recounting the Nativity with children playing the parts. Though they may be adorable only to the parents, we partake in them as fondly as we do Aunt Martha's annual fruitcake, and we do so with dignity and . . . Hey, who are you?

We apologize as the first writer has been sacked in favor of someone more interesting

The fact is, British panto is a theatrical style known and loved for centuries. The misconception that pantomime is solely about Frenchmen in invisible boxes is understandable, given the rampant popularity of Marcel Marceau, but it has little to do with Christmas and less to do with panto. So, what is the to-do here? For one, panto is a hysterical send up of fairy stories. Jack and the Beanstalk, Cinderella, and Aladdin are all popular targets, er, um, titles for panto theatre at Christmastime. What makes these adaptations of classic children's stories different and popular? Let me tell you!

Why panto is different and popular

For one, panto has been around since at least the 18th century, with singing and dancing coming into play in 1723 and the addition of dialogue coming in 1814. Having moved away from boxed-in Frenchmen, audiences figured that the players in these pantos should not have all the fun and so began to participate. Though Americans seem to reserve such shenanigans solely for the *Rocky Horror Picture Show,* panto crowds jeer, heckle, and join in the fun. This fun includes, as a matter of tradition of course, a woman in the part of the Principal Boy. Like Mary Martin in the role of Peter Pan, this is not just an excuse to ogle young women's legs in fancy tights but a perfectly reasonable tradition, unlike some other unreasonable traditions held by panto groups the world over.

The world over? Seriously? Yes, quite seriously!

We all know that football (known as soccer in the States, though no one seems to get socked) is an export from the British Empire that is now popular everywhere but America. Panto is like that too, except that there are no tournaments, no governing body of world panto players, the concessions are far more affordable, and most of the pantos around the world are staged by British expats who just want a taste of home without having to sing "God Save the Queen" over and over again.

But what about those unreasonable traditions you mentioned?

Oh, those? Well, first you have to understand what the reasonable traditions are, I suppose. Besides the gender reversal already mentioned, men often dress as women in pantos. The shows are often finished quickly, though this may be the fault of the male members.

OK, so here are the stranger things about panto. Did I mention that double entendre is part of the tradition? It is, but that aside, each panto is often no longer than 20 minutes. For this reason, panto groups often bunch several stories into a performance. After all, if you are inciting the crowd to be rowdy, then you really ought to give them their money's worth. In modern times, however, it has become tradition to include television and sports personalities as guest players.

Some panto groups have begun performing outside the traditional Christmas time frame, like the University of Western Australia's Pantomime Society, which performs once a semester and actually dares to incorporate modern elements such as zombies and television shows.

Sounds like fun. Where do I sign up?

Oh, here we go again with Americans wanting in on the fun. I suppose we should have seen this coming when *Spamalot* debuted in Chicago before it ever went to London's West End. The truth is,

Chicago itself is home to at least two American pantos. The Piccolo Theater in particular has been putting on pantos since 2002. Meanwhile, in Dallas, Texas, Theatre Britain has been performing pantos just as long. There are, of course, older groups around America that perform pantos, and some of them eschew the Christmas aspect of the panto all together. In West Des Moines, Iowa, a high school group known as The Baker's Dozen has been performing pantos since 1969.

Kindly leave the stage...to us!

If American teenagers are performing pantos, we know it must be popular. Why, we will probably see American comedy troupes similar to Monty Python next, and they may as well start paying English athletes to play soccer in cities like Los Angeles. As long as they don't start calling French fries "chips" or eating bangers and mash, British panto should be safe. Americans have their own ways of misappropriating classic children's stories, such as Fractured Fairytales or Hollywood films such as *Hoodwinked,* but they will never quite enjoy the same popularity as these traditional Christmastime farces for children and families.

"In the old days, it was not called the Holiday Season; the Christians called it 'Christmas' and went to church; the Jews called it 'Hanukkah' and went to synagogue; the atheists went to parties and drank. People passing each other on the street would say 'Merry Christmas!' or 'Happy Hanukkah!' or (to the atheists) 'Look out for the wall!'"

—Dave Barry

Jive Turkey

*Did the Pilgrims start a tradition by eating turkey at
the first Thanksgiving—or was that Tiny Tim's doing?*

Which came first, the turkey or Thanksgiving?

Governor William Bradley's journal from
around that time indicates that "besides
waterfowl there was great store of wild turkeys,
of which they took many." Another record notes that "our governor
sent four men on fowling...they four in one day killed as much fowl,
as with a little help beside, served the company almost a week."

Of course, "fowl" doesn't necessarily mean turkey, so the best we
can say is that the Pilgrims may have eaten it. The only food we
know for certain they ate was venison, and that was provided by their
guests, the Native Americans (who may have been a little surprised
by the meager spread their hosts had laid out). They probably also
ate codfish, goose, and lobster, but not a lot of vegetables—you can
catch fish and fowl, but it takes time to grow crops. And mashed
potatoes? Nope—potatoes hadn't yet been introduced to New
England.

So how did the gobbler become the centerpiece of Thanksgiving celebrations?

It may have had something to do with the prevalent diet at the time
the national holiday was founded in 1863. Beef and chicken were too
expensive to serve to a crowd. Even if you had your own farm, you
needed the animals' continuous supply of milk and eggs. Venison
was an option, but you couldn't always count on bagging a deer in
time for the holiday. Turkey was readily available, not too expensive—and very popular, perhaps in part due to the scene at the end
of Charles Dickens's *A Christmas Carol* in which Scrooge buys "the
prize turkey" for Bob Cratchit's family. The novel, published in 1843,
was immensely popular in America and may have secured the
humble fowl's center-stage spot on the Thanksgiving, and oftentimes
Christmas, table.

The Art of Christmas

*Some of the world's greatest painters have celebrated
the holiday season in their art.*

These days, the phrase "Christmas painting" may bring to mind thoughts of Thomas Kinkade's precious, glowing cottages, but Christmas has been used as a subject by many acclaimed, distinguished artists.

- Kinkade may be rolling in dough, but he will probably never overtake Norman Rockwell as America's favorite painter of Christmas. Rockwell's holiday covers for *The Saturday Evening Post*—often portraying Santa getting ready for the big day—are treasured by millions in the United States and around the world, and Rockwell's art has slowly but surely been undergoing a critical reevaluation.

- Like Rockwell, Joseph Christian Leyendecker often painted for the holiday covers of *The Saturday Evening Post,* but his vision was a bit more realistic; one might even say it was a bit darker. The cheeks of his Santas were not quite as rosy, the boughs of his Christmas trees were not quite as full, and the use of black and gray in his paintings is notable.

- Though not many people know it, pop artist Andy Warhol was a devout Catholic who adored the winter holidays and the celebrations and gift giving of the season. In 1958, he painted *Christmas Tree,* an abstract yet warm pyramid of ornaments. By mixing unexpected colors such as pale pink and sky blue in with the usual green and gold, Warhol created a whimsical winter delight. Decades later, in *Poinsettias* (1983), he painted a more traditional Christmas image using just red and white.

- Harriet M. Bennett was a late 18th-century English watercolor painter who not only illustrated many children's books but exhibited many paintings at the Royal Academy in London. Her *Five Children Fetch Home a Very Big Yule Log* is a wonderful example of the way she used bright colors sparingly—and therefore to great effect—amongst a backdrop of earth tones. Sadly, little is known about this pioneering female artist.

- Early 18th-century sporting artist Henry Thomas Alken was most famous for his hunting scenes, but his work also depicted such activities as horse racing and steeplechasing. To our modern eyes, his world seems stark, cold, and at times even cruel. In his painting *Christmas Deliveries,* a rather joyless carriage driver and his equally joyless (but quite healthy looking) white horse make their holiday rounds. Their red carriage is quite pretty, though.

- One of the most famous images of Santa is Thomas Nast's 1889 engraving *Merry Old Santa Claus.* Though born in Germany, Nast became a renowned cartoonist in New York, working for such publications as *Harper's Weekly* and the *New York Illustrated News.* He was the first to portray Santa not as a tall, thin, serious man but as the pipe-smoking, roly-poly, fun-loving guy we know today. This and other important works (including the Republican elephant and the Democratic donkey) made Nast famous.

- In 1896, artist Charles Green painted the lovely *Christmas Comes but Once a Year!* for the Pears' Christmas Annual (Pears was the most popular soap in Britain). Using soothing greens and blues, he depicts an upper-class English family gathering for Christmas dinner, two servant girls and a butler attending to their every need. The family members smile as a steaming plum pudding is carried across the dining room to the head of the table, but their domestics look a tad nervous.

- C. Coles Phillips was a successful American painter and illustrator in the early 20th century. His Christmas painting *Let's Party!* for the December 1926 cover of *Live* magazine portrays a red-clad flapper waving her paycheck in front of a Christmas tree. It is the perfect example of the kind of carefree, fun art that was so popular during the Jazz Age. Unfortunately, Phillips's promising career was cut short when he died of kidney failure at just 47 years old.

Poor Santa!

♨ ♨ ♨

*Mall Santas are resilient. They spend the holiday season sitting
in hot red suits and hotter white beards, listening to squirming
kids demand gifts. And through it all they maintain a cheerful and
ready "Ho ho ho." But even the most jolly fellow might get a little
Grinch-ish after what some of these Santas have gone through.*

Perhaps the most resilient of all mall Santas was Ken Deever, a Santa
from Des Moines, Iowa. In 2005, a few days before Deever's annual
Santa visit to a local elementary school, a fire destroyed his family
house, incinerating not only all of his personal possessions, but
almost 500 wrapped gifts that were meant to be distributed to the
schoolchildren. Deever spent the next two days replacing and
rewrapping the gifts in time for the school visit.

Even for Santas who haven't experienced major tragedies,
everyday life in Santa's Village can be a challenge. In 2006, Auntie
Anne's Pretzel Company conducted a survey of several hundred mall
Santas. Here were some of their findings:

• Number of Santas who had been peed on by a child: 34 percent

• Number of Santas coughed or sneezed on more than ten times per
day: 60 percent

• Nine out of ten Santas have their beards pulled at least once per
day by children

• Average Santa boot size: Between 10 and 11.5

• Average number of Santas who said those boots were stomped on
by kids at least once per day: 50 percent

Don't tell Mrs. Claus

With all this lap-sitting going on in malls across the country, impro-
prieties are bound to happen, but this 2007 incident was a little
surprising. A Danbury, Connecticut, woman asked to pose with a
Santa at the Danbury Fair mall—a normal enough request. But once
on his lap, the woman began fondling him inappropriately. She was
charged with fourth-degree sexual assault.

Christmas Around the World

JAPAN

Though Japan is home to few Christians, the Japanese love a good celebration—especially at Christmas!

Christmas is not a holiday generally associated with Japan. After all, less than one half of one percent of the nation's population are Christian. But as it turns out, this doesn't really matter. While the Japanese may not be into the religious aspects of the holiday, they can't get enough of the celebration!

Indeed, Christmas is amazingly popular in the Land of the Rising Sun. While December 25 is not a national holiday there as it is in the United States, the people still like to go all-out in the spirit of the season. On Christmas Eve, for example, it's traditional for the entire family to enjoy a special Christmas cake, which the father purchases on his way home from work.

Christmas Eve is also promoted as a day for romance. Young lovers use the holiday as an excuse for a romantic interlude, filling fancy restaurants and expensive hotels, while those at the beginning of a relationship may use it as an opportunity to express their true feelings. As a result, asking someone out on Christmas Eve has implications far deeper than just dinner and a movie.

A dinner most fowl
Speaking of dinner, chicken has become the meal of choice on Christmas Day for many Japanese—thanks to some savvy marketing by Kentucky Fried Chicken! In fact, so popular has the Christmas chicken dinner become in Japan that families often place their orders well in advance so they don't miss out.

Gifts are also given on Christmas Day. Parents commonly give gifts to their children, but children usually do not give gifts to their parents. The reason? Tradition states that only Santa Claus delivers presents.

Jesus may not have a significant role in Christmas in Japan, but that doesn't make the holiday any less important to those who celebrate it. Ultimately, a kind and generous spirit is the heart of the Japanese celebration.

Dickens Saves the (Christmas) Day!

Surely one of the best-known stories in all of English literature is Charles Dickens's A Christmas Carol. *The tale of Scrooge's journey from "Bah! Humbug!" to Christmas enlightenment resonates with even those most resistant to holiday cheer. In fact, the story is so powerful that it may have single-handedly put Christmas back in vogue at a time when it was close to disappearing for good.*

If you were living in England at the beginning of the Victorian era, Christmas was in trouble. There were medieval pagan traditions (e.g., yule logs, wassail) and Christian ones too, but any and all Christmastime festivities were coming under harsh scrutiny by Oliver Cromwell's Puritan insurgents.

Also, Christmas carols had disappeared around the turn of the century, and Christmas cards wouldn't be invented for another 40 years or so. Some people tried to hold Christmas feasts in secret and observe their traditions, but the government bans, combined with the Industrial Revolution that kept everyone working 24/7 and a disproportionate number of poor and needy, made for a holiday that was losing its shine. Late December was becoming a vague, not-so-special time of year for the vast majority of Victorian England.

Saving the day

Then a few things happened that changed history. First, Prince Albert, a huge fan of the German Christmas tree tradition, put that trend in vogue. People dusted off old Christmas carols, and in 1840, Christmas cards began appearing in mailboxes.

But more than any of these events, the boost Christmas needed was delivered with the 1843 publication of *A Christmas Carol* by the already mega-popular Charles Dickens. Dickens had gained huge popularity at home and had recently taken a trip to America, where he was treated like royalty. (He wrote *A Christmas Carol* in between making hundreds of appearances and traveling nearly every day.)

Dickens said later that he too loved the story he wrote, and he gladly gave readings of it often. One observer said he "wept, and laughed, and wept again, and excited himself in a most extraordinary manner in the composition."

The reception

The public reaction to the story was far beyond anyone's expectations. People all over the world wrote to Dickens telling him how the story had touched their hearts and changed their lives. The letters proved the power of Dickens's short holiday tale; people responded deeply to the celebration of human kindness, mercy, rebirth, and joy portrayed by beloved characters Tiny Tim, Bob Cratchit, and the jolly Mr. & Mrs. Fezziwig.

Dickens's deft writing was the key ingredient, of course. Mouthwatering descriptions of food, delightful dancing scenes, creepy ghosts, and an almost sci-fi premise (Scrooge goes back and forth in time, a fairly revolutionary idea at the time) made for a story that is still enjoyed, well into its second century of existence.

In the story, Christmas itself seems to be a character: The happy shoppers, the food purveyors in the town displaying their holiday goods, the continual "Merry Christmas" greetings called on the street, and the excitement built around the characters as Christmas approaches all had a huge impact on the millions of people who read the story. Suddenly, they remembered—or perhaps realized for the first time—how special the holiday really was.

They also warmed up to the romantic scene of Christmas that the author had painted and soon were emulating it. Garlands, gifts, cards, and Christmas feasts quickly came back into fashion for nearly every family, rich or poor.

Dickens's impact

A *Christmas Carol* is only the first of five Christmas-themed books written by Dickens. The stories are similar and follow some of the same ideas, but none have enjoyed the enduring popularity of *Carol*.

Since its first printing, there have been countless theater, film, television, radio, and opera adaptations, retellings, modernizations, and parodies of the classic story, and since the story continues to resound with pretty much any human being who reads it, those retellings don't show signs of stopping any time soon.

Crazy Canadian Cuisine

*On Christmas Eve, Newfoundlanders love
to belly up to a big bowl of bangbelly!*

Food is an integral part of the Christmas holidays. Depending on where you live, you might enjoy a Christmas goose, turkey, ham, or duck. If you're British, you might cap off your holiday meal with a yummy figgy pudding.

And if you're Canadian, well, there's always bangbelly.

The history of this unusual dessert is rather sketchy, as is the list of ingredients. At its simplest, bangbelly is kind of half pudding/half pastry culinary hybrid. Depending on which recipe you use—and there are a lot of them—the ingredients may include such eclectic items as salt pork, molasses, flour, raisins, spices, fruit, eggs, and even seal fat. (Good luck finding that at your local grocery store.) Some recipes call for soaking stale bread in water, which makes the dessert a second cousin to bread pudding. The ingredients are mixed together and then baked for more than an hour, resulting in a dish that is flaky on the outside and pudding-y on the inside.

Bangbelly is traditionally served on Christmas Eve, though how that custom got started is yet another mystery. Think of it as the Canadian equivalent of American fruitcake—a weird foodlike thing you see only around the holidays.

Other unusual dishes

As odd as bangbelly may sound, it's not the strangest thing Canadians put in their mouths. There's flipper pie, for example—which is made with real seal flippers. (Look for them in your grocery store next to the seal fat.) And let's not forget fish and brewis, a popular Newfoundland meal prepared from salt cod made with hardtack, soaked in water, and served with molasses and salt pork.

Of course, the food on your plate at Christmastime isn't as important as the people you're sharing it with. Friendship is what Christmas is really all about.

Please pass the bangbelly, dear friend!

An Alabama First!

*Christmas is an international holiday, but Alabama
was the first state to grant it legal status.*

It's commonly believed that Christmas has been a legal holiday in
the United States since the nation was established, but that's not
correct. While the birth of Christ has been celebrated worldwide for
nearly two millennia, no mention of it appears anywhere in the
establishing documents created by our country's founders.

As a result, it wasn't until 1836 that Christmas was finally granted
legal recognition in the United States. The first state to do so?
Alabama!

By 1890, all the remaining states and territories, plus the District
of Columbia, had followed Alabama's lead in establishing Christmas
as a legal holiday. Interestingly, Christmas is also the only religious
holiday to receive this kind of official secular recognition in America.

No cause for celebration

Despite this historic first step, Alabama celebrates Christmas pretty
much like all the other states; nothing special is done to observe the
Yellowhammer State's foresight in making Christmas something
more than just a religious observance. But that shouldn't stop those
who know about the first-of-its-kind legislation from feeling just a
little superior.

The Christmas holiday aside, Alabama has hosted many other
important achievements over the years. Among them:

• Alabama introduced Mardi Gras to the Western world. (Sorry,
New Orleans!)

• Montgomery established the nation's first electric trolley system.
It premiered in 1886.

• The first open-heart surgery in the Western Hemisphere was
performed by Dr. Luther Leonidas Hill of Montgomery in 1902.
He saved a boy's life by suturing a stab wound in the youngster's
heart.

Holy Days and Holidays

Celebrating Christmas in the land where it all began.

So intense and bloody have the battles between Jews and Muslims in the Holy Land been over the last six decades that the Christian minority is often almost completely forgotten. Out of a population of about 7.5 million, approximately 2 percent of Israel's citizens identify themselves as Christian. Though the history of Christ's followers in the Holy Land has been twisted and turbulent, they continue to practice their faith in the place where it began more than two thousand years ago.

Crusades and controversy

To say that Christianity never really "caught on" with the Jews of ancient Israel would be an understatement. Though Christ's first followers and apostles were obviously Jews, after his death they had trouble making any significant inroads among their own people, who were still burdened by Roman occupation and economic struggles. This new religion traveled well, however, and spread quickly through Greece, Rome, and upward into Europe. By the end of the 4th century, it had made its way back to the Holy Land, which became and remained predominantly Christian for the next 300 years or so. When Arab armies conquered Palestine in the 7th century, the persecution of Christians began and reached its height with the destruction of the Church of the Holy Sepulchre in 1009. This oppression led to Christian outrage in Europe and planted the seed of the Crusades.

The Crusades were Church-approved military campaigns conducted between 1095 and 1291. Though Palestine was only one of its targets, it was certainly the most meaningful. Here, after all, was the place of Jesus' birth, ministry, and crucifixion. It seemed so wrong to Medieval European Christians that it should be in the hands of Muslims. The Crusaders also wanted to make sure the Holy Land never fell into the hands of Jews again, and they persecuted Jews throughout Europe and the Middle East as they attempted to gain control of Palestine. All these things happened at what seems to us a snail's pace, covering hundreds of years and creating deep resentments that continue to affect the political landscape today.

Pious pilgrims

Though the Crusades were ultimately unsuccessful in restoring Christian rule to the Holy Land, a small Christian community remained there after the last Crusade and Christian believers continued to make their pilgrimages to Bethlehem, Nazareth, and Jerusalem. Most of the Christian communities that exist in the Holy Land today could be categorized into one of four groups: Catholic, Protestant, Orthodox, and non-Chalcedonian. Despite their theological differences, most Christians in the Holy Land speak Arabic and most descend from the early Byzantine Christian communities.

In theory, Israeli and Palestinian Christians are free to worship as they please. The State of Israel declared in its 1948 Declaration of Independence that it would " . . . be based on freedom, justice and peace as envisaged by the Prophets of Israel; it will ensure complete equality of social and political rights to all its inhabitants irrespective of religion, race or sex; it will guarantee freedom of religion, conscience, language, education and culture . . . " Of course, this is easier said than done in a land so plagued by religious strife, and Christians have at times been the object of bigotry by both Jews and Muslims. Some Christians—especially tourists—have also been insensitive to the local Jews and Muslims.

Still, most Jews and Muslims realize that Christian tourism—and the Christian citizens of their country who facilitate it—are an important part of their economic survival. Bethlehem, which has been governed by the Palestinian National Authority since 1995, relies heavily on tourism, which makes up 65 percent of the city's economy. And 25 percent of Bethlehem's working population works in the tourist industry. Everyone who lives in Bethlehem—Christians, Muslims, and Jews—realizes the importance of creating a safe space for Christian pilgrims who travel to the Church of the Nativity and Manger Square every Christmas season.

Very Special Christmas Episodes

🕯 🕯 🕯

Christmastime means a change of pace for television viewers every year. Almost since the dawn of television, our favorite programs have produced special holiday episodes for the season. This is in addition to a number of specials and made-for-TV movies that have become perennial classics. Sweeps may take place in spring, but we're all watching our televisions at Christmas.

America meets Parson Brown

One of the first shows on television to produce a Christmas special was Perry Como's. America's favorite baritone started making Christmas specials in 1948, and he kept them coming for decades, the last one airing in 1987. That first special helped cement the song "Winter Wonderland," already a hit for Como, as a Christmas classic that is still one of the most performed holiday tunes to this day. A snowman, though prominently featured in the song, wouldn't find himself in his own Christmas special until 1969.

Animated wonderland

Of course, Rankin and Bass first hit it big with TV audiences in 1964 with *Rudolph the Red-Nosed Reindeer.* This first hit allowed them to bring us more specials, including *The Little Drummer Boy* (1968), *Frosty the Snowman* (1969), and *The Year Without a Santa Claus* (1974). Rankin and Bass weren't the only animators to get in on the holiday special craze though. In 1965, Bill Meléndez brought Charles Schulz's *Peanuts* character to life in *A Charlie Brown Christmas.*

This huge hit, sponsored by Coca-Cola, spawned over 75 other

Peanuts specials. A year after that, Looney Tunes alum Chuck Jones got into the Christmas special game himself with *How the Grinch Stole Christmas!* based on the Dr. Seuss book of the same name. All these still air regularly around the world during the holidays.

We now return to your regularly scheduled programming

Specials aside, regular series have been continuing the tradition started by Perry Como. Across nearly every genre, many shows have chosen to create episodes showing how some of our favorite characters have celebrated, or at least coped with, the holiday season. In some cases, these have been retellings of already classic stories, recast with a show's characters. In others, show producers have set out to create new memories for us to cherish. Both takes on Christmas episodes have met with mixed results.

Carol of the network stars

One tradition that seems to have developed in the short history of television broadcasting is that of re-creating stories we already love within the confines of our favorite shows. In some cases, the episodes bear little resemblance to the classics for which the episode is cleverly named. On *The Honeymooners*, for example, the episode called "'Twas the Night Before Christmas" had nothing to do with sleeping children or dancing sweets. Instead, the episode follows a plot closer to the O. Henry classic *Gift of the Magi*, showing the exploits of Ralph Kramden as he decides to sell his beloved bowling ball in order to buy a last-minute gift for his wife, Alice. In other cases, the plot of the titular classic is lifted directly and adapted to the format of the show. On *Family Ties*, Alex Keaton took the place of Ebenezer Scrooge in "A Keaton Christmas Carol," and *Xena: Warrior Princess* took the same plot and retrofitted it to fit in that show's setting of ancient Greece in the episode "A Solstice Carol."

In with the new

Some of the best Christmas episodes are ones that attempt to tell us a new story. These new entries sometimes come to hold just as much meaning for us at the holidays as their "based-on-a-classic" counterparts. The first season of *M*A*S*H* featured a Christmas episode called "Dear Dad," where Hawkeye Pierce narrates a letter home to his father detailing the ups and downs of the holiday in a war zone. The episode records the only appearance of a wartime Santa/surgeon hybrid in television history. Then there's the series *Lost,* which used the spirit of Christmas to bring home a message of love in an episode called "The Constant." Though it didn't air during the holidays, the association is clear.

Sometimes the Christmas episodes we love most don't have much to do with Christmas at all, as the show *Seinfeld* proved. In its last season, *Seinfeld* viewers learned of a brand new holiday called Festivus in an episode called "The Strike." Festivus, though a made-up holiday, has gained in popularity since the episode aired in 1997. During the holidays, Americans of all creeds can be found observing the traditions laid out on the show. The Wisconsin Historical Museum even features a "Festivus Pole" used by Governor Jim Doyle in the executive residence in Madison in 2005.

Flat screens instead of yule logs

Like it or not, television is just as much a part of the fabric of American culture as Christmas and apple pie. Some networks have made it a tradition to run films such as *A Christmas Story,* *A Christmas Carol,* or in years past, *It's a Wonderful Life* with such regularity that many people can now quote the films almost word for word. Many more specials and episodes exist than are mentioned here, and everyone seems to have their favorite. However we decide to celebrate the holiday, regardless of whether we live in snowy and cold Alaska or sunny Florida, Christmas reaches out to us and our families from the television reminding us why we love the holiday so much.

"I will honor Christmas in my heart, and try to keep it all the year."
—*Ebenezer Scrooge, in Charles Dickens's*
A Christmas Carol

What Carol Is This?

Check out these lines, and see if you can pick out which popular carols and songs they come from.

1. *That makes each toy to sparkle bright*
   a. "Santa Claus Is Coming to Town"
   b. "Suzy Snowflake"
   c. "O Christmas Tree"
   d. "Do You Hear What I Hear?"

2. *Frankincense to offer have I*
   a. "Good King Wenceslas"
   b. "We Three Kings"
   c. "Joy to the World"
   d. "Away in a Manger"

3. *Look at her tumblin' down*
   a. "Baby, It's Cold Outside"
   b. "Grandma Got Run Over by a Reindeer"
   c. "Suzy Snowflake"
   d. "All I Want for Christmas Is My Two Front Teeth"

4. *Oh, just see what a glorious fill!*
   a. "Here Comes Santa Claus"
   b. "Over the River"
   c. "The Marvelous Toy"
   d. "Up on the Housetop"

5. *And there it did both pause and stay*
   a. "O Little Town of Bethlehem"
   b. "The First Noel"
   c. "O Christmas Tree"
   d. "Away in a Manger"

6. *Until the other kiddies knock him down*
   a. "Winter Wonderland"
   b. "Frosty the Snowman"
   c. "Grandma Got Run Over by a Reindeer"
   d. "Run, Run Rudolph"

Answers: 1. c; 2. b; 3. c; 4. d; 5. b; 6. a

A Fairy Tale Come True

Too many cooks didn't spoil this Christmas soup.

Most entertainment for children is, of course, written by adults, so it is not surprising that the problems and fears of the grown-up world often seep into stories for youngsters. It's hard to believe, but *The Nutcracker*—a two-act, three-scene ballet that has delighted children for generations—began as a bleak, depressing book for adults that used a child's world of toys as a metaphor for an adult world in which personal hopes are often crushed by larger forces and dreams die in the face of reality. (Merry Christmas! Woo-hoo!)

The Nutcracker is based on an 1816 novel called *The Nutcracker and the Mouse King,* written by a German romantic writer named E. T. A. Hoffmann. As a young man working as a civil servant in Prussian Poland, Hoffmann broke up the monotony with such cheerful hobbies as drawing sketches of filthy peasants and himself drowning in a sea of mud. Legal disputes, debt, alcoholism, syphilis, the War of the Sixth Coalition, political intrigue, and various lost loves ensured him a life of almost constant despondency and stress. But the guy could write, even if what he wrote was depressing as heck. In *The Nutcracker and the Mouse King,* the little protagonist, Marie, is terrorized and even physically injured to the point that she winds up in a pool of blood after being caught up in a battle between her Christmas nutcracker, which has come to life, and the Mouse King and his rodent army.

Bring in the bomb squad

Unsurprisingly, *The Nutcracker and the Mouse King* didn't exactly fly off the shelves. Hoffmann had what we would now call a "demographic problem": Adults didn't want to read about a little girl getting hurt, and children didn't want to read such a long novel about anything. But Hoffmann's publisher realized there was potential in the story and didn't want to give up on it, so he asked French author Alexandre Dumas to "clean it up" and commercialize it. Dumas shortened it, lightened up the story overall, and gave it a happy ending. *The Nutcracker and the Mouse King* was now a children's fairy tale, and the book began to sell in much larger numbers.

In the late 19th century, Marius Petipa, the ballet master of the Russian Imperial Ballet, read the Dumas version of *The Nutcracker and the Mouse King* and decided to adapt it for the stage. Petipa is widely regarded as one of the most talented choreographers who ever lived, a man who created over 50 ballets and whose influence is still felt today. He felt that his good friend, the composer Peter Ilyich Tchaikovsky, would be the best man to write the score of *The Nutcracker.* He asked the director of the Imperial Theatres, Ivan Vsevolozhsky, to help him convince Tchaikovsky to do it. Tchaikovsky had just finished another ballet, *The Sleeping Beauty,* and he didn't really care for the source material for *The Nutcracker,* but he accepted the commission anyway and slogged through the work.

Took you long enough

The Nutcracker premiered at the Imperial Mariinsky Theatre in St. Petersburg, Russia, on December 18, 1892. It had been a long, 76-year journey from Hoffmann's dark novel to this bright, beautiful ballet; indeed, the finished product was barely recognizable as Hoffmann's work. The wounded, terrorized Marie was now Clara, a wide-eyed innocent who, in the end, rides off to a life of happiness with a nutcracker prince. The gloom and doom of the book was replaced by the joy of the waltzing flowers, the Spanish dancers, and the beautiful Sugar Plum Fairy.

Though *The Nutcracker* was fairly well known over the next five decades, it was not until the New York City Ballet performed George Balanchine's staging in 1954 that *The Nutcracker* really took off in America. Now it is performed all over the United States, every year, to the delight of both children and adults.

Kris Kringel Delivers!

*Kris Kringel of North Pole, Alaska, lives up to
the reputation of his much more famous namesake.*

It's one thing to look like Santa Claus, but it's even more impressive when you also share his name and live in his hometown.

Just ask Kris Kringel. Not only is his name similar (the real Santa also goes by Kris Kringle), but Kringel lives in North Pole (Alaska, just outside of Fairbanks) and delivers goodies for a living. In Kringel's case, however, it's pizzas instead of toys, and in lieu of a reindeer-driven sleigh, he gets around in an old Ford Tempo.

Actually, pizza delivery is Kringel's second job. During the holiday season, his primary occupation is portraying St. Nick at North Pole's famous Santa Claus House. It's the perfect gig for Kringel because his silver hair, white beard, and protruding belly make him look just like the jolly old elf!

Ho! ho! hot! pizza

Kringel strives to make pizza delivery fun. He often wears a bright red robe when on the job, and more than a few children have watched, wide-eyed, as "Santa" brought their families a piping hot pie. When asked, he tells the youngsters that he is just checking on them to see if they are being naughty or nice. Many parents have found that his arrival means better-behaved children and specifically request him when ordering a pizza.

Kringel's current hometown, which has a population of fewer than 2,000 people, has never hesitated to cash in on its association with Santa Claus. It promotes itself as the place where Santa lives, and as a result, its post office receives bundles of letters addressed to St. Nick every holiday season.

Despite its name, however, North Pole, Alaska, isn't even close to the earth's geographic North Pole. In fact, it's about 1,700 miles away—as the sleigh flies.

TURKEY

*Though predominantly a Muslim nation,
Turkey goes all out for Christmas!*

The city is bustling as Christmas draws near. Storefronts are decorated with bright holiday lights and signs reading "Merry Christmas," and the sidewalks are crowded with smiling shoppers in search of last-minute gifts. Are we in New York? London? Nope—we're in Ankara, Turkey!

It may seem odd that a nation with a population that is 99 percent Muslim would celebrate Christmas with such enthusiasm, but that's what makes Turkey so special. Officially a secular nation, Turkey's Muslim majority get along well with their Christian neighbors and are happy to celebrate their cherished holiday with them.

Let's go shopping!

Christmas in Turkey isn't as big a religious celebration as it is in other parts of the world; manger scenes and angels are understandably few. It's the gift-giving aspect of the holiday—with a strong emphasis on Santa Claus—that makes Christmas here what it is.

This makes sense, considering that the real St. Nicholas was born in Demre (formerly Myra), Turkey. In his homeland, St. Nick is fondly referred to as Noel Baba, or Father Christmas, and thousands of devout Orthodox pilgrims from around the world visit his birthplace every year.

The city is extremely proud of its St. Nick connection, and vendors there sell his image on everything from plates to rugs. In 1955, Turkey issued a Santa Claus stamp to draw even more attention to the nation's best-known saint, and starting in 1981, a variety of St. Nick–themed events have been held under the auspices of the Turkish Ministry of Culture and Tourism.

Christmas in Turkey is a very special holiday, celebrated by people with a unique connection that can be claimed by no others.

Christmas in the White House

In the over 200 years that American presidents have been living in the White House, many Christmases have come and gone. You might think then that the president's abode would be steeped in holiday traditions, but you'd be wrong. Though it is presently the first lady's honor to follow through on several Christmas traditions, many of those in practice today are actually very modern.

Even the Christmas tree, which many would say is a universal tradition, hasn't necessarily been a White House tradition. When President Warren G. Harding's wife fell ill in 1922, for example, the *Washington Post* reported that the first family was celebrating the season quietly and without a tree, and President Teddy Roosevelt didn't order one once or twice. If we want true consistency in White House Christmas traditions, however, we really can't go back much further than the 1960s.

"Christmas is not a time nor a season, but a state of mind."—Calvin Coolidge

The presentation of the White House Christmas tree by the National Christmas Tree Association (NCTA) dates back only to 1966. Every year since then, the first lady has accepted the tree on behalf of the nation and then displayed it in the Blue Room within the executive residence. Though it might sound simple, the first family doesn't just go out to a tree farm like the Parkers or the Griswolds. The selection of the tree involves a series of contests (similar to state and national beauty pageants) held by the NCTA. Once the tree is presented, the real work of decorating begins, and since 1961, the first lady has designated a particular theme for the tree. Jacqueline Kennedy's first theme was "The Nutcracker Suite," and the theme in 2009, as designated by Michelle Obama, was "Reflect, Rejoice, Renew."

This aspect of the tradition is no stranger to controversy, however. Often, artists and others from outside the White House create the decorations, and sometimes those making them seem to have a sense of humor. The Clinton family was criticized in 1995 for keeping an ornament that depicted then Speaker of the House Newt Gingrich's Christmas stocking as being full of coal. On the other side of the aisle, the Bush family faced similar disapproval from the public in 2008 when they chose to exclude an ornament they received that featured the phrase "Impeach Bush." Thankfully, other White House Christmas traditions seem to escape public rancor.

Nixon should have been a gingerbread man

Several modern traditions stem from Pat Nixon, who in 1969 charged the White House Pastry Team to create the first White House gingerbread house. Since then, this has become a full-blown replica of the presidential residence itself. The intricacy of the gingerbread White House has grown over the years; it has become a 400-pound behemoth, complete with working lights, shadowbox rooms with scale furniture made from dark chocolate, and even marzipan replicas of the gardens and the first family's dog. More than 150 pounds of gingerbread dough is baked and then cut with a band saw before being assembled with the same white chocolate that will give the building its signature finish. This is one of many attractions awaiting visitors to the White House during the holidays.

Candles, cards, and a crèche

Pat Nixon also started the tradition of offering candlelight tours of the White House during the 1969 holiday season. These tours, scaled back somewhat since 2001, are the same as the tours that take place during normal operating hours, but admission times are extended until about 7:00 P.M. People on the tour can marvel at the gingerbread replica of the White House, see the decorations on the White House Christmas tree up close, and even view the White House crèche in the East Room. Though the crèche itself dates to the 18th century, the tradition of displaying it in the East Room began in 1967, when Lady Bird Johnson received it as a gift from billionaire Charles W. Engelhard Jr.

What the public will not see on these tours, however, is perhaps the oldest of the modern White House Christmas traditions. Starting in 1953 with President Eisenhower, the White House has sent out official Christmas cards from the president, extending the holiday cheer of the presidential mansion around the globe for all to share.

Christmas in the Big Apple

There's only one place in the world with as much Christmas spirit as the North Pole—New York City. Not only is the Big Apple where the "real" Santa sets up shop during the days leading up to Christmas, but it's the setting for many of the season's best books and movies.

The tree at Rockefeller Center

The next time you complain about stringing lights on your Christmas tree, consider what it takes to decorate the towering fir in Rockefeller Center. The first Christmas tree appeared on the site in 1931, when workers in the Great Depression placed a tree in the dirt. That year, the tree symbolized the indomitable human spirit as much as it did Christmas. In 1933, the tradition as we now know it began with a tree adorned with 700 lights and placed in front of the eight-month-old RCA Building. The Rockefeller Plaza Outdoor Ice-Skating Pond opened in 1936.

The celebrations have varied from year to year. In 1941, two live reindeer borrowed from the Bronx Zoo were housed in cages beside the Prometheus Fountain. During World War II, three living trees—all without lights due to wartime restrictions on electricity—graced the Center. In 1949, the tree was painted silver. In 1951, the entire nation witnessed the tree lighting ceremony when it was televised on the *Kate Smith Show.* And by 1964, the ceremony had become an annual event, with celebrities such as Johnny Carson, Hugh Downs, Ed McMahon, Barbara Walters, Marlo Thomas, and Phil Donahue hosting the show. Today, the tree is recycled after the holidays, providing three tons of mulch.

Radio City Music Hall Christmas Spectacular

In New York, the Christmas season officially "kicks off" with the first showing of the Radio City Music Hall's *Christmas Spectacular.* Originally performed as a holiday gift to the audience before movie screenings, the show expanded to its current 90-minute live stage production in 1979. For nine weeks each year, the show attracts over a million people to its performances, and gazillions more see the show on its holiday tour to major cities around America. No doubt its over-the-top presentation is a major reason why it's the number-one live show in the country. Some examples:

- The cast changes costumes eight times during each show, with as little as 78 seconds between numbers to do so. In all, there are 1,300 costumes worn.

- The Wurlitzer Organ that plays for all performances of the *Spectacular* boasts 4,328 pipes and 1 million moving parts, all of which are housed in 11 rooms honeycombed around the theater.

- During the "Music Hall Menagerie," two donkeys, three camels, five sheep, and a horse make a special appearance. The animals have their own staff of trainers offstage.

- A real ice rink built on a movable platform is used during the "Christmas in New York" scene, made from an artificial surface with the same properties as real ice.

- The "Here Comes Santa Claus" number features every member of the cast dressed as Santa to explain how Santa can actually deliver gifts to every boy and girl in the world, all in one night.

- Over 2,500 pounds of "snow" fall upon the Great Stage during the show's run.

Santaland and street celebrations

In the season of spend, spend, spend, here's some good news about celebrating the holidays in New York City: Some of the best sights and sounds of the season are free—yes, FREE. For starters, there are scads of holiday lights to ogle, the most visible of which is the light show compliments of the Empire State Building. During the holidays, the building glows red and green to celebrate Christmas, changing to a blue and white combo for Hanukkah. Along Park Avenue, two miles' worth of holiday trees all twinkle with white

Christmas lights—an especially breathtaking sight at night when the fog has rolled in. At Grand Central Terminal, the restored Sky Ceiling features a five-minute musical laser-light display every half hour during the holidays. And in Little Italy, weekends in December set the scene for parades, free entertainment, and street vendors on Mulberry Street between Canal and Broome streets.

Peeping for free

Another freebie is the ultimate spectator sport of window peeping. It seems that every department store in the city tries to outdo the others with outrageous, decadent, and unbelievable window displays. Live musicians and ballerinas, muppet and celebrity appearances, recreations of entire winter wonderlands, working trains and sleighs, couture clothing, and every other fantasy imaginable are among the eye candy awaiting window peepers. Fifth Avenue boasts the crème de la crème of window displays, with creations by Saks Fifth Avenue, Bergdorf Goodman, Lord & Taylor, Tiffany & Co., and FAO Schwarz, to name a few. Go after closing time to avoid the crowds and get an up-close view of the windows.

And it's not over until you see the jolly old elf himself. Santa Claus arrives in full pomp and circumstance at the tail end of Macy's Thanksgiving Day Parade to—of course—reign over Macy's Santaland in the 34th Street flagship store for the entire month of December. If you're lucky, you'll not only get to sit on Santa's lap (the lap is free but a picture will cost you), but you might even catch a glimpse of Buddy, the lovable elf played by Will Ferrell in the movie *Elf*, who works and falls in love in the toy department.

"Let us keep Christmas beautiful without a thought of greed, that it might live forevermore to fill our every need, that it shall not be just a day, but last a lifetime through, the miracle of Christmastime that brings God close to you."

—*Ann Schultz*

Ageless and Evergreen

🕯️ 🕯️ 🕯️

*It took a Jewish girl from Brooklyn to make
the perfect Christmas album.*

Back in the day, many Jewish stars changed everything from their names to their noses in order to hide their ethnic heritage and be more "presentable" to mainstream audiences. But young Barbra Streisand, who became a huge star in the early '60s with her hit albums and her Broadway show and movie *Funny Girl,* refused to change a thing about herself. She was who she was, she liked what she liked, and she wanted what she wanted. And if she wanted to make a Christmas album, she wasn't going to let anyone tell her she couldn't just because she was Jewish.

A Christmas Album was recorded in London and Los Angeles in 1966 and 1967. Producers Jack Gold and Ettore Stratta and arranger/conductor Marty Paich were some of the top talents in the business, and their musical knowledge and guidance were invaluable assets to Streisand on this project. Streisand decided to split the album in half, with side one featuring secular holiday songs and side two featuring songs that emphasized the religious nature of Christmas.

Like buttah

One of the most memorable songs on *A Christmas Album* is Streisand's version of "Jingle Bells?" The cheeky question mark was added to the title because in its new arrangement by Gold and Paich, the traditionally mid-tempo tune was bumped up into a frenetic ditty that used Streisand's comedic skills as well as her vocal skills. But naturally, nothing could outshine those pipes, especially on the religious songs. Young Streisand's voice is a knockout on such songs as "O Little Town of Bethlehem" and "Sleep in Heavenly Peace (Silent Night)."

Though *A Christmas Album* originally only peaked at number 108 on the *Billboard* charts, it has gone on to become one of the best-selling Christmas albums of all time. Not bad for a Jewish girl from Brooklyn.

From Germany to England

The phrase "Christmas in England" brings to mind Father Christmas, Ebenezer Scrooge, roast turkey, plum pudding, and of course... a beautifully decorated Christmas tree. You might be surprised to learn, though, how relatively new the Christmas tree is to jolly olde England and how it arrived on British shores as a result of one of that country's most legendary romances.

Queen Victoria ascended to the throne of England on June 20, 1837, at the tender age of 18. Her uncle, King William IV, had died of heart failure, leaving behind only the ten illegitimate children he had sired with the actress Dorothea Jordan. Victoria was a confident young woman, and though she could hardly be called a feminist, she had no doubt in her leadership abilities as a woman. Still, like generations of women after her, she longed to "have it all." Taking a husband and bearing children was a monarch's duty, of course, but it was a duty she was happy to fulfill. She would have married out of political obligation alone if it had come to that, but instead she was lucky enough to find happiness in that rarest of relationships: a royal love match.

Marry me?

Unions between first cousins were nothing out of the ordinary in those days, especially among royals and aristocrats, so Victoria felt no need to hold back her feelings upon meeting her cousin Prince Albert of Saxe-Coburg and Gotha. The young German prince was handsome, kind, and intelligent, and Victoria quickly fell in love. She also knew that the sooner she married, the sooner she would be out from under the control of her domineering mother, with whom, as a proper 19th-century young lady, she was required to live. In any case, as queen she couldn't wait around for Albert to propose—his lower rank made that impossible. So Victoria proposed to Albert, and they were married on February 10, 1840. Albert's new, formal title was His Royal Highness Prince Albert.

Like Victoria, Albert was eager to start his own family, perhaps because his childhood had been full of heartache. His parents, Ernest I, Duke of Saxe-Coburg-Saalfeld, and Louise of Saxe-Gotha-Altenburg, had fought constantly over their infidelities. Many historians believe that Albert was the biological son of Baron von Mayern, the chamberlain at the court of Saxe-Coburg-Gotha. When Albert was seven years old, his parents mercifully divorced, and he settled into a comfortable life of study and play. But he was never allowed to see his mother again—

surely a terrible ordeal for any small child to go through. Albert clung to the things he still had, and two of those things were German culture and the Lutheran Evangelical Church.

Missing home

The newlyweds Victoria and Albert were blissfully happy and very much in love, but Albert was homesick. Though still a Protestant, he'd obviously been forced to leave Lutheranism for the Church of England when he'd married the Defender of the Faith. And so many other things were different, too, including the language, eating and drinking habits, and childrearing methods. Albert felt out of his element, and Victoria noticed that this homesickness hit him especially hard during religious holidays. She encouraged him to keep his German traditions, even if he had to practice them far from home.

Though the Christmas tree was not unheard of in England—the gossipy diarist Henry Greville recounted that the German Princess Lieven decorated three at her 1827 holiday party in London—the English had shown no interest in adopting this German symbol for themselves. That all changed 13 years later when Victoria and Albert began their family, and Albert placed a Christmas tree, with presents beneath it, in the nursery for their children. The British press eagerly reported this cozy scene, the English promptly fell in love with the Christmas tree, and what was at first thought a "fad" is now a beloved institution.

Going Out, Not Stressing Out

Christmas in a restaurant? Why not?

Not everyone feels the need to cook a big dinner and celebrate Christmas at home. The number of Americans who trade the traditional home-centered festivities for a relaxing dinner in a restaurant on Christmas Eve or Christmas Day grows every year, but some may be loath to admit it. Friends and relatives who continue to "keep Christmas" in the customary manner often react with shock. "What?! Christmas in a restaurant? It's just not right." For those who choose the restaurant route, however, their reasons are many and varied.

A relaxing choice

The stereotype of the Christmas restaurant patron is that of a lonely, friendless recluse, venturing out only because he or she is too depressed to even pop a TV dinner into the microwave. Well, don't tell that to a whole new generation of diners who've decided that the stress of cooking at home affects their holiday more negatively than positively. They are thrilled that in every city in America, they now have more choices than ever when it comes to eating out on Christmas Eve or Christmas Day.

It used to be that urban Christmas diners would simply take a tip from their Jewish friends and head to the nearest Chinese restaurant, and Asian restaurants are still a great alternative. But in recent years, restaurants have responded to their patrons' requests for more traditional American and European fare. In New York, Chicago, and many other major metropolitan areas, an upscale roast goose or turkey dinner can be found with just a few phone calls. An Italian restaurant, serving a traditional fish dinner on Christmas Eve, makes a great choice for couples looking for something a bit more romantic. Whatever the choice, though, the relaxation means "luxury," not "loneliness."

The Cinnamon Bear

Paddy O'Cinnamon, Crazy-Quilt Dragon, the Wintergreen Witch.... Children couldn't bear to miss an exciting episode of this Christmas-themed radio show!

The Cinnamon Bear was a popular radio show that originally aired in 1937 and was produced by Transco (Transcription Company of America). It was a special syndicated holiday serial, broadcast between Thanksgiving and Christmas, and developed by a group of retailers as a holiday ad promotion. The campaign worked: The show was broadcast for many years after (even to this day on old-time radio shows), and the bear with shoe-button eyes captured the imagination of children around the world.

The program follows the adventures of twins Judy and Jimmy Barton who wander through the magical world of Maybeland to reclaim the Silver Star that has gone missing from their Christmas tree. Cinnamon Bear helps them in their quest, and along the way, they meet such eccentric characters as the Wintergreen Witch, the Crazy-Quilt Dragon, and the Roly-Poly Policemen. They also discover enchanted places such as Root Beer Ocean, the Lollipop Mountains, and the Wishing Woods. Of course, Santa himself shows up as well. The plot was intended to be in the vein of *Alice's Adventures in Wonderland* and *The Wonderful Wizard of Oz.* Glanville Heisch, with assistance from his wife, created the songs and story in only six weeks.

The characters in *The Cinnamon Bear* were voiced by popular radio talents of the day. The Cinnamon Bear was voiced by Buddy Duncan, a vaudeville comedian and little person; Lou Merill portrayed Santa Claus; Barbara Jean Wong lent her voice for Judy Barton; while the actor who performed the role of Jimmy Barton remains something of a mystery (some credit it to Walter Tetley).

The Cinnamon Bear was especially popular in the Northwest—namely in Portland, Oregon, where it was broadcast on two AM stations, KXL and KALE. In 2005, Portland Spirit Cruises introduced a holiday Cinnamon Bear Cruise where children can come onboard and meet characters from the radio show.

Let It Snow!

Do you crave a white Christmas? There are plenty of places throughout the United States that receive more than a little snow.

To many, a Christmas without a blanket of snow outside is a dreary Christmas indeed. But if you're willing to put in the miles, there are plenty of places in the United States that won't disappoint. In fact, several regions receive more than 100 inches of snowfall each year, so if you go, don't forget your shovel!

Take the Rainier Paradise Ranger Station in Washington State, for example. It averages 676 inches of snow annually—enough to make an entire army of snowmen! Other American locales that see 100 or more inches of snow a year include

- Mt. Baker Ski Area, Washington: 647 inches

- Valdez, Alaska: 326 inches

- Mt. Washington, New Hampshire: 261 inches

- Blue Canyon, California: 240 inches

- Yakutat, Alaska: 191 inches

- Marquette, Michigan: 144 inches

- Syracuse, New York: 118 inches

- Sault Ste. Marie, Michigan: 117 inches

- Talkeetna, Alaska: 115 inches

- Caribou, Maine: 112 inches

- Mount Shasta, California: 105 inches

- Flagstaff, Arizona: 101 inches

- Lander, Wyoming: 100 inches

Interestingly, the Mt. Baker Ski Area also holds the world record for the most snow in a single year: 1,140 inches, or 95 feet. This landmark meteorological event occurred between July 1, 1998, and June 30, 1999. In total, weather stations in 10 states have recorded more than 30 feet of snow in a single 12-month period.

How about the most amount of snow to fall in a single day? That record goes to Georgetown, Colorado, which saw a heart-attack–inducing 63 inches fall on December 4, 1913. Thompson Pass, Alaska, comes in second—barely—with 62 inches on December 29, 1955, followed by Giant Forest, California (60 inches on January 19, 1933), Millegan, Montana (48 inches on December 27, 2003), and Gunn's Ranch, Washington (48 inches on January 21, 1935).

That's *snow* joke!

More on Christmas Cards!

- *Christmas cards account for 60 percent of all card sales each year. More than two billion boxed and individual cards are purchased annually.*

- *The first official White House Christmas card was mailed in 1953 by President Eisenhower. In 1961, the White House mailed out 2,000 cards; by 2008, the number had increased to 2.25 million.*

Baby, It's Cold Outside: Life at the North Pole

*Things are snowy and sparse at the
northernmost point on earth!*

Even though we know the real North Pole is frozen and barren, it can still be difficult to shake our childhood imaginings of it as the home of Santa Claus and Mrs. Claus—a mysterious and magical Christmas wonderland with toy workshops, snow-covered cottages, and smoke spiraling out of chimneys. Countless Christmas movies and stories reinforce this vision, and it's such a pleasant one that maybe we don't *want* to shake it. But the reality of life at the North Pole is pretty fascinating too. It's a land that's not in any time zone (or, to look at it a different way, in *every* time zone), not owned by any country, and actually not even *land*—and that's just the tip of the iceberg! Read on to find out how things look at the very top of the world.

Pole position
We'll begin by complicating matters: There are actually two North Poles. (Three, if you count North Pole, Alaska, but we'll leave that small city out of this discussion!) We usually think of the geographic North Pole or terrestrial North Pole—the northernmost point on earth—but there's also the magnetic North Pole, the point at which all compasses point (it shifts a bit each day). According to *National Geographic,* some scientists think the earth's magnetic field is undergoing a reversal, which will eventually cause compasses to point south rather than north.

Shifty behavior
The geographic North Pole is situated in the Arctic Ocean and surrounded by Russia, Greenland, Canada, and Alaska. It's not a landmass, but rather a floating ice cap roughly six to ten feet deep. Below the ice is only ocean—13,000 feet deep! The sea ice constantly moves and shifts, expanding and shrinking depending on the season.

There is scientific evidence that ice covering the Arctic has thinned over recent years, a trend likely caused by global warming. The situation is such that a great deal of the habitat of polar bears and other animals has already vanished, and some predict that summer sea ice will completely disappear from the Arctic sometime between the years 2060 and 2080.

North Pole residents

We mentioned polar bears, but what else lives at the North Pole? The occasional Arctic fox has been spotted, and there are a variety of birds in the area. One example is the Arctic tern, a brave seabird that journeys from pole to pole, breeding in the Arctic and migrating to Antarctica in winter (the longest regular migration of any animal!). The Arctic is also home to a range of aquatic life, including orcas, beluga whales, walrus, seals, sea otters, and Arctic cod. Don't expect to find any penguins up there, though: They reside almost exclusively in the Southern Hemisphere.

While no people live at the actual North Pole, thousands of Aleuts, Eskimos, and other indigenous people live in the snowy territories of nearby Alaska, Canada, and Russia.

Day and night

Can you imagine spending half the year in darkness? Half the year in sunlight? As earth rotates around the sun, the planet's axis stays constant, so the North Pole spends six dark months away from the sun (late September through late March) and six bright months facing the sun. Sunrise happens around March 21, the spring equinox, a day on which all the polar bears surely don their sunglasses! Winter temperatures at the North Pole average between −45°F and −15°F, while summer temps hover around freezing (32°F).

Santa's zip code

In Canada, the zip code for the North Pole is the oh-so-clever H0H 0H0. Every year, volunteer postal workers in Canada—approximately 15,000 of them!—come to Santa's aid by writing personal responses to more than one million letters addressed to the jolly old elf. How's that for getting into the Christmas spirit? Now if only there were a real Polar Express that zoomed to the North Pole . . . . (Ah well. Our inner child can only wish!)

A Different Kind of Christmas Show!

Most holiday concerts are light and airy. Not so TubaChristmas, which is exactly like it sounds.

Christmas concerts are plentiful over the holiday season, with most featuring the same old songs played on the same old instruments. But over the past three and a half decades, a different kind of Christmas concert has occurred, one that spotlights a handful of instruments given short shrift at Christmastime. The show is called TubaChristmas, and it's unlike any concert you'll ever see—or hear.

TubaChristmas, which showcases the tuba, baritone, sousaphone, and euphonium, was conceived by Harvey Philips, a student of William Bell, a top tuba player of the early 20th century. Born on Christmas Day 1902, Bell performed with the John Philip Sousa Band, the Cincinnati Symphony, and the New York Philharmonic. Bell's death in 1971 saddened the low brass community, and three years later, Philips started TubaChristmas in his honor.

A different holiday sound

That first TubaChristmas concert in 1974 took place at New York's Rockefeller Plaza, and it was very well received. In the years that followed, free TubaChristmas concerts started popping up throughout the United States, drawing hundreds of performers (most of whom perform gratis) and thousands of audience members.

Because most Christmas music, aside from "We Wish You a Merry Christmas," has little use for the tuba and related instruments, the selections performed during a TubaChristmas concert have been specially adapted for the event. The goal is to have fun, and many musicians decorate their instruments with ribbons and even battery-powered lights for the concert. Audience members are also encouraged to join in the merriment by jangling their car keys during the orchestra's rendition of "Jingle Bells."

If you ever have an opportunity to attend a TubaChristmas concert, take it. It's a special holiday experience you'll never forget.

Crunching the Christmas Numbers

- **2,314:** Number of people who live in Santa Claus, Indiana

- **1223:** Year that St. Francis of Assisi first displayed a crèche, or miniature nativity scene, in Grecchio, Italy

- **30.5 billion:** Retail sales in dollars in December 2007

- **1892:** Year *The Nutcracker* was first performed at the Mariinsky Theatre of Russia

- **100 million:** Number of copies of the song "White Christmas" that have sold around the world

- **594 million:** Value in dollars of imported Christmas tree ornaments from China

- **1931:** Year the Christmas tree first appeared on the site of Rockefeller Center in New York

- **1,175:** Number of carolers present for the world's largest caroling service on December 20, 2003; the event was organized by the city of Cambridge in Ontario, Canada, and the carolers sang in the square for 28 minutes

- **100,000:** Number of people who work in the Christmas tree industry in the United States

- **450:** Number of figures in the world's largest diorama of the Nativity in Einsiedeln, Switzerland

GREECE

The Greeks love their customs and traditions—
especially when it comes to Christmas!

Greece is no different from many other countries when it comes to celebrating Christmas. There's plenty of religious pomp and pageantry, pretty decorations, and lots of shopping!

But Christmas in Greece has its unique aspects as well. For example, St. Nicholas is the holiday's patron saint—but he's also the protector of sailors, so you're just as likely to see a boat decorated with colorful lights as a traditional Christmas tree.

A monthlong season
In Greece, the traditional Christmas holiday begins on December 6, St. Nicholas Day, and ends on January 6 with the Feast of the Epiphany. Things really get hopping around December 20, however, and continue to build as Christmas draws nearer.

But unlike the United States, where gifts are traditionally given on Christmas Eve or Christmas Day, in Greece they are given on New Year's Day. As a result, Christmas shopping continues long after Christmas itself. Shops are packed during Christmas week as people look for last-minute presents to give friends and loved ones.

If you love holiday festivities, Greece is the place to be. Almost all of the major cities host a wide variety of Christmas events, including concerts, pageants, and theatrical performances. In Athens's colorful Syntagma Square, you'll find one of the largest Christmas trees in Europe, as well as a Christmas village where children can receive candy and enjoy a variety of holiday-themed activities.

Tradition rules!
As noted, Greece is big on tradition. For example, while Christmas carols may be sung anytime during the holiday, there are actually three official caroling days: Christmas Eve, New Year's Eve, and January 5, which is the Eve of the Epiphany. On these occasions, children carrying triangles go from house to house singing carols, and they are given money or treats as rewards.

Some people hang a pomegranate above the front door of their house so that it has dried by New Year's Day. To ensure good luck during the coming year, the dried pomegranate is thrown on the ground so that it breaks, then everyone steps into their homes with their right foot first.

Feasts and fun

As in the United States, food plays a big role in the Greek celebration of Christmas. In years past, the traditional Christmas meal has been roast pork. But in recent years, turkey has become equally popular.

The Greeks also love their holiday cookies, especially *meloma-karona,* which are made with semolina, cinnamon, and cloves and drenched in honey; and *kourabiedes,* which are rosewater and butter cookies sprinkled with sugar. Kourabiedes are traditionally served on New Year's Day, as is a special pastry called *vasilopita* or St. Basil's pie. What sets vasilopita apart from your average cake, however, is that a foil-covered coin is inserted into the batter before it is baked. Good luck will come to whomever finds the coin in his or her piece.

A holy holiday

Greece is a deeply religious country, so Christmas is a holy and important holiday. Most Orthodox Christians attend services on Christmas Day but may also go to church several times throughout the holiday season. On January 6, local waters are blessed and a wood cross is thrown in. Then dozens of young men jump into the frigid waters in an attempt to retrieve it. Why? Because whoever reaches the cross first will have a year of good luck.

"Christmas gift suggestions: To your enemy, forgiveness. To an opponent, tolerance. To a friend, your heart. To a customer, service. To all, charity. To every child, a good example. To yourself, respect."

—Oren Arnold

SANTA WHO?

AGIOS VASSILIS

*St. Nicholas is revered in Greece, where he's the protector
of sailors. But then there's Agios Vassilis...who?*

In the United States, St. Nicholas is most commonly associated with Santa Claus. In fact, to most Americans, St. Nick is another name for the jolly old elf who brings presents to all good girls and boys.

St. Nicholas is the patron saint of sailors, which is why most Greek fishing vessels and naval ships carry his picture whenever they go out to sea. According to Greek tradition, St. Nicholas's clothes are soaked with seawater, and his face is covered with perspiration from the ceaseless effort of protecting vessels from the hazards of the ocean. December 6 is St. Nicholas Day, and gifts used to be given to children on this day. Also, boats were often decorated instead of Christmas trees. Today, Greeks decorate trees. Those larger ships were hard to fit in the living room!

Then there's that other Greek Santa Claus figure. He is Agios Vassilis (St. Basil), who is called Father Christmas. He delivers presents on New Year's Day, the feast day of St. Basil, rather than Christmas Day.

Evil elves

These Greek elves/pixies aren't the sweet counterparts to Santa's elves. In fact, they love to play tricks. So homeowners keep the fireplace lit during Greece's version of the 12 days of Christmas: December 25 to January 6. This is to keep out those trouble-some goblins, which are called *kallikantzari* (singular is *kallikantsaros*). These troublemakers enter homes through the chimney, and they tease the housewives and put out the fire. They will also eat the special Christmas food, and even urinate on it if it isn't covered! Santa would never approve!

ALL ABOUT *RANGIFER TARDANDUS*, OTHERWISE KNOWN AS *REINDEER*

- *The word "reindeer" is in no way related to the word "reins." Rather, the Old Icelandic word* hreinn *(meaning reindeer) is the source of the first syllable, but its original spelling was lost in translation.*

- *Because a reindeer can pull twice its weight for miles over snow-covered terrain, the Saami people of Lapland have used its muscle power for 5,000 years as a primary means of transportation.*

- *Antlers are made of the fastest-growing tissues know to humans, growing up to an inch a day. Antlers appear within weeks of a reindeer's birth. Regardless of age or sex, every reindeer grows a new set of antlers each year. Antlers are actually bone, while horns are made of keratin, a protein similar to a human's fingernails.*

- *The secret's out: Reindeer aren't equipped with built-in GPS. Instead, it's their supernatural sense of smell—so keen that they can detect food up to 3 feet below snow—that helps guide Santa's sleigh.*

- *Blessed with nature's version of an orthopedic shoe, reindeer have wide splayed hooves that distribute their weight evenly. That way, reindeer can walk across snow without sinking, with their hooves working in much the same way as snowshoes.*

- *The furry layer on a reindeer's antlers is called* velvet. *Each fall, reindeer rub the velvet off their antlers to signal the rutting, or mating, season.*

- *If only red-blooded American* homo sapiens *could be as lucky as reindeer. In the antlered set, dominant male reindeer called bulls keep harems of females, or cows, throughout the winter for mating purposes. Calves are born each spring, and most cows have one or two. Interestingly, reindeer twins are more common in Europe than North America.*

These Crackers Aren't for Your Soup

In America, we celebrate Christmas with tinsel and wrapping paper, bows and ribbons, and our friends across the sea do much the same. In the United Kingdom, however, they like to add a little bang to the mix. For more than a century, it has been traditional in the UK for children and adults alike to share Christmas crackers with one another. Two people each grab an end of the cracker and pull on it until it explodes and a prize falls out.

Pop goes the present

These little novelties are cardboard tubes filled with candy or small gifts festively wrapped. The small piece of mildly explosive paper, similar in power to a cap gun, gives this holiday treat its name. Though they don't pack much punch, they are usually packed with an assortment of small gifts. Christmas crackers are a staple of the holiday in the British Commonwealth and other parts of the world. A more powerful version of these treats even makes an appearance in the popular *Harry Potter* books.

A brief history

Though pervasive in England and parts of Europe, America hasn't adopted the Christmas cracker as a integral part of the season quite yet. Part of this is due to the fact that the inventor of the cracker was British, and the company that invented them remains the largest producer of the product to this day. In 1847, Tom Smith invented the treat as a way of improving on the French bonbon. Bonbons in Smith's time were little more than wrapped sugared almonds, and though they sold well seasonally, he wanted to make more of the small treats. Sitting next to a crackling fire, he came upon the idea that the treats should make a similar sound, and he set about perfecting the small friction-powered chemical explosion that gives a cracker its characteristic snap today.

Surprising prizes

At first, the Christmas crackers Tom Smith produced contained only verses of love poetry. It was Tom's youngest son, Walter, who began adding contemporary sayings to the treats. Soon, crackers would contain cartoons and finally they would graduate to the cheesy jokes and riddles for which they are now known. Walter also began experimenting with small gifts such as scarf pins, bracelets, and even the paper hats that are still part of the regular selection of prizes. Though classics like riddles and paper hats are still found, the prizes have expanded in our time to include small toys such as simple magic tricks, yo-yos, toy cars, and stickers. Crackers aren't just for kids though, and a wide selection of prizes for adults, including cuff links, makeup compacts, and even miniature flashlights are available. Crackers that can be filled after purchase are even sold, which means the selection of prizes a cracker may contain is truly limited only by one's imagination.

Bigger is better

Though these prize-filled tubes are usually only about four inches long, larger ones have been made. The records of the Tom Smith factory show at least one order for a six-foot cracker that was used to decorate the Euston Street subway station in London; though it is doubtful this one was used as traditionally intended. In Australia, however, one group made a Christmas cracker to put all others to shame. In 1998, a group in Sydney built a cracker that was nearly 182 feet long and more than 11 feet tall. While they held the world record for largest Christmas cracker for several years, the record would come home to England in 2001. That year, the students of Ley Hill School in Buckinghamshire helped build the biggest of all: a cracker measuring more than 207 feet long and 13 feet tall! While crackers are sold as a novelty in America, especially from the Tom Smith company Web site, it is clear that nowhere is the Christmas cracker more a beloved tradition than in England.

Fake Forests

Take a walk in a polystyrene wonderland!

Christmas wouldn't be Christmas without the sweet plastic smell of a fake tree. Or the slick shiny tinsel that will never melt in your hand like a real icicle. Or the white felt skirt that surrounds the towering faux pine instead of real snow.

The original

There are six general types of fake trees. The original is the German feather tree. These were made of goose or turkey feathers dyed green. The technique was invented in the 1800s when deforestation was a big problem in Germany. The feather trees were sparse to mimic the local white pines. Plastic versions are available if you're not only concerned about deforestation but also degoosification.

The classic

This is your standard green plastic tree. It's a lot fuller than the feather tree and can even hold those heavy ceramic ornaments grandma gives you every year. You can't throw them out until she dies, but fortunately the tree can handle them on its wiry limbs.

The midget

The midget is a small fake tree popular among single folks and urban couples. The former don't even take the lights off so that they can pull this baby out of the box and get their Christmas decorations up in under 16 seconds. The latter use the tree's small size to make their Amazon.com–wrapped gift boxes look larger by comparison.

The Snow White

You know how snow falls from the sky and lands on the tops of tree limbs? If you hate that, and prefer snow to cover every inch of the tree, then the Snow White is the way to go. Every inch of the tree is white. It's what Christmas will look like during a nuclear winter or after an asteroid hits earth covering everything with a fine pale ash. This bleak version is sometimes called the Cormac McCarthy.

The hipster

This is for the "too cool for school" kids. Any proper hipster knows it's not cool to take anything seriously. They need a tree that's as ironic as they are. The solution? A single Christmas tree air freshener hanging from a nail in the wall. Instant Christmas but without the sincerity.

Tinsel and flock

Tinsel is a classic. Properly hanging tinsel on a tree involves the time-honored tradition of getting a strand stuck to every surface in the living room—except the tree—until one gets completely frustrated and just clumps the rest on one branch. People who spend time applying it strand by strand will have an epiphany on their deathbed about how they wasted their life on tinsel designs that nobody noticed anyway.

For a more realistic snow and ice effect, forget tinsel and forget white trees. Flocking is the answer. From homemade soap flakes to store bought sprays, this is how Martha Stewart would want you to spend your holiday season: not with friends, not with family, but on a 6-foot ladder spraying chemicals onto your tree.

The abomination

Nothing says "I don't care about Christmas" more than the Abomination. This is for those parents too lazy to drag themselves down to the garden center so they have to pick up the last lonely tree at their local Wal-Mart. All the good trees are gone, as are all the halfway decent ones. All that's left is a skinny eyesore sitting naked and alone in what will next month become the Valentine's Day aisle. It's the pink aluminum tree.

For all their faults, fake trees have their good points. Every year that you lug it down from the attic represents another real, oxygen-giving tree saved. You don't have to water it. Most importantly, it doesn't shed needles that you continue to vacuum up six months later.

From Show Tune to Standard

It's a song we all know and love, sung by many musicians over the years to extol the joys of being with loved ones at Christmastime. "Have Yourself a Merry Little Christmas" has been recently performed by the likes of Coldplay and The Pretenders, and classically by Ol' Blue Eyes himself, Frank Sinatra. When Hugh Martin and Ralph Blane wrote it, however, it was meant to be a melancholy tune for Judy Garland.

"Let your heart be light"

In the 1944 film *Meet Me in St. Louis,* Judy Garland sings the song to seven-year-old Margaret O'Brien, who plays her sister. Originally, the song opened "Have yourself a merry little Christmas; it may be your last; next year we may all be living in the past." Undeniably gloomy, Martin thought it fit well with the scene he'd read from the script, but Garland and director Vincent Minnelli disagreed. The scene in question takes place on Christmas Eve night, and the sisters are commiserating because the family has decided to move to New York. The younger is concerned that Santa won't be able to find the family once they're gone, and the elder sister knows that her budding romance will never survive the long distance. Initially, Martin's song was meant to show the girls commiserating over their fates, but Garland's protests caused Martin to do the requested rewrite. This changed the tone of the scene so that the elder sister is actually providing comfort to the younger. When the song and movie were released at Christmastime that year, a new classic was born.

Still too blue

When Frank Sinatra decided to rerecord the song in 1957, he felt that the lyrics still needed a pick-me-up. According to Hugh Martin, Sinatra called him specifically about rewriting a line near the end of the song that goes, "Until then, we'll have to muddle through somehow." He reportedly pointed out that the title of the album he was working on was *A Jolly Christmas,* so Martin changed the line for him to "Hang a shining star upon the highest bough." A perennial hit for Sinatra, the song has been reissued several times in various formats as we've progressed from LPs to MP3s. Of course, most of us probably don't notice the different versions because Frank Sinatra's version has also become one of those songs our favorite artists love to cover.

Play it again, Gomer

When Sinatra reissued his album in 1963, The Chipmunks and Johnny Mathis also released the song. In the 1970s, Jim Nabors (of *Gomer Pyle, U.S.M.C.* fame) covered the tune, but he wasn't alone. That decade, the Jackson 5 released a version that likely sold more copies than the version released in 1978 by Frank Oz and Jim Henson as Ernie and Bert from *Sesame Street.* In 1987, The Pretenders released the version that sees the most radio play today, but that hasn't stopped anyone from recording new versions. Artists as disparate as Mel Tormé (in 1990) and Twisted Sister (in 2006) have also celebrated Christmas by recording their own versions of "Have Yourself a Merry Little Christmas," all with the same lyrics. Not to say that there wasn't room for change, mind you, as Hugh Martin would again change the song in 2001.

Christmas blessings

Working with gospel artist Del Delker at the beginning of the 21st century, Martin altered the lyrics yet again. This time, he kept the same tune, but changed the lyrics drastically to fit a more religious tone. Though this version may fit the religious origins of the holiday more closely, it doesn't take away from how beloved the song is overall. No matter the age or taste in music, listeners the world over will likely continue having a merry little Christmas for generations to come.

How Do You Say That?

MERRY CHRISTMAS!

Luxembourgish: Schèine Chreschtdaag

Macedonian: Sreken Bozhik

Maltese: IL-Milied It-tajjeb

Manx: Nollick ghennal

Maori: Meri Kirihimete

Mime:

Navajo: Merry Keshmish

Norwegian: God Jul *or* Gledelig Jul

Papiamento: Bon Pasco

Papua New Guinea: Bikpela hamamas blong dispela Krismas

Pennsylvania German: En frehlicher Grischtdaag

Filipino: Maligayang Pasko

Pig Latin: Erry-May Istmas-Cray

Polish: Wesołych Świąt Bożego Narodzenia *or* Boze Narodzenie

Portuguese: Feliz Natal

Pushto: Christmas Aao Ne-way Kaal Mo Mobarak Sha

Rapa-Nui (Easter Island): Mata-Ki-Te-Rangi. Te-Pito-O-Te-Henua

Romanian: Craciun fericit

Russian: Pozdrevlyayu s prazdnikom Rozhdestva

Sami: Buorrit Juovllat

Samoan: La Maunia Le Kilisimasi Ma Le Tausaga Fou

Sardinian: Bonu Nadale

Scots Gaelic: Nollaig chridheil huibh

Jingle Bells, Batman Smells!

As kids, our first exposure to Christmas song parodies is usually "Jingle bells, Batman smells..." That's great for third graders, but as we get older, we need more, ahem, sophisticated comedy.

For pure silliness, no Christmas song parody beats "Grandma Got Run Over by a Reindeer," the 1979 song by Elmo and Patsy (Shropshire). Grandma gets drunk on eggnog. Santa runs her over during her walk home. Her body is found Christmas morning with hoof prints on her head and "Claus marks on her back." The rest of the song is about how the family copes without her, debating what to do with her presents. Grandma got to live in the music video and then got run over a few more times in the forgettable 2000 cartoon special.

If that humor isn't black enough, try "Weird Al" Yankovic's "Christmas at Ground Zero." Christmas "under a mushroom cloud" is fun, dark comedy as "Weird Al" huddles by the mistletoe while the nukes start to drop from the sky.

Twisted Christmas

Radio DJ Bob Rivers released *Twisted Christmas* in 1987. Among some of the "Twelve Pains of Christmas" are rigging up the lights and finding parking spaces. Several follow-up albums included "It's the Most Fattening Time of the Year" and "Chipmunks Roasting on an Open Fire."

In fulfilling the old adage that where there's parody there's porn, *Rated Xmas* was eventually pulled from shelves after the songs' rights owners hired the gift that keeps on giving: lawyers.

George Lucas ruined Christmas...again

As if 1978's *The Star Wars Holiday Special* isn't seared into the memories of kids that year, Lucas ruined Christmas again in 1980 with *Christmas in the Stars: Star Wars Christmas Album.* Although we technically have to categorize this under *unintentional* parody, listening to C3PO sing (complete with random *Star Wars* sound effects) will have you adding earplugs to your Christmas list!

Santa Is a New Yorker

Everyone knows that old St. Nick lives at the North Pole.
The problem is, there is overwhelming evidence that
Santa actually lives in New York City! Even if he spends
some of the year in the Arctic Circle, the fact that there are
so many solid connections between the Big Man and
the Big Apple can't be a coincidence.

Macy's has long laid claim to hosting the one true Santa Claus. Every year since 1924, the start of the Christmas season has been marked by the arrival of Santa Claus at the end of Macy's Thanksgiving Day Parade held in New York. Now, considering all the work Santa has to do before Christmas Eve, it would only make sense for him to spend the last month he has to prepare for his annual voyage in Macy's parade if he happened to be a New Yorker. Some might argue that this just isn't the case, that he is just another chubby old man with a beard in a red suit, but that question was resolved in 1947!

"Just because every child can't get his wish that doesn't mean there isn't a Santa Claus."
—Kris Kringle, *Miracle on 34th Street*
In fact, it was decided in 1947, and then again in 1955, 1959, 1973, and 1994, in the film *Miracle on 34th Street*. Sure, there are plenty of 34th streets around the world, but Santa only ever calls the one in New York City his home. After all, what is really on trial in that film is Santa himself, and the court, of course, rules on the side of Kris Kringle every time. If that isn't enough, keep in mind that the original film was nominated for a Best Picture Oscar, and actually won three Academy Awards, so it must have merit—and be true.

"The most real things in the world are those that neither children nor men can see."
—Francis Pharcellus Church, *Yes, Virginia editorial*
Of course, there are those who will argue that the film(s) got it wrong, and that there is no such thing; that Santa simply is not real. New York, as we should expect, is also source to the most famous

rebuttal to that argument, the "Yes, Virginia..." letter. In 1897, Virginia O'Hanlon wrote the *New York Sun,* at the suggestion of her father to ask if Santa Claus was real. Her father's reasoning, according to legend, was "If you see it in the *Sun,* it's so." She received a response in the form of an editorial by Francis Pharcellus Church on the morning of September 21 that same year. In it, Church made one of the best arguments for the existence of Santa, leaving out only the part about his living in New York. The article would be reprinted numerous times, and the catchphrase "Yes, Virginia, there is a Santa Claus" has become prevalent in popular culture even today.

NORAD guest Santa trackers have included Ringo Starr, Kathy Griffin, and George Lopez

Still, for some that may not be enough, so we need to look at the other evidence. According to NORAD's 2008 tracking of St. Nick's journeys, Santa's reindeer have an affinity for the Statue of Liberty, and they spend extra time in the Big Apple. This indicates that while Santa lives in New York, he must keep the reindeer up north at his Arctic base of operations. Speaking of the reindeer, the famous poem "'Twas the Night Before Christmas" was first published in a New York newspaper about three hours north of Santa's American home. It was an ingenious way of revealing the names of Nick's beloved beasts of burden, as well as other secrets, to the world.

Before Santa drank Coke

Evidence further suggests that Santa moved from this smaller New York town to the big city a few decades later. He enlisted the help of New York City artist Thomas Nast in the 1860s to reveal his image, red suit and all, to the public via illustrations in *Harper's Weekly.* As the center of world commerce and communication, only a city like New York could help him stage such a revelation. Besides, who but a resident of the "city that never sleeps" would even dare to take on the task of delivering all those presents to the entire world in one night? No, dear readers, consider the North Pole story a refuted myth. Santa Claus, without a doubt, hearts New York.

Toymakers Toil at Christmas

So often have we seen the image of workshop elves scurrying around the week before Christmas to finish making all the toys that we assume real-life toymakers, such as Hasbro and Mattel, must be doing the same. The truth is they're already at work designing toys for the following *Christmas.*

Very few—if any—elves are involved in the modern toy manufacturing process. The entire process—from initial idea to finished toy sitting on a shelf at Toys "R" Us—typically takes anywhere from 12 to 24 months. Toys are first drawn up in a concept sketch. This could be drawn from scratch, based on detailed notes, or based on an existing licensed property (see below). When the sketches are approved, an artist (or team of artists) creates more detailed drawings called turnarounds. These are depictions of the toy from the front, back, and sides.

Sculptors and/or engineers build a rough prototype from these drawings. Meanwhile, executives call factories (usually in China) for price quotes. The factory will produce another prototype that the toymaker's engineers and designers can fine-tune if there are any problems. The factory manufactures steel tools that will be used to make the final product. These are very expensive so it's important that any major adjustments in the shape or function of the toy be made as early in the process as possible. There is a lot of back-and-forth with the factory to ensure the design, functionality (e.g. movable parts), and paint applications (colors) are exactly what the toymaker wants.

Meanwhile, the prototypes and concept art are used to sell the toy to stores around the country. Most toys are sold before the final product is even complete.

Licensing

A lot of popular toys (Elmo, *Star Wars*) are not invented from scratch. They are licensed from other companies; that is, Hasbro (the licensee) buys the rights from Lucasfilm (the licensor) to make *Star Wars* action figures and play sets. The difference between licensed and nonlicensed toys is the approval process. A company sends concept art, prototypes, and every stage of the toy to the licensor for approval. They want to make sure all the colors, designs, and—in the case of movie-based toys—actors' likenesses are accurate.

Video games

Video games also have a long development time. The producer and the team begin composing detailed notes of what is to happen at every stage in the game, sometimes even two years before it's slated to hit stores. Once graphic artists finish the concept art, 3-D modelers transform the 2-D images into 3-D space. Programmers, meanwhile, work on the "guts" that define how the user and game objects all interact. In order to get a perennial hit like EA Sports' Madden onto shelves each year, the company has two separate teams working on different versions. So one team is finishing the 2011 version while the second begins work on the 2012 version.

Christmastime

The Christmas season is mostly a time for the public relations and marketing people to shine. They're busy getting the word out on the hot new toy for Christmas. You think the hosts of those TV morning shows picked out those new toys at random? Nope. They were strategically placed by savvy PR people.

Elsewhere in the toy company, various managers are tracking shipments from China, orders, inventories, and fulfillments to make sure enough product is getting to stores on time and in the right quantities.

The designers, inventors, and marketing departments, meanwhile, are busy looking toward future toys and future Christmases.

Companies have their own practices, and some of these steps may occur at different stages or in different order, but that's the general principle of toymaking. By comparison, Santa's elves have it easy!

Christmas Around the World

BRAZIL

Here Comes Papai Noel... with a suntan! Brazilian Christmas takes place during the sizzling summer.

Brazilians don't associate Christmas with snow and "Jack Frost nipping at your nose." That's because it's summer in the South American country, and even Papai Noel (the Brazilian version of Santa Claus, imported from North America in the 1950s) has to dress in a lightweight silk suit to keep cool. Some people celebrate the holiday by hitting the beach and watching fireworks or having a BBQ.

Leave that baby alone!
Since Brazil was once a colony of Portugal, many Christmas traditions in the country are of Portuguese origin, including the popular *presépio* or nativity scene. Derived from the word "presepium" (meaning a bed of straw where the Christ child lay), elaborate presépio pop up in many places throughout the Christmas season. Some Brazilians enact the traditional play *Los Pastores* ("The Shepherds"), which is also performed in Mexico—except Brazil's version features shepherdesses instead of shepherds and a gypsy who sneaks in and tries to snatch baby Jesus from his straw bed!

Who am I?
Christmas decorations include giant illuminated trees and fresh flowers. Many Brazilians celebrate the holiday by exchanging clues with an *amigo secreto* (a "Secret Santa" of sorts) whose identity is not revealed until Christmas, accompanied by the giving of a special gift. Up until that point, participants conceal their identity by corresponding with fake names (or *apelidos*).

The Christmas meal is often a lavish affair, featuring roast turkey and ham, seasonal fruits and vegetables, beans, and rice. Some families attend mass on December 24 and then eat their special dinner at midnight. Others attend midnight mass or *Missa do Galo* (*galo* meaning "rooster," since the service traditionally ends at 1 A.M.), although this mass is no longer as widely observed. As is the tradition in many countries, on Christmas morning, children open presents that were delivered in the night by Papai Noel.

The 20 Most Performed Modern Christmas Songs

The subject of Christmas has been a favorite of musicians for centuries. From the most tone-deaf street carolers to well-trained professional recording stars, everyone loves to sing about their favorite holiday. After all, you don't hear too many songs about Halloween!

What follows are the 20 most performed modern Christmas songs of the first decade of the 21st century according to the American Society of Composers, Authors and Publishers. See if your favorite is on the list, and if not, start calling your local radio station to make requests when they begin playing holiday music, which seems to happen earlier and earlier every year.

1. "Winter Wonderland"
2. "The Christmas Song" ("Chestnuts Roasting on an Open Fire")
3. "Sleigh Ride"
4. "Have Yourself a Merry Little Christmas"
5. "Santa Claus Is Coming to Town"
6. "White Christmas"
7. "Let It Snow! Let It Snow! Let It Snow!"
8. "Jingle Bell Rock"
9. "Rudolph the Red-Nosed Reindeer"
10. "Little Drummer Boy"
11. "It's the Most Wonderful Time of the Year"
12. "I'll Be Home for Christmas"
13. "Rockin' Around the Christmas Tree"
14. "Silver Bells"
15. "Feliz Navidad"
16. "Frosty the Snowman"
17. "A Holly Jolly Christmas"
18. "Blue Christmas"
19. "It's Beginning to Look a Lot Like Christmas"
20. "I Saw Mommy Kissing Santa Claus"

Dickens Meets *Star Trek!*

🕯 🕯 🕯

*There have been many stage versions
of* A Christmas Carol, *but none entirely in Klingon!*

Star Trek fans are a devoted group, embracing all aspects of their favorite television show while eagerly creating new, original works of their own. Trekkers are especially fond of all things Klingon, so it should come as no surprise that someone finally wrote a stage production of Charles Dickens's *A Christmas Carol* performed almost entirely in the fictional alien tongue.

A Minnesota favorite

The Commedia Beauregard Theater, in conjunction with the IKV RakeHell of the Klingon Assault Group, has produced *A Klingon Christmas Carol* at various venues in Minnesota's Twin Cities since 2007. In 2009, the play was performed at the avant garde Mixed Blood Theater in Minneapolis, and Commedia Beauregard plans to take the production to other cities.

The premise of the show is that the audience is attending a production at the Vulcan Institute of Cultural Anthropology, where Klingon stories and their human counterparts are being studied. The Imperial Klingon Players perform a decidedly Klingon version of *A Christmas Carol* while a Vulcan anthropologist narrates. Rightly assuming that most members of the audience do not speak fluent Klingon, English subtitles are projected on an overhead screen.

In this version of the Dickens classic, a Klingon with neither honor nor courage is visited by the ghost of a dead comrade. Later, he is visited by the spirits of three Klingon warriors, who help him find the bravery he lacks.

Interestingly, this isn't the first *Star Trek* connection to *A Christmas Carol.* In 1999, actor Patrick Stewart, who played Captain Jean-Luc Picard on *Star Trek: The Next Generation,* portrayed Ebenezer Scrooge in a television production of the Christmas holiday favorite. That time, though, the dialogue was in easy-to-understand English.

You'll Shoot Your Eye Out!

*An unlikely classic becomes a
must-watch at Christmastime.*

Nine-year-old Ralphie Parker wants a Red Ryder BB gun for Christmas. That, in a nutshell, is the entire plot of *A Christmas Story*. Wrapped around that is a tapestry of oddball characters and themes that draws viewers in to pre–World War II America. Rose-colored nostalgia is wryly adjusted by the ever-present narrator: Ralph as an adult looking back both fondly and not so fondly. The oddball characters in the movie aren't even so strange; they're more a commentary that normalcy is just too rare.

Oh, fudge

Ralphie's dream for the Red Ryder BB gun is scuttled by his mother, teacher, and Santa, who all scold, "You'll shoot your eye out." So consumed is Ralphie with the gun that he daydreams about submitting an A+ essay about the rifle and defending his home against intruders. Ralphie's quest is sidetracked by other humorous moments of suburban childhood. School kids "triple dog dare" a classmate to stick his tongue on the frozen flagpole. His father (an artist with obscenity and affectionately named the "Old Man") hears Ralphie accidentally repeat one of his own favorite words ("the queen mother of dirty words, the f-dash-dash-dash"). Ralphie launches into his own screed of foul language when he stands up to the bully with yellow eyes. Younger brother Randy is layered so tightly in sweaters and a snowsuit by his mother that he can't move his arms. Ralphie's parents wage war over a grotesque lamp in the shape of a woman's leg in netted stockings. Neighborhood dogs trash the family's holiday turkey, sending the Parker tribe to a Chinese restaurant where waiters horribly mispronounce seasonal songs. From start to finish, *A Christmas Story* mashes the familiar with the bizarre.

"My Old Man was one of the most feared furnace fighters in Northern Indiana"

Several scenes reveal a more cynical view of Christmastime. When Ralphie finally gets his Little Orphan Annie secret decoder badge, he is dismayed to learn the encrypted message from the radio show is little more than an ad for Ovaltine. But there are warm moments, too. Ralphie's mother changes the subject after telling the Old Man about the fight in order to keep Ralphie out of trouble. Later, Ralphie's disappointment over not getting the BB gun is erased when the Old Man brings out one last present.

The climax—when Ralphie fires his gun and really does almost shoot his eye out (thanks to a ricochet)—launches into the turkey/Chinese restaurant disaster. The family bursts into laughter, and despite all the lies, swearing, and back-stabbing, we're still treated to a happy ending.

Triple dog dare

Ralphie is the creation of Jean Shepherd, a writer and radio host. He largely invented the talk radio format with his long, discursive monologues. Shepherd's semiautobiographical stories and monologues would become the foundation for the movie.

Before he brought Shepherd's stories to screen, director Bob Clark cut his teeth on horror films, including *Black Christmas,* in which a killer stalks a sorority house. He later scored a hit writing and directing the sex farce *Porky's* (and its sequel). Perhaps it was *because* and not *in spite* of his previous work that *A Christmas Story* retained an edge uncharacteristic of holiday fare. Clark brought Shepherd's stories to the big screen, collaborating with the author on the script and enlisting him in narration duties as well. The idea of an adult narrating his childhood would later inspire *The Wonder Years* television series.

BB gun mania knows no loyalty

Shepherd's real life was as far from a fairy tale as the movie was. He married three times, divorced twice, never graduated Indiana University, and had little contact—if any—with his son and daughter.

A *Christmas Story* House: Live the Dream

For many holiday movie buffs, A Christmas Story *is the holiday film by which all others are measured. But did you know you can visit the house where the movie was filmed? Yes, Virginia...*

In 2004, an ad popped up on eBay offering a house for sale in Cleveland: A 4-bedroom, 2-bathroom farmhouse built in 1895 was listed at $99,900.00. The house just happened to be used in the filming of *A Christmas Story* in 1983, and movie fan Brian Jones's bid won the auction. His goal was to "restore" the house to the way it looked for the film, open it as a tourist attraction, and keep *A Christmas Story* dream alive.

Renovation, expansion, leg lamps

Jones began renovating the house in 2005. It wasn't easy. Much of the house had to be gutted, the props from the movie recovered or duplicated as closely as possible. There was wallpaper to replicate and 1940s memorabilia to hunt down; Jones knew fans of the movie would be sticklers for the details.

Several of the cast and crew from the original film helped to bring in pieces from the original set. Actor Ian Petrella, who played Ralphie's little brother, Randy, was among the first to donate. By 2006, the house and museum were ready to open to the public. Less than three years later, the house celebrated its 100,000th visitor.

There are actually two parts to the *A Christmas Story* tourist experience. If you find yourself in the Tremont neighborhood, you'll first visit the *Christmas Story* museum. The museum features original props and set pieces, as well as over 100 behind-the-scenes photos from the filming. After that, you cross the street for a guided tour of the actual house and yard.

And be careful with that Red Rider BB gun! You'll shoot your... well, you know.

Nipping at Your Nose

*Jack Frost, an eponymous part of the holiday season
and winter as a whole, has taken many forms over
the years. He's appeared as a Norse giant, a woodland
sprite, and even as a mutant killer snowman. Jack's origins
date back to a time before Christmas was widely celebrated,
but as our favorite holiday took over the entire winter season,
this ancient character was adopted as well.*

Fortunate son

One of the earliest references to Jack seems to be in the form of a giant named either Jökul or Frosti. The Norse revered Frosti as the son of Kári (wind) and father of Snær (snow), and it is easy to see how the name would have been anglicized over the years. Even today, tradition holds that Jack Frost is responsible for leaving crystalline patterns on our windows on cold winter mornings. While the Norse revered Jack, L. Frank Baum made him a true prince. Baum, famous for *The Wizard of Oz,* wrote several stories featuring Jack as the son of the Frost King, and he embellished his trickster side. On the coldest day of the year, Jack's father encourages him to prank to his heart's content and specifically mentions that the imp should go for any exposed skin the humans might be showing. When our parents made us wear hats in winter, it seems they were only protecting us from Jack and his dad!

The many faces of Frost

Unfortunately, that's really about all there is to Jack's history. Much of what we know today is a modern invention, and it is one that seems to evolve every season. Jack Frost has appeared in every form of media one can imagine. In the comic book *Jack of Fables,* not only is Jack the consort of the Snow Queen, but he is also most every fairy-tale character named Jack. In film, Jack has worn many different guises. In one film named for him, he appears as a father reincarnated as a snowman, seeking to make amends to his son. In another, he is a reincarnated serial killer, which results in a horror film that is more comedic than scary. In both, however, the whimsical nature of Jack is certainly a central theme.

You know, for kids!

Rankin and Bass used Jack at least twice in their beloved series of Christmas specials for children. In his first appearance, in 1976, Jack appears as a jealous sprite in *Frosty's Winter Wonderland*. At first, Jack Frost tries to spoil the fun Frosty has with the children he plays with, but he quickly comes to be a friend to them all and attempts to keep winter going all year round.

Parson Brown has to have a sit down with the sprite and the snowman to convince them to let spring come once again. A couple of years later, in 1979, Rankin and Bass would give Jack his own special, simply titled *Jack Frost*. Featuring Mel Tormé's "The Christmas Song" ("Chestnuts Roasting on an Open Fire"), this adventure saw Jack take on a temporary human form in order to pursue the girl he had fallen in love with.

We do know Jack

No matter where we find Jack, in stories, films, television, or even our own windows in winter, he's always recognizable. While he may not have started out as a member of the Christmas pantheon, he certainly helps characterize the season for us all. Generation after generation, we have known this merry prankster and his mischievous ways bring a certain reminder that Christmas is about children. Besides, it just wouldn't be Christmas without Jack nipping at our noses.

"It is Christmas in the heart
that puts Christmas in the air."
—W. T. Ellis

Hopping Up the Wrong Tree

Planes, trains, automobiles, and Christmas trees?
Some North American frogs unintentionally
discovered a new form of transportation.

When relocating to a new home, most people rent a moving van, but when Pacific Chorus frogs want to move, apparently they just hitch a ride on Christmas trees bound for Alaska. In December 2009, the *Anchorage Daily News* reported that some of these critters were showing up in the Anchorage area during the holiday season, having traveled discreetly on trees imported from Oregon. (Who knows, maybe they just wanted to see the Northern Lights or go whale watching!)

Unfortunately for the Pacific Chorus frogs (so-named because of their raspy vocal trills), city officials didn't exactly leap for joy at their arrival. In Alaska, these amphibians are nonnative and have the potential to carry the disease-causing chytrid fungus, which has caused amphibian population declines around the world. Although the frogs didn't appear to be invasive, the Alaska Department of Fish and Game encouraged residents to take precautionary measures by killing the frogs (euthanizing them with a toothache anesthetic, such as Orajel) or putting them in the freezer. Then locals were supposed to bring in the frozen frogs for inspection. Not a very "hoppy" Christmas for these critters!

This wasn't the first time that Pacific Chorus frogs traveled far from home. In 2007, members of this North American species showed up in Guam—again riding Christmas trees. (Maybe this time they were in search of sandy beaches and mangrove forests!) They also found their way to the Queens Charlotte Islands in British Columbia, where they spread fairly quickly, thus raising the possibility that the Pacific frogs could eventually become established in Alaska, too. But in order to do so, they'll have to steer clear of toothache medication and subfreezing temperatures!

Christmas Around the World

ENGLAND

In with the old, in with the new . . . . A storied history gives England plenty of reasons to celebrate the holidays.

Keeping Christmas in merry olde England features many of the same traditions celebrated in other parts of the world—with one notable exception. The English hold on to the superstition that decking the halls with greenery before Christmas Eve brings bad luck. Consequently, festivities held the night before Christmas center around decorating the house. Pine boughs and holly with red berries, believed to ward off witchcraft, are draped across mantels and doorframes. Mistletoe—its romantic symbolism began in England—is also used for decorating.

Crackers and caroling

Christmas Day dawns with families attending mass, where the reading of scripture lessons are interspersed with the singing of well-loved carols—many of which were written in the 19th century by English musicians and writers. Church is followed by Christmas dinner, a lavish feast with goose or roast beef as the main dish. For good luck, mincemeat pie is served, along with Christmas pudding with raisins and prunes, made the Sunday before Advent by the entire family. As ingredients are added, each member stirs the pudding with a wooden spoon in honor of Jesus' wooden crib. The highlight of the meal—at least for children—is popping open the English "crackers" placed beside each plate. These colored paper tubes are filled with a hat, candy, and small presents (see page 226).

Inside the box

In the old days, English servants were required to work on Christmas Day but were given reprieve on December 26. As they left to visit their families, their employers would send them off with a box containing gifts and food, hence the English holiday "Boxing Day." Today, the tradition is kept alive by people who take the day off to visit family and friends. Others mark the day by giving small gifts to the postman, paperboy, grocer, and other people who have helped them out throughout the year.

Santa? Can I Have Your Autograph?

🕯 🕯 🕯

*There have been countless people who have donned
the famous red and white costume of Santa Claus,
but there are a few that have gone above and beyond
(sometimes just beyond) the call of duty...*

Louis Prang: Santa's costume designer (and part-time Macy's Santa)

When we think of Santa, we think of him in that iconic red velvet suit, right? Well, before Louis Prang, all Santa ever wore was fur. Prang was a German immigrant working as a printer in Boston in 1856, and he designed a Christmas card in 1885 with Santa Claus on the cover. Instead of the usual outfit of fur and bells and a cane or wreath in his hand, Prang made him decidedly chubby, gave him a cap and a belt, and put him in a red suit with white fur trim. This image enchanted the Victorian public: Santa was cleaner, looked friendlier, and was generally more adorable than ever, making Santa a marketing hit. Rumor has it that Prang walked the walk, too; some sources say he moonlighted as a Macy's department store Santa for several years.

Charles Howard: dean of Santas

In 1937, a former Macy's Santa named Charles Howard founded the Santa Claus School in Michigan on the firm belief that being St. Nick demands a lot more than a red suit and a fake beard. For decades, the school has been training men and women who want to "further define and improve their individual presentations of Santa Claus." The school teaches skills that range from vocal lessons for caroling to beard grooming. Santas take lessons in child psychology, sign language, and are instructed in media for talk-show appearances and call-in shows.

Billy Bob Thornton: a very *Bad Santa*

Just in time for the holiday season in 2003, Columbia Pictures released *Bad Santa,* a strangely heartwarming story of a man at the end of his rope who is redeemed—sort of—by the true meaning of Christmas. Under the direction of Terry Zwigoff, Billy Bob Thornton plays Willie, a conman who works with his buddy Marcus (a little person), robbing department stores across the country. Willie dresses as Santa; Marcus is his "little helper." Together, they steal, drink, womanize, and generally run amok.

But when Willie gets involved with Sue, a beautiful bartender, and a young boy he calls The Kid, the plot thickens. Willie's behavior starts to nag at his conscience and his priorities are in danger of shifting. For an audience interested in seeing a rated-R Santa behaving badly, the movie provides a surprisingly satisfying pay off.

James Martin: post office Santa

He didn't wear a red suit to work, but James Martin will forever hold the distinction of being the man who received untold numbers of letters to Santa in the 1920s.

The town of Santa Claus, Indiana, was originally Santa Fe when it was formed in 1846. Legend has it that when the town applied for a post office they were denied, since "Santa Fe" was taken. Details are murky, but in May 1856, "Santa Claus" was recognized by the U.S. Postal Service, and the town's post office opened for business. In the 1920s, postmaster James Martin spread the word that there really was an address for Santa Claus—in Indiana. Martin got mountains of letters from children around the world, eventually prompting the U.S. Postal Department to forbid any future towns from calling themselves "Santa Claus."

Marshall Ratliff: the Santa Claus criminal

A few days before Christmas in 1927, ex-convict Marshall Ratliff, out on parole and backed up by a posse of four, decided to rob Cisco's First National Bank using a Santa Claus costume as a disguise.

Ratliff's plan was simple: Pretend to be Santa during the bustling holiday shopping season, enter the bank, and fool everyone into letting him get close to the money, then stuff all the cash into his satchel. Things didn't go as smoothly as Ratliff would've hoped, however; a shootout commenced and townspeople, police, and criminals sustained injuries—three were dead. Ratliff and his cronies took two little girls as hostages, which didn't help their case when they were caught the next morning. It didn't end well for Ratliff: He was hanged a year later by an angry mob after he tried to escape from prison.

Macy's Santa: the grand finale Santa

In 1920, a group of employees from Macy's department store in New York decided to launch a Christmas parade. Many of the employees involved were German immigrants wishing to celebrate the season by recalling festivities from home.

Since then, the Macy's Thanksgiving Day Parade has grown exponentially; the eagerly anticipated annual event features float after float, hundreds of acts and parade participants, celebrities, and lots of special effects. But from the first parade to the latest—which recorded 2.5 million spectators along the parade route and over 44 million viewers at home—there's always been the same grand finale: Santa Claus. When the famous Macy's Santa rolls out on his lavish float, everyone knows the Christmas season has officially begun.

A "Deer" Gesture

Veterinary surgeon performs life-saving procedure on reindeer just in time for Christmas.

You could call it a Christmas miracle: After years of being bullied by other male reindeer and showing abnormal antler development, Eskimo, an eight-year-old tundra reindeer at the Edinburgh Zoo in Edinburgh, Scotland, received groundbreaking surgery. Since birth, Eskimo had a testicle lodged in his abdomen, and beside having the potential of becoming tumorous and giving off abnormal hormones, it also appeared to be affecting his testosterone levels. He was showing submissive behavior and getting picked on by the seven other deer in the herd (who apparently couldn't "rein" in their harassment)! Enter surgeon Romain Pizzi, of the Royal Zoological Society of Scotland, who in December 2009 performed life-saving surgery on Eskimo that is highly uncommon in veterinary medicine.

The key(hole) to a healthier deer

The surgery is referred to as keyhole, or laparoscopic, surgery, and it involves making small incisions rather than operating through a large incision. Magnified images on TV monitors help guide surgeons through the procedure. While it is routine in human patients, it's rare in animals. In fact, Dr. Pizzi's was the first keyhole surgery performed on a reindeer (he has operated this way on cats, dogs, and exotic pets). Rather than undergoing open abdominal surgery, which would have caused slower recovery and greater pain, Eskimo's keyhole procedure allowed him to be up and at 'em and munching on lichen within a few minutes of recovery from anaesthesia.

"He hardly seemed to notice he had even had surgery," Pizzi told *The Courier.* "This would simply not have been possible with traditional open abdominal surgery, as the long wound would have been much more painful." Whether or not Eskimo was feeling well enough to pull Santa's sleigh is another story, but luckily, that task traditionally falls to Dasher, Dancer, Prancer, Vixen, Comet, Cupid, Donder, and Blitzen!

How Do You Say That?

MERRY CHRISTMAS!

Serbian: Hristos se rodi

Singhalese: Subha nath thalak Vewa. Subha Aluth Awrudhak Vewa

Slovak: Vesele Vianoce

Slovene: Vesele Bozicne Praznike Srecno Novo Leto *or* Vesel Bozic in srecno Novo leto

Southern: Merry Christmas, y'all!

Spanish: Feliz Navidad

Surfer: Whoa, dude! Merry…wait, what? . . . oh yeah! Christmas!

Swedish: God Jul

Tagalog: Maligayamg Pasko. Masaganang Bagong Taon

Tamil (Tamizh): Nathar Puthu Varuda Valthukkal (good New Year, not Merry Christmas)

Trukeese (Micronesian): Neekiriisimas annim oo iyer seefe feyiyeech!

Thai: Sawadee Pee Mai *or* souksan wan Christmas

Turkish: Noeliniz Ve Yeni Yiliniz Kutlu Olsun

Ukrainian: Srozhdestvom Kristovym *or* Z RIZDVOM HRYSTOVYM

Urdu: Naya Saal Mubarak Ho (good New Year, not Merry Christmas)

Valley Girl: So I'm like, Merry Christmas! And she's all like, totally! And I'm like, whatever!

Vietnamese: Chuc Mung Giang Sinh

Welsh: Nadolig Llawen

Yoruba: E ku odun e ku iye'dun!

Christmas Around the World

ICELAND

What could be better than Christmas? Maybe 12 days of Christmas, but why settle for that when you could have a full 26 days to celebrate! You'll need to give up Santa Claus....Oh yeah, and you'll need to go to Iceland to celebrate Yule, or as they call it, Jól.

One of the most notable differences between our Christmas celebration and that of Iceland is that Santa really doesn't have a presence there. Instead, the *Jólasveinar,* or "Yule Lads," begin showing up on December 12, and each morning children find candy, fruit, and other small treats in their shoes (see page 254).

Cats, kids, and church bells

The children of gods Grýla and Leppalúði aren't the only ones who get in on the holiday spirit. Their child-eating cat, known as the Yule Cat, is said to devour anyone unfortunate enough not to receive clothing on Christmas. With the Yule Cat taken care of, most of Iceland focuses on children and family. Most children get two to three weeks for Christmas break, and drinking alcohol is frowned upon for the duration of the holidays. This focus on family also means that big Christmas dinners are customary, and people usually feast on ham, smoked lamb, or ptarmigan. We know ptarmigan by another name: partridge. (Guess we know now why it flies to the pear tree!) The feast is preceded by a special service in the Lutheran Cathedral of Reykjavík, signaled by the ringing of the church bells.

Most of the country shuts down the night of Christmas Eve. At home, children rush to clean the table and wash the dishes so they can open gifts that are under the Christmas tree. After, most people settle in for the night with a new book in a new sweater (don't forget the Yule Cat) and later to watch an evening mass on television.

New Year's is a huge party, and now is the time in the celebration to raise a glass of spirits. Fireworks are lit, and the celebration stands in stark contrast to the quietness of Christmas. On January 6, Icelanders celebrate Twelfth Night with another family dinner. The last of the fireworks are usually lit, and another Jól comes to a close for the people of Iceland.

SANTA WHO?

YULE LADS

Iceland. It is a beautiful land of impish pop singers, active volcanoes, and 13 "Santas." Snow-swept mountains in a land known for holding Nordic traditions lost to the rest of the world, Iceland's lack of one old man with a beard and furry red suit may seem strange to outsiders, but their gift-giving elves have been well loved by Icelanders for more than four centuries.

Gifts and potatoes
The Icelandic call them *Jólasveinar*, or "Yule Lads," and all are mischievous troublemakers who bear gifts at Christmastime for good children and potatoes for the naughty. They are themselves the children of two mountain-dwelling ogres from Dimmuborgir named Grýla and Leppalúði, who eat naughty kids at Christmastime. The lads manage to escape their parents during the holidays, one a day until Christmas, and bring not only gifts but their own form of tomfoolery as well. When their legend first spread, they were feared for their fiendish brand of humor, but today their jokes are mostly humorous and harmless. Each has a name that tells precisely what kind of hijinks he will be up to.

What's in a name?
The first to visit, on December 12, is Sheep-Cote Clod, who likes to harass sheep for their milk but is hindered by bad knees; he is sometimes called Gimpy because of it. The next is Gully Gawk, who waits in gullies for milkmaids to start flirting with cowherds so he can sneak into barns and steal milk. Stubby (also known as Shorty), the shortest, follows the next night to steal dirty pans to eat the crumbs, followed by Spoon Licker (also called Ladle Licker), whose skinny frame is due to the sparse amount of food left on spoons. Pot Scraper likes to knock on the front door and then run around to the back. While kids are checking for guests, he's scraping what he can from the pots in the kitchen. Bowl Licker is next, stealing from bowls left for pets, and the night after that Door Slammer starts slamming doors when least expected.

Skyr, a type of Icelandic yogurt, is a favorite of Skyr Gobbler on the eighth night, and Sausage Swiper (or Snatcher) sneaks into smokehouses for his food of choice starting on night nine. On the tenth, Window Peeper shows up and takes whatever he manages to peep through windows, and by the eleventh night families must deal with the further invasion of Door Sniffer using his enormous nose to search for baking leaf bread. Meat Hook is second to last, and he fishes for any meat Sausage Swiper has left untouched, followed, finally, by Candle Beggar, who loves to steal tallow candles from children in the dark. After the lads have all arrived, left their gifts or potatoes, and played their pranks, they begin leaving in the same order they arrived. By Twelfth Night (January 6), the lads have all departed for Dimmuborgir once again, and life returns to normal.

Modern trappings

Today, the Yule Lads still live in Dimmuborgir and often still wear the same clothes from the Middle Ages, though they sometimes don the same garb as Santa. Hundreds of tourists make the trek each year to visit the lads in their mountain home between the end of November and December 23. On December 6, the 13 brothers take their annual Christmas washing in Mývatn nature bath, and more than 200 people typically join them. Though the hot spring is certain to be a bit crowded, there are other activities for those who want to stay dry. Local women teach classes on making leaf bread, and guests can visit the Yule Lads in their home from 1 to 3 in the afternoon. No, it isn't the same as visiting Santa at your local mall, but then Iceland isn't like anywhere else in the world. And the people there, and their 13 Santas, like it just fine that way.

"My idea of Christmas, whether old-fashioned or modern, is very simple: Loving others. Come to think of it, why do we have to wait for Christmas to do that?"

—*Bob Hope*

Christmas in Space!

For a few shining minutes, the crew of Apollo 8
offered Christmas cheer to a tumultuous world.

The year 1968 was rough for the United States and the world. The war in Vietnam was ramping up, and civil unrest was rife on college campuses. But one bright spot that year was a televised Christmas address from the crew of *Apollo 8*.

Apollo 8's mission—to orbit the moon and return safely—was vital to the American space program, but it barely registered on the public consciousness at the time. That changed on December 24 when Commander Frank Borman, Command Module Pilot Jim Lovell, and Lunar Module Pilot William Anders greeted the world with a holiday message from lunar orbit.

Vast loneliness of space

During the presentation, the astronauts showed pictures of the earth and the moon as seen from their space capsule. "The vast loneliness is awe-inspiring," said Lovell, "and it makes you realize just what you have back there on earth."

Anders took the mic: "For all the people on earth, the crew of *Apollo 8* has a message we would like to send you." The astronauts then took turns reading the first ten verses of the book of Genesis.

Though *Apollo 8* didn't garner nearly as much attention as *Apollo 11*, which landed the first men on the moon, the Christmas message from its crew was viewed by an estimated one billion people around the world, making it the most widely watched television broadcast at the time. There was, however, a bit of controversy: Atheist activist Madalyn Murray O'Hair sued NASA because of the overtly religious broadcast. The case was eventually dismissed by the Supreme Court because of lack of jurisdiction.

Interestingly, *Apollo 8* was not the only mission to have a religious component. During *Apollo 11*, Edwin "Buzz" Aldrin quietly received communion on the lunar surface shortly after he and Neil Armstrong made their historic landing.

🎥 CHRISTMAS MOVIE QUIZ

Match the line to the Christmas movie it came from.

1. "You smell like beef and cheese! You don't smell like Santa."
   a. *A Christmas Story*
   b. *Jingle All the Way*
   c. *Elf*
   d. *Mixed Nuts*

2. "Mother always taught me: 'Never eat singing food.'"
   a. *Mixed Nuts*
   b. *The Muppet Christmas Carol*
   c. *We're No Angels*
   d. *Scrooged*

3. "Can we take a direct flight back to reality, or do we have to change planes in Denver?"
   a. *The Santa Clause*
   b. *A Christmas Story*
   c. *How the Grinch Stole Christmas*
   d. *Christmas with the Kranks*

4. "In some ways, you're far superior to my cocker spaniel."
   a. *White Christmas*
   b. *The Muppet Christmas Carol*
   c. *Elf*
   d. *Fred Claus*

5. "Blast this Christmas music. It's joyful and triumphant."
   a. *Ernest Saves Christmas*
   b. *Fred Claus*
   c. *Scrooged*
   d. *How the Grinch Stole Christmas*

Answers: 1. c; 2. b; 3. a; 4. a; 5. d

I'm Gettin' Nuttin' for Christmas

On Christmas morning 1977, thousands of American children woke up to find an empty box under the tree, and to them, it was the greatest gift ever. But this box wasn't exactly empty: It contained a certificate for the first four toys in a line that would become one of the most popular ever. These children were the first generation of Star Wars *fans.*

A maker of classics

Prior to obtaining the license to produce *Star Wars* action figures, Kenner was a small toy company from Ohio owned by General Mills. Its most popular products up until then were classics such as Play-Doh, the Easy-Bake Oven, and the Spirograph. In 1975, the company achieved some success with licensed properties when it made the *Six Million Dollar Man* toys. These were 13-inch-tall dolls, similar in size to Barbie or G.I. Joe, and they sold well enough to help Kenner break the $100 million mark for the first time. It wasn't too much of a surprise then that the company would take a chance on George Lucas's little science-fiction adventure a couple of years later.

Low expectations

Unfortunately, Kenner wasn't expecting the film to do well and hadn't begun production on any *Star Wars* toys when the film came out, and several months later it still wasn't ready to meet the demand for Christmas. *Star Wars* had already broken all box-office records, but without a toy to put under the tree, it looked like Kenner and *Star Wars* would miss the chance to capitalize on the biggest movie phenomenon since *Gone with the Wind.* With nothing to lose, Kenner decided to sell little more than the promise of a toy. The IOU came in the form of a certificate good for four action figures to be shipped between February and June of 1978. The company sold it as the "Early Bird Certificate Package," which included little more in the package than the certificate and a few stickers. Demand was high for *Star Wars* toys though, so Kenner did all it could to get the word out to the good little boys and girls of the world. In the next year, the company's profits would double thanks to *Star Wars*.

Selling air

Kenner started an advertising campaign that included television commercials, print ads, and a catalog. TV spots showed two happy children, gleefully extending Luke Skywalker's lightsaber, twisting R2-D2's dome, and posing the wookie Chewbacca with Princess Leia. The Kenner catalog had more details though, and it listed the certificate and stickers, as well as a *Star Wars* Club membership card. The commercial alerted kids to a delivery date between February and June of the following year, and the catalog revealed another important fact: The soon-to-be famous "*Star Wars* Empty Box" would only be sold until December 31, 1977. It wasn't long before print ads began running as well. One Kenner ad even upped the ante, promising delivery of all toys by February 15, 1978, a much quicker timeframe than the prospect of getting the toys nearly a year after the film debuted.

Collectors rejoice

When the figures arrived, they were 3¾ inches tall, helping cement a new standard for action figure size over the next decade. Today, the *Star Wars* Early Bird Certificate Package can be difficult to come by in its original condition. Nearly all those purchased in 1977 were torn open, the stickers stuck to lunch boxes, and the certificates mailed away for the promised figures. Those four toys that came, however, still fetch a good price on Web sites such as eBay. It's easy to see

why so many would pay so much for something so little. For many, remembering the excitement that came from opening an empty box on Christmas morning is priceless.

Christmas Jeers!

*A Christmas card intended to be humorous
set off a furor by poking fun at redheads.*

Christmas cards are supposed to make people feel good by invoking the spirit of the holiday. That's why, in 2009, when British mom Davinia Phillips spotted a holiday card making fun of redheads, she saw, well, red and blasted the store that sold it.

The card, which was manufactured by a British company called Quitting Hollywood, showed a young red-haired boy sitting on Santa's lap. The caption read: "Santa loves all kids. Even ginger ones." The term *ginger* has become a pejorative term for people with red hair, light skin, and freckles.

Kids confused

"Maybe I am just being naive, but they shouldn't be able to make fun of ginger children like that," Phillips, who has red hair, as do her three daughters, told a British newspaper. "I showed my nine-year-old twins the card and they were confused. They asked me why it didn't just say 'Santa loves all kids.' It's quite upsetting. Kids do get bullied for looking different, and people making cards like this encourages the bullies."

Phillips contacted the Tesco supermarket where she found the card and filed a formal complaint. The store was sympathetic and immediately removed the cards from its shelves. Quitting Hollywood, however, refused to comment on the cards or apologize to Phillips.

Gingers a target

The taunting of so-called gingers has become increasingly common in recent years. Incidents spiked following an episode of the popular animated television series *South Park,* in which one character espoused the bizarre belief that "gingers have no soul." In November 2009, two 12-year-old boys and a 13-year-old were arrested for bullying at a California middle school after assaulting several red-haired classmates as part of "Kick a Ginger Day."

The Giant Straw Goat of Gävle

Every year at Christmas, the Southern Merchants of Gävle, Sweden, erect a straw goat. Nearly every year, vandalism gets their goat.

You'd think it would be the final straw: On December 22, 2009, in Gävle, Sweden, just three days before Christmas, an unknown culprit snuck up to the 43-foot-tall straw goat in the town square and set fire to the big ol' billy. The tradition of building a Swedish Yule goat began in 1966, and the tradition of vandalizing it started shortly thereafter. In fact, this was the *24th* torching of the famous Gävle goat. Some years the goat goes up in flames mere hours after it's erected. Other goats have been smashed, run over by cars, and had their legs removed. Thus far, only ten of the goats have survived past Christmas. Still, the town continues the tradition. If the goat is destroyed before St. Lucia Day (December 13), it is often rebuilt.

Advertising man Stig Gavlén came up with the idea of building the goat to attract people to Gävle businesses. The Southern Merchants, a local association, provided financing for the first goat—which was built by the local fire department—on December 1, 1966, and it went up in flames at midnight on New Year's Eve. Successive goats were also vandalized, to the point that the Southern Merchants stopped building them for 15 years, and the task fell to the Natural Science Club of the School of Vasa. Their goats, too, often succumbed to flames. Today, there are two Gävle goats—one by the Southern Merchants and one by the Natural Science Club.

In 2001, a tourist from Cleveland, Ohio, was apprehended and spent 18 days in jail for setting fire to the goat, but often the culprits are never caught. The city has experimented with fireproofing chemicals, but they discolor the straw. There have been Webcams on the goat, but vandals have tampered with those as well. It's safe to say that at this point, the Gävle goat is an endangered species!

Christmas Greetings from the White House!

*Modern presidents send out thousands of
Christmas cards every year. Back in the day,
it was a completely different story.*

The presidential celebration of Christmas has evolved greatly since George Washington first took office in 1789. Back then, Christmas wasn't what it is today, and few really cared how the nation's commander-in-chief observed the holiday. Today, of course, it's a whole different story. Here's a brief holiday history lesson.

George Washington spent eight Christmases as president, none of them in the White House, which didn't become the official residence of the president until 1800. However, the Washingtons were joyous celebrants of the holiday, and they hosted numerous parties for friends and family. There were, however, no Christmas cards—that tradition didn't begin in the United States until the mid-19th century.

Party down!

When John Adams finally moved into the newly completed White House, it was so cold and drafty that it took 13 fireplaces to make the place livable. But that didn't stop Adams from hosting the very first White House Christmas party in honor of his granddaughter, Susanna. (The illustrated invitation for the event is considered by some historians to be the first White House Christmas card.) The party included music in the grand ballroom, cake, punch, carols, and games. By all accounts, it was a rousing success.

Thomas Jefferson, the nation's third president, also hosted some fun Christmas soirees in the White House, attended by his grand-children and close friends. Because Jefferson was a widower by the time he was elected president, the first such affair was hosted by Dolly Madison, the wife of Secretary of State (and future president) James Madison.

Every president has celebrated Christmas in the White House in his own way, but most have made at least some attempt at a public overture. Andrew Jackson, for example, sent illustrated invitations to local children inviting them to a special holiday event in the East Room on Christmas Day. The shindig included singing, dancing, and plenty of food.

Wartime holiday

The Civil War occupied most of Abraham Lincoln's time, even during the holidays, but he still tried to spend at least some time with family and friends. Christmas 1861, for example, started with a morning cabinet meeting, but the president was able to host a dinner party that evening at the White House. It's interesting to note that Thomas Nast, one of the era's most skilled illustrators, gave us the caricature of Santa Claus as we know him today, which was first seen in the January 1863 issue of *Harper's Weekly*. It was an illustration created at Lincoln's request.

It was during Ulysses S. Grant's presidency that Christmas became a national holiday—via legislation that did the same for New Year's Day, July 4, and Thanksgiving Day. Despite that great achievement, however, little is known today about how Grant celebrated Christmas during his two terms in the White House.

Our 30th president, Calvin Coolidge, started a unique White House holiday tradition that continues today—what Coolidge called the National Community Christmas Tree. The first such tree, erected on the White House grounds in 1923, was a 48-foot Balsam fir from Coolidge's home state of Vermont. The following year, with the passing of Coolidge's son, Cal Jr., from blood poisoning, the White House received a record-setting 12,000 Christmas cards from the American people. The Coolidges themselves sent cards only to close friends and family.

An avalanche of cards

In 1933, Franklin Delano Roosevelt set a new record for the number of Christmas cards received from the public: 40,000 total. In fact, so many cards came pouring into the White House that extra staff was hired to handle it all. The Roosevelts, like the Coolidges before them, sent cards only to family and friends—the first featuring an etching of the White House engraved by artist A. B. Tolly. The Roosevelts also gave gifts to the White House staff, as did most presidents before them.

Dwight D. Eisenhower took the White House Christmas card to a whole new level by creating his own. During his first Christmas in the White House in 1953, Ike tapped the Hallmark company to produce a card that featured a portrait of Abraham Lincoln painted by Eisenhower himself, which was given to White House staff and others. Original paintings by Eisenhower also graced the 1954 and 1955 White House Christmas cards.

Tragic collector's item

John F. Kennedy also turned to Hallmark for the creation of the White House Christmas card during his two Christmases in the White House. Kennedy was assassinated on November 22, 1963, and that year's official White House card was never distributed. However, approximately 30 cards were signed by the president and first lady just days before that fateful trip to Dallas, and those cards have become extraordinary collector's items.

With Christmas 1963 falling just a month after Kennedy's assassination, neither Lyndon Johnson nor the nation were in a mood to celebrate. Nonetheless, Johnson, at the suggestion of the State Department, sent holiday cards to several heads of state and other dignitaries with whom his predecessor had close ties. In the years that followed, Johnson turned to American Greetings Corporation, rather than Hallmark, to create the official White House Christmas card because Irving Stone, the company's president, had been a financial supporter of the Johnson campaign.

All modern presidents have sent special Christmas cards, each looking to put his own unique mark on the tradition. Some cards have been ornate, others simple and dignified. All share the spirit of the holiday.

Christmas Around the World

ETHIOPIA

*Rise and shine! The Ethiopian Christmas celebration
starts in the wee hours of the morning.*

Christmas in the African country of Ethiopia is called *Ganna* and takes place on January 7, since Ethiopians observe the ancient Julian calendar. It is largely a religious celebration. The day before Ganna, people fast and then, early the next morning, dress in white clothing. Some also don a traditional *shamma,* a thin cotton cloth resembling a toga that has colorful stripes along the hem.

Standing for Christ

For the faithful in Ethiopia, there's no sleeping in on Christmas morning: Mass takes place at 4 A.M.! In rural areas, services are often held in ancient churches carved out of volcanic rock, while in urban centers, mass is held in modern churches designed in three concentric circles. Upon entering the church, each person is given a candle and then solemnly circles the sanctuary three times before taking his or her place in the second circle (the choir occupies the outer circle). Men and women are separated, and in the inner circle, the priest serves Holy Communion. The mass can last up to three hours, and everyone stands throughout. After church, young men play a game—also called *Ganna*—which is similar to hockey.

The Christmas feast includes traditional Ethiopian foods such as *injera,* a spongy sourdough flatbread and *wat,* a hearty stew of meat, vegetables, and spices. Rather than use utensils, people use the injera to scoop up the wat.

Twelve days after Christmas, on January 19, Ethiopians observe *Timkat,* a three-day celebration of the baptism of Christ. The priests wear white and red robes and carry intricately embroidered umbrellas. This time, the young men play a jousting game called *yeferas guks,* and once again, everyone enjoys a great deal of food. In Ethiopia, gift-giving is not a large part of the celebration, though children do receive simple presents. Instead, families partake in religious rituals, games, and shared meals.

The Boys in Blue

Funny hats? Check. Short stature? Check. Lead by an elder who wears a red hat and white beard? Check. Helpful to and beloved by children the world over? Check and double check! Very little seems to separate the toy-makers of the North Pole, Santa's elves, from the keepers of the Magic Flute, the schtroumpfs. Of course, in America we know these blue-skinned Franco-Belgian forest dwellers by another name: Smurfs.

Smurfing the Smurf

Despite the obvious similarities in disposition and clothing style, there's actually very little connection between the Smurfs and Santa's elves. The Smurfs date back only to 1958, when Belgian comic-book artist Peyo (née Pierre Culliford) introduced the small blue elves to the world as part of his ongoing adventure series *Johan and Peewit*. Set in the Middle Ages, these comic books follow Johan, a young page, and his sidekick on their sword-and-sorcery adventures, one of which introduced them to the Smurfs. These little blue creations, led by Papa Smurf, soon had a following all their own, and by the 1980s they would star in their own television series.

Smurfy Smurf is the smurfiest

Santa's elves, on the other hand, appeared in popular culture long before that. The magazine *Godey's Lady's Book* first published images of Santa's helpers in 1873, depicting St. Nick as knee deep in knee-high helpers. From there, the elves, similar to the Smurfs, took on a life of their own. Today we see elves with Santa all the time, and numerous films and books present them as part of the indelible landscape of Santa's North Pole hideaway. Still, the junior servants of Father Christmas look more like lawn gnomes or Norse dwarves than the Belgian forest protectors ever have.

Smurfing the part

In considering Smurfs and elves, their similar looks cannot be ignored. First, there's their peculiar choice in headwear. Both wear conical hats called Phrygian caps. While this style of headdress can be seen throughout history, even being worn by the likes of King Midas himself, fashionistas of our time would be hard-pressed to find any non-Smurf or elf groups sporting Phrygian caps today. Of course, there is the small matter of one group having blue skin, but we don't know much, if anything, about the physiology of Santa's elves. For all we know, they could tan blue in the sun. After all, it isn't like the North Pole gets that much sunlight, so it just might be possible.

Also, we shouldn't ignore the shared stature of these two groups. While everyone agrees both are short, neither Smurfs nor elves have ever been measured properly. Visual representations often place both somewhere between as small as a mushroom and as large as a Macy's Parade balloon. It would have to be quite a coincidence for there to exist two large and separate populations of extremely short individuals who share the same taste in hats and a propensity for being extremely kind to children.

The smurf is in the pudding

That said, there is one final bit of evidence that points to the two having no direct connection whatsoever. In 1982, Hanna-Barbera released video footage (some called it an animated holiday special) featuring the Smurfs at Christmastime. *The Smurfs' Christmas Special* featured the little blue people celebrating Christmas in their own way, and not once did they pack a sleigh or tend to reindeer.

Though we might read into Gargamel's hatred for both Smurfs and Christmas, the Smurfs clearly spend more time thwarting his villainous plans than making toys. It is also clear that while the children in the film mistake Papa Smurf and his kin for Santa and his elves, none of the adults make the same error. No, when it comes to Smurfs and elves, there is little more to their relationship than a highly understandable case of mistaken identity.

Depressing Holiday Returns!

Many Christmas movies have been huge moneymakers. Others, not so much.

Christmas has been an incredibly popular genre among filmmakers since the establishment of the commercial motion-picture industry in the early 1900s. Every year, it seems, more and more new holiday flicks are unleashed on a popcorn-hungry public eager for some end-of-year cheer. More than a few of these films have become cult classics, such as *It's a Wonderful Life* (1946), *Miracle on 34th Street* (1947), *White Christmas* (1954), and *A Christmas Story* (1983), and many have gone on to make hundreds of millions of dollars at the box office.

Not so classic

And then there are those Christmas movies that didn't. Frequently costing a small fortune to make and starring popular performers, they simply failed to find an audience and quickly disappeared. Don't feel bad if you missed these top ten worst-grossing Christmas movies:

1. *Christmas at Maxwell's* (2006): $12,350
2. *Christmas in Wonderland* (2007): $78,566
3. *Santa with Muscles* (1996): $220,198
4. *Christmas in the Clouds* (2005): $279,225
5. *Noelle* (2007): $257,868
6. *Nutcracker: The Motion Picture* (1986): $781,727
7. *The Nutcracker Prince* (1990): $1,781,694
8. *The Nutcracker* (1993): $2,119,994
9. *The Perfect Holiday* (2007): $5,812,781
10. *Trapped in Paradise* (1994): $6,017,509

Holiday blockbusters

And which Christmas movie has grossed the most over the years? That record is held by the live-action adaptation of Dr. Seuss's *How*

The Grinch Stole Christmas (2000), directed by Ron Howard and starring Jim Carrey and Taylor Momsen. To date, it has grossed more than $350 million.

The next top highest-grossing Christmas movies are:

2. *The Polar Express* (2004): $181,320,482
3. *Elf* (2003): $173,398,518
4. *The Santa Clause* (1994): $144,833,357
5. *The Santa Clause 2* (2002): $139,236,327
6. *A Christmas Carol* (2009): $137,855,863
7. *Four Christmases* (2008): $120,146,040
8. *The Santa Clause 3: The Escape Clause* (2006): $84,500,122
9. Tim Burton's *The Nightmare Before Christmas* (1993): $75,082,668
10. *Christmas with the Kranks* (2004): $73,780,539

More Reinder Facts!

- It's one thing to crave a burger, but a reindeer burger? In Scandinavia, reindeer is commonly found on dinner menus with burgers, casseroles, and chops being among the favorite ways to serve them.

- Early on, Laplanders hunted reindeer for both food and other uses. Their meat and milk were eaten. The hide made clothing and shelter. Their sinews served as thread and twine. And their bones and antlers were carved into weapons and utensils.

- Reindeer live farther north than any other animal except muskoxen, well past the timberline of the Arctic. Wolves, bears, and the wily wolverine are their predators in the Arctic tundra.

- The earliest depiction of a reindeer was found in Sagelva, Norway, on a rock carving dating sometime between 2000 and 500 B.C.

The Tremendous Tinkertoy

*If you have kids, know kids, or ever were a kid,
you know that even when surrounded by expensive, designer
toys, children are often perfectly happy banging pots and pans
together or playing with a box. This was the principle behind
Tinkertoys, a Christmas gift favorite for over a century.*

Hey, kid: good idea!

Once upon a time in the early 1900s, two guys were on their way to work. Their names were Charles Pajeau and Robert Pettit, and they were on a train headed from the Chicago suburb of Evanston into the city. While they rode, they talked about how bored they were with their jobs: Pajeau was a stonemason, Pettit worked at the Board of Trade. Neither man felt satisfied. The talk turned to inventions, and Pajeau shared an idea with Pettit.

Prior to their conversation, Pajeau had seen some kids playing with pencils and spools of thread. They invented moving parts, made up stories to go along with what they engineered, and generally seemed to have a blast with their improvised toy. Pajeau figured he could design a toy on the wooden spool/pencil concept; Pettit knew he could market his new friend's brilliant idea.

Ladies and gentlemen … Tinkertoys!

In his line of work, Pajeau was used to dealing with angles, math, and basic engineering principles. The first Tinkertoy set was entirely handcrafted, and it consisted of 2-inch-diameter wooden spools with holes drilled every 45 degrees around the perimeter, plus one through the center. The perimeter holes in a Tinkertoy spool don't go all the way through, but the center hole does. This allows for the spool to move freely around the "axle," which is made with any of the various lengths of wooden sticks in the set. Ever the math whiz, Pajeau based the toy on the Pythagorean progressive right triangle, and he made sure everything was exact.

Pettit helped get the toy to the American Toy Fair, but the set didn't really take off until the pair tried a unique marketing scheme: the Toy Tinkers (which is what they called their company) hired a group of dwarves dressed in elf costumes to play with Tinkertoys in a Chicago department store window. The idea paid off: Customers came in droves to see the elves and bought Tinkertoy sets by the hundreds. Within a year, over a million sets had been sold and the two working stiffs from Chicago were on the toymaker map for good.

Tinker adapts

By the late 1940s, more than 2.5 million Tinkertoy construction sets had been produced. The Tinkertoy continued to sell, but the inventors were both in their seventies. When Pettit passed away, Pajeau decided to sell the rights to his creation to A. G. Spalding Bros., Inc., a company that grew the line by adding color and additional pieces to play with.

The Tinkertoy continued to find its way under Christmas trees around the world, even garnering press as a tool for professional engineers. Students of computer science and robotics at Cornell and MIT used the toy as a model to develop complex machines.

Then, in 1985, game giant Playskool purchased the rights. In 1992, they released a revamped Tinkertoy set to commemorate its 80th anniversary. The new sets were all plastic, with easy-to-assemble parts including "flags," "pulleys," "elbows," and of course, "rods" and "spools." Available in both junior and jumbo versions, kids (and adults) can now build bigger structures than ever before. Every set includes instructions on how to create machines that move and building structures with intricate moving parts.

Until the 1960s, the company averaged sales of over 2.5 million sets per year. While that number has decreased significantly, Tinkertoys, that classic toy of motion and construction, continue to be a hit for Christmas, birthdays, and ordinary trips to the toy store.

Zoot Suit Santa

The Pancho Claus legend lives in Texas!

In Houston, where there's never a snow white Christmas, you might see a jolly Santa in a zoot suit. He's been organizing toy drives and drop-offs for decades. In real life, his name is Richard Reyes, but in December he is Pancho Claus.

The legend of Pancho Claus

Pancho Claus was the subject of a 1950s Lalo Guerrero song of the same name. Guerrero made a career of performing socially conscious parodies that dealt with issues in the Chicano community.

Guerrero's Pancho was a riff on the "'Twas the Night Before Christmas" poem. The *story* of Pancho Claus, however, is a little different. In Lubbock, Texas, the American GI Forum built a program for giving needy kids gifts apparently based on a song by Cuco Sanchez. In the song, Pancho is a cousin of Santa raised in the South Pole and aided by Spanish-speaking elves who moonlighted in mariachi bands. The legend has a strong base in Texas, where there is a sizable Hispanic population.

A Christmas superhero

As his alter-ego Pancho Claus, Reyes and his elf helpers travel to poor neighborhoods in the Houston area to give out gifts to children with nothing under the tree. In zoot suits and a small fleet of low-riders, Pancho and his troupe are indeed a spectacle. Santa's cousin has been even busier the last couple of years due to the economy. Reyes also serves as a youth mentor for at-risk kids. Pancho can be found on the Web at PanchoClaus.com.

Like Santa Claus, there are many Pancho Clauses (and more than a few are veterans). But there is only one Richard Reyes, who was hampered by a heart attack in November 2009. It slowed him down, but only a little. Whether it was a new aspirin regimen or the zoot suit that got him back on his feet, only Reyes knows.

Fast Facts

CHRISTMAS TREES!

- In 1856, Franklin Pierce became the first president to place a Christmas tree in the White House.

- The National Christmas Tree Association has donated a Christmas tree to the president and his family every year since 1966.

- Theodore Roosevelt declined to set up a National Christmas tree on environmental grounds.

- Calvin Coolidge started the National Christmas Tree Lighting Ceremony in 1923.

- In 1963, the National Christmas Tree was not lighted until December 22 because of a 30-day period of mourning following the assassination of President Kennedy.

- In 1979, the National Christmas Tree was unlighted, except for the top ornament, in honor of the American hostages in Iran.

- Christmas tree farms are good for the environment. For example, the trees provide a habitat for wildlife.

- Christmas trees help remove pollen and dust from the air.

- There are an estimated 4,000 Christmas tree recycling programs nationwide. More than 90 percent of tree buyers dispose of their trees through some sort of community program.

- Recycled Christmas trees are commonly used as barriers against soil erosion and as habitats for fish in ponds and lakes.

- Nearly 80 percent of the world's artificial Christmas trees are manufactured in China.

- The use of candles to illuminate Christmas trees dates back to the 17th century.

Hallmark Ornaments: Manufacturing Memories

🕯 🕯 🕯

Of course, not all Christmas tree ornaments are made by memento giant Hallmark, but there's bound to be one on your tree at some point. Read on for a little background on those whimsical, ubiquitous additions to American Christmas decor.

Decking the halls (and the tree)

According to Hallmark's research, 88 percent of us decorate a Christmas tree during the holidays. This wasn't always the case. In fact, decorating the Christmas tree with ornaments wasn't in style until the turn of the 20th century. A couple hundred years prior to that, German immigrants brought the custom to America. Some folks were early adopters, but it wasn't until the late 1800s that you could buy tree ornaments at Woolworth's department store. Even then, the selection was limited—Mr. Woolworth wasn't convinced they'd sell.

But ten years later, Woolworth's was doing $25 million annually in Christmas tree ornaments alone, all of which were priced at about ten cents apiece. The European tradition had become a fad: Christmas tree ornaments were suddenly part of the American Christmas experience.

Trying their hand

In 1973, Kansas City–based greeting card company Hallmark Cards decided to make a foray into the ornament business. They were already producing cards, wrapping paper, and other Christmas-themed items for what had become their biggest season, so exploring tree ornaments was a logical step. Specialty glass and ceramics company Corning had entered the ornament market before World War II, but that was pretty much it as far as American competition went. The market was wide open—and Hallmark came in swinging.

Instead of producing plain old ornaments that would get used year after year, the marketing geniuses at Hallmark introduced an entirely new idea: collectible ornaments. Their debut collection offered six glass balls and twelve yarn figures, all of which were labeled to be the first collection of the Hallmark Keepsake Ornaments. The ornaments bore the year in which they were made, and they were only available for a short amount of time before Christmas. This caused a consumer feeding frenzy around the product (think "Tickle Me Elmo"). Hallmark sold out of the ornaments in no time. It did the same the next year and have been on top of the ornament business ever since.

The mark of Hallmark

Hallmark's Keepsake Ornaments have come a long way since those first yarn figurines. More than 3,000 pieces have been produced since the first launch, and over the years, they've gotten increasingly more intricate—and thoroughly modern.

The product lines are typically planned up to two years in advance. Licensing takes place where necessary, allowing designers to incorporate images and characters from movies, television, and other media: Star Wars, Barbie, Mickey Mouse, etc. Illustrators and sculptors work to create a prototype; once the design is approved, it's sent to the manufacturer and the limited quantity is produced—and all ornaments always bear the date stamp and official Hallmark logo. In order to keep the ornaments in demand and worth collecting, any pieces not sold by the end of the short selling season are sent back to Hallmark and destroyed (though a few are kept for their archives).

Many of the ornaments created under the Keepsake umbrella are actually part of a larger series. There have been more than 100 different series launched since 1973; some, like *Frosty Friends,* are still active and receive new additions each year.

Those crazy Christmas collectors

Maybe you're a collector, or maybe you know one. If so, you might be interested in joining the local chapter of the national Hallmark Keepsake Ornament Club. Over 600 groups are active in the United States and Canada, gathering to share their collections, shop for the next season (starting in July, mind you), and enjoying the spirit of the holiday—or any day, for that matter. Some ornaments aren't strictly holiday-themed, and some consumers hang their Keepsake ornaments around their house or in their car year-round.

Tree Thief

It's the unkindest cut of all!

The holidays are stressful. Between buying gifts, planning dinners, and visiting relatives, it's understandable that some things get pushed off to the last minute. Maybe the tree hasn't been bought yet, and the ones remaining are spindly little things.

Idiot ruins Christmas

One Scrooge snuck onto Seattle's Washington Park Arboretum in December 2009 and cut down a rare Chinese keteleeria tree worth over $10,000. David Zuckerman, the horticulturist for the University of Washington Botanic Gardens, was shocked that this particular tree was cut. "It's a Charlie Brown tree," he said. Many firs, which are more traditional Christmas trees, are prevalent throughout the arboretum. The keteleeria is a sparsely branched tree, not as bushy as firs. It's also much more rare.

The keteleeria tree, native to China, is endangered. It was planted at the arboretum in the hopes that its seeds would be used to help propagate the species.

The theft wasn't even a last-minute panic decision on Christmas Eve. The perpetrator cut down the tree sometime on December 9. That's 15 solid tree-shopping days that don't necessitate cutting down the nearest endangered keteleeria.

Those who worked at the arboretum to cultivate the tree from a sapling to a fine seven-foot specimen were particularly hurt by the act. The local botanic gardens might have to watch their flowers around Mother's Day.

This was not even the first time a tree had been stolen from the Washington Park Arboretum. Several Christmases ago, a fir was cut down and displayed in a restaurant. The perpetrator was caught, but trees that are cut down are dead and can't be repaired. Staffers at the arboretum are considering covering the trees with bright, nontoxic paint during December that can be washed off after the—apparently deadly—holidays are over.

Funny Christmas Web Sites

They make you feel better about your in-laws coming over for the holidays!

It's great to see the neighborhood decorated with lights and wreaths during the holidays, but sometimes . . . sometimes a house just doesn't look right. UglyChristmasLights.com is dedicated to those residents who "have no sense of decency in how they choose to celebrate." Nor any sense in how they're gonna pay their electric bill. This site documents the A to Zs (well, mostly the Gs: gaudy, garish, and grotesque) of Christmas lights. It's hard to pick a favorite, but a 2008 picture of a house with a Seattle Seahawks sign as the centerpiece should tell you about the priorities of the victims—I mean *inspirations*—of this Web site.

Everyone likes to get their picture taken with Santa, right? No. No, they don't. We don't know why Santa is so popular given how many kids scream and cry sitting on his lap. The site divinecaroline.com/22059/40140-photos—scary-santa has compiled a selection of some of the best "kids who want no part of Santa" photos throughout the years. There's even a picture of a kid freaking out when he sees a *statue* of Santa Claus.

The groan-worthy TheHolidaySpot.com/christmas/jokes has some of the best so-bad-they're-funny jokes. What do you give a reindeer with an upset tummy? Elk-a-seltzer. Why does Father Christmas go down the chimney? Because it "soots" him. That's the caliber of humor here. Perfect for after-dinner LOLs.

Some humor is intended for adults (even though your kids know more than you think). LettersFromBadSanta.com features letters Santa would write if he were a complete misanthrope. The highlight of the site, however, is Santa's bag of evil toys. Offerings include the My Little Pony Glue Factory and the Easy Bake Oven Meth Lab, and then it only gets worse from there.

This Verse Is Worse

Here are some later verses of well-known Christmas carols.
See if you can guess the song.

1. **Lo! star led chieftains, Magi, Christ adoring,**
   Offer Him incense, gold, and myrrh;
   We to the Christ Child bring our hearts' oblations.
   a. "O Come, All Ye Faithful"
   b. "What Child Is This?"
   c. "Hark! The Herald Angels Sing!"
   d. "Away in a Manger"

2. **Now the goose is on the table/And the pudding made of fig/**
   And the blue and silver candles/That would just have
   matched the hair in Grandma's wig.
   a. "Sleigh Ride"
   b. "Have Yourself a Merry Little Christmas"
   c. "It's the Most Wonderful Time of the Year"
   d. "Grandma Got Run Over by a Reindeer"

3. **Now the ground is white/Go it while you're young/**
   Take the girls tonight/And sing this sleighing song.
   a. "Sleigh Ride"
   b. "Jingle Bells"
   c. "Winter Wonderland"
   d. "Home for the Holidays"

4. **As for me, my little brain/Isn't very bright;/**
   Choose for me, old Santa Claus,/What you think is right.
   a. "I Saw Mommy Kissing Santa Claus"
   b. "Jolly Old Saint Nicholas"
   c. "Grandma Got Run Over by a Reindeer"
   d. "Santa Claus Is Coming to Town"

Answers: 1. a; 2. d; 3. b; 4. b

Orson Welles in *Christmas Tails*

*Even from beyond the grave, the legendary
Orson Welles still has "tails" to tell.*

Although he passed away in 1985, filmmaker Orson Welles—often dubbed "the greatest filmmaker of all time"—is making a new movie. Or well, not exactly *making* a movie, but he is narrating one with his deep, authoritative voice. Titled *Christmas Tails,* it's a 3-D live-action/animation film based on an obscure, self-published book of the same name. Welles's friend Robert X. Leed wrote the children's holiday story, and just a few months before his death, Welles narrated the book for him on five reels of tape—heretofore stashed in a closet in Leed's Las Vegas home. Eventually, various sources got wind of the lost tapes, which are believed to be Welles's last professional recording project, and unearthed them in December 2008.

Christmas Tails tells the story of Santa's reindeer becoming ill, so the jolly old elf might have to call off Christmas, but then his dog enlists the help of other dogs to come to Santa's rescue. Drac Studios, a special effects company that provided effects and virtual makeup for *The Curious Case of Benjamin Button* (2008), is at the helm of the project. "It's a movie about how Santa's dog saves Christmas, but on one level, this is a story about the discovery of Orson's lost tapes," Drac Studios president Harvey Lowry told *The Hollywood Reporter.* "This is a substantial find. It's something that a filmmaker dreams of."

As actor Boris Karloff's voice was used in the 1966 film adaptation of *How the Grinch Stole Christmas,* so too will Welles's voice be scattered throughout the film, narrating the action of the CGI (computer-generated imagery) canines on their quest to save the day. There's an irony in Welles's career "going to the dogs": Given some of the filmmaker's less-than-popular late-career decisions, such as being a spokesperson for sparkling wine and frozen peas, his narration for *Christmas Tails* should be much more warmly received.

Ron Howard's *Grinch*

Dr. Seuss's How the Grinch Stole Christmas *is
right up there with Dickens's* A Christmas Carol *when
it comes to tried and true Christmas stories.
A-List director Ron Howard took on a live-action
version of the story in 2000—and the results were
as mixed as the bowl of nuts at your office holiday party.*

Improving on perfection

Dr. Seuss's *How the Grinch Stole Christmas* started, of course, as a
book. Theodore Geisel (aka Dr. Seuss) wrote what quickly became a
classic in 1957. The story of the mean, nasty old Grinch and how his
anti-Christmas heart is melted by the magic of the season is fiercely
beloved by millions.

Just under ten years later, the book was made into an animated
special, narrated by none other than Boris Karloff, the actor who
played Frankenstein's monster in the classic 1931 movie. The
animated *Grinch* was a direct adaptation; artistically, it took no risks,
which made everyone happy—including Dr. Seuss himself, who kept
a tight grip on the licensing of his creation.

But in 2000, long after Geisel's work had passed into the hands of
lawyers and businesspeople, Universal Pictures got the green light to
tackle a live-action version of the story. This had never been done
before. Director Ron Howard was given $100 million and the ability
to execute artistic license—and that's when things started getting
complicated.

Uber-famous actor Jim Carrey signed on to play the lead. Sir
Anthony Hopkins narrated the film using Seuss's poetry—the
producers still wanted to include the book's text. But aside from that,
not much of what Howard and his team created resembled the
original *Grinch*. The movie has earned over $350 million worldwide,
so it can hardly be considered a commercial failure, but the world
that Howard created struck most people as nightmarish rather than
purely fantastical or unique.

It's possible that Dr. Seuss's drawings aren't meant to translate to
live-action. It could be that the heart of the story was lost in the

midst of such an enormous budget. However you see it, one thing is certain: Ron Howard's *Grinch* is a much different version of the Dr. Seuss story.

Trouble in Whoville

Howard and his producer, hit-maker Brian Grazer, knew from the start they wanted Jim Carrey to play "Mr. Grinch." Carrey's vocal variation and physical abilities made him an obvious choice for the kind of Grinch (and the kind of movie) they wanted to make: big, glitzy, frenetic, and fun.

Though he was paid millions to take the job, Carrey probably didn't bank on the trauma he would endure to play the part. The heavy makeup and costume he needed to wear to achieve the director's vision proved almost unendurable—and took three hours to put on every day. At one point, Carrey actually met with a Navy Seal to learn techniques used by soldiers to withstand torture—that's how bad it was under the layers of fur, wax, and rubber. As a testament to his dedication and physical ability, however, Carrey managed to deliver a wild performance, mugging, dancing, jumping, and interacting as a Grinch no one had ever seen before.

Every "Who" in Whoville had full makeup too, including a young Taylor Momsen, who played Cindy Lou Who, the girl who saves the day. Not since *The Wizard of Oz* in 1939 had so many actors been in full makeup. Approximately 8,000 makeup appliances were used to get the job done, and on the busiest days, nearly 50 makeup artists were on set for the project.

The set offered its own issues, some more stressful than others. There were over two million feet of foam used to create Whoville, as well as the movie's various props. Around 152,000 pounds of crushed marble was used for the snow on the exterior sets, and the movie spread itself across a whopping 11 soundstages.

Screenwriters Jeffrey Price and Peter Seaman (*Who Framed Roger Rabbit*) added a subplot to the original story, giving the Grinch a crush on a Whoville resident and making Cindy Lou Who a beefier character.

Critics, not so much

These changes to the script and the wanton use of a seemingly bottomless budget may have scored ticket sales, but the critics weren't buying. In fact, the reviews for Howard's *Grinch* were downright awful. Stephen Holden from *The New York Times* began his scorching review with one word: "Ugh." He called the film a "shrill, overstuffed, spiritless cinematic contraption," in the first paragraph, and it didn't get any better from there. Roger Ebert called it "dank, eerie, [and] weird." Nearly all the critics—and plenty of audience members—commented on how cynical the movie turned out to be. Ironically, cynicism is exactly what Dr. Seuss originally intended to stamp out.

For some, the spectacle is enough to make Dr. Seuss's *How the Grinch Stole Christmas* a worthwhile holiday flick. For others, it doesn't hold a candle to the book or the animated version from the 1960s. However you like your Grinch, you can find a few versions available once the holiday season kicks into gear.

"Next to a circus there ain't nothing that packs up and tears out faster than the Christmas spirit."
—*Kin Hubbard*

"There's nothing sadder in this world than to awake Christmas morning and not be a child."
—*Erma Bombeck*

A Flintstones Christmas!

Fred Flintstone has had a lot of adventures over the years—including a brief stint as Santa's helper!

The Flintstones holds a very special place in popular culture. Created by Bill Hanna and Joe Barbera, the cartoon is notable for being the first 30-minute animated series to air in prime time. It also drew raves for showcasing such popular celebrities as Ann-Margret, Tony Curtis, Elizabeth Montgomery—and Santa Claus.

The latter appeared in a very special season five episode titled "Christmas Flintstone," which aired on December 25, 1964. The story opens with Fred (Alan Reed) taking a job at the Macyrock Department Store to earn some extra money for Christmas. However, he's so bad at his job that his boss is about to fire him. At the last minute, Fred is asked to fill in for the store's Santa Claus. He does such a wonderful job that the real Santa, bedridden with a cold at the North Pole, sends two elves, Twinky and Blinky, to have Fred replace him on his annual route.

Family forgotten

Fred quickly gets into his new role, and with the help of Twinky and Blinky, he delivers toys to all of the world's good boys and girls. But at the end of the night, Fred realizes that he has forgotten to deliver gifts to his own family. Arriving empty-handed, he finds that the real Santa has saved the holiday with an unexpected last-minute delivery.

"Christmas Flintstone" is the only holiday episode to air during *The Flintstones* original six-season run, but it's a delightful story that perfectly captures the spirit of the season. Santa is voiced by veteran voice actor Hal Smith, who was usually tapped to play various incidental characters. In the Christmas episode, Smith also voices a man, a bird, and an animal.

The Flintstones is considered a television classic for a number of reasons. "Christmas Flintstone" is one of them.

Tudor Tinsel

*Beheading was, like, sooo over and moderation
was the new black as Elizabeth I and her
people partied like it was 1599.*

For 44 years, beginning on November 17, 1558, Queen Elizabeth I ruled over England during a time of unprecedented economic growth and military might. And although Christmas looked rather different during the Elizabethan period, then—as now—the holiday season was celebrated in a robust and joyous manner. For the aristocracy and landed gentry, especially, Christmas and New Year's balls were highlights of the year.

Setting the scene

These glittering galas were held both in the city and the country. The setting in either case was likely to be a timber-framed home (usually oak) with walls made of plaster (lime, sand, and animal hair). The ball would be held in a great room or hall that was decorated brilliantly for the season. Wall paintings were very popular at this time, often portraying scenes from nature or the Bible. Though wall paintings were more or less permanent, tapestry wall hangings and painted cloths could be rotated to match the time of year, and during Christmas they were especially popular. In very wealthy homes, decorators used gilt leather to line the walls of dining rooms and ballrooms, as it did not retain the smells of smoke and food the way cloth did.

Guests at an Elizabethan Christmas ball would have enjoyed strolling around the hall, looking at the host's prominently displayed coat of arms and shining armor; marble or plaster cherubim and nymphs; and glittering chandeliers hung from high, painted ceilings. All furniture, which would have been made of heavy walnut or oak, would be pushed against the walls to leave the middle of the room cleared for the exuberant dancing that was to come. Gold and silver ribbons and bows would have been everywhere, shimmering in the glowing candlelight.

The dining hall and the great hall were sometimes one and the same, but often they were two connected rooms. Guests would meet and greet in the great hall, move into the dining hall for the Christmas or New Year's feast, and then move back into the great hall for music and dancing. Musicians might be stationary, or they might move through the crowd, joking with the men and flirting harmlessly with the women between their numbers. Jesters and fools might also be employed by the host to fill the evening with laughter and colorful movement.

Primping and pageantry

Color wouldn't be lacking in any event. The guests, in their gorgeous, "best" clothing for the holiday occasion, would see to that. Rarely have wealthy women been so elaborately garbed as in the Age of Elizabeth. To our eyes, even the poor women of that day appear overdressed and hopelessly weighed down. But the women of the upper classes—why, they look perfectly *costumed* rather than clothed! It's quite apparent from primary source material, however, that many rich women took immense pleasure in their wardrobes, spending a great deal of money on them and working closely with designers and tailors to achieve exactly the look they wanted.

The most characteristic article of clothing in the Elizabethan wardrobe is, of course, the ruff. Though everyone constantly complained about them, everyone—men, women, and sometimes even children—wore them. Ruffs were gathered collars worn about the neck. They were literally a pain in the neck to wear and to clean, and they were outrageously expensive. But if one aspired in any way to "decent" society, one had to wear a ruff. Most in the upper classes wore them constantly, every day, and they definitely would have been worn at a holiday ball.

From the neck on down, the men's and the women's clothing would be very different. Male clothing in the Elizabethan Age was not kind to men whose legs were less than perfect. Men's breeches were short—at or even above the knee—and their calves were covered only by thin stockings made of wool, linen, or silk. Women wore floor-length, heavy skirts, and unmarried women, especially, wore very low necklines. The corsets women were forced to wear are often commented upon in our time, but in truth, men's fashion was nearly as uncomfortable. Unsurprisingly in a society where beer and wine were consumed from morning until night on a daily basis, many men had beer bellies, and they crammed themselves into ridiculously tight girdles to hide their expanded girth.

A feast fit for a queen

Food and drink were among the most important components of an Elizabethan Christmas or New Year's party, and hosts and hostesses worked tirelessly with their large kitchen staffs to make sure the timing of the courses was just right and the food was cooked properly. In the country, the cooking would take place in an outbuilding and was brought into the main house, while in the city, the kitchen would most likely be attached and would provide extra warmth to the guests in this cold, damp season. The dining hall, where the hostess' impressive collection of silver, platinum, and crockery would be on display in a large, wooden cupboard, was usually a long room that accommodated a long, heavy table with massive legs.

Knives were used by all adult diners in this era, but forks hadn't become too popular yet. People used their hands to eat, whether they were eating a piece of dry bread or a slab of greasy meat. Hence, the guests at a holiday party would have made a big to-do out of washing their hands (in basins set around the dining hall) in front of their hosts and the other guests. With that public display over, they would have sat down at the table, prayed, and begun eating and drinking with gusto. Wine, beer, and strong spirits would be passed around the table, and servants would present large trays piled with roasted beef and game birds.

Once sated with food and drink, the Christmas partiers would really let loose, with revelers often seeing the break of dawn.

Away in a *Really Big* Manger: World's Largest Nativity Scene

Tired of Christmas at your parents' house? Try Switzerland! While you're there, stop by Einsiedeln, a town about 25 miles southeast of Zurich, where you can find the biggest nativity scene on the planet.

In the early 1930s, crib maker Ferdinand Pöttmesser embarked on a project. Pöttmesser lived in Tyrol, the alpine region that comprises parts of Austria and Italy. Pöttmesser made a huge wooden crib and carved close to 500 figures to fill out a nativity scene. Then he took his show on the road. People loved it, and the crib scene toured for over a decade. By 1953, Pöttmesser was ready to sell the figurines and crib, and did, to the Swiss town of Einsiedeln.

More is better!

After the sale, a curator for the Bavarian National Museum in Munich stepped forward with a plan to make the impressive crèche extraordinary. Dr. William Döderlein, a doctor and savvy entrepreneur, hired artists and artisans to create a dazzlingly ornate diorama, using Pöttmesser's figures as a starting point. He called it "The Diorama Bethlehem" and spared no expense in making it stand out.

He commissioned a 100-foot-long painted backdrop, which begins with the angels waking the shepherds after the birth of the Christ child and follows the story through to the Holy Family's flight into Egypt. Döderlein hired sculptors to create the 3-D elements of the set out of plastic, plaster, chicken wire, and various other materials. The entire scene spanned hundreds of square feet, and Döderlein knew it was special. Lighting effects were added, and the doors to the nativity scene opened to the public the following year.

If you want to visit the diorama today, you'll have company. Each year, about 20,000 people travel to see Einsiedeln's nativity, mostly around Christmastime. The Diorama Bethlehem is situated in the center of town, easily accessible by train or car.

Christmas Disasters!

*A lot of train wrecks seem to occur
around the Christmas holidays.
Thank goodness Santa rides a sleigh.*

Be cautious when taking the train around Christmastime. Historically, that's when a lot of accidents occur. According to experts, a variety of factors contribute to the high number of train disasters, including poor weather conditions, driver fatigue, and the stress of trying to stay on schedule over the holidays.

Here's a rundown of the most devastating yuletide train wrecks over the past century:

- **December 26, 1902:** In Wanstead, Ontario, a miscommunication places two trains on the same track, resulting in a head-on collision. A total of 28 people are killed.

- **December 29, 1906:** An express train strikes the back of another train during a blizzard in Elliot Junction, Scotland, killing 22.

- **December 24, 1910:** Six separate train accidents occurred worldwide. They include two collisions in England, three in France, and one in Upper Sandusky, Ohio. The following day, a seventh accident involving a train and a horse-drawn carriage occurred in Chateaudun, France, killing six.

- **December 23, 1933:** A train accident in France occurs when the nation's largest steam-engine locomotive, traveling at 60 miles per hour, plows into a stopped train at the Lagny-Pomponne station. The standing train is reduced to splinters; 230 people are killed and 300 are injured.

- **December 24, 1938:** A troop train and a local train collide head-on when accidentally directed to the same track in Etulia, Romania. A total of 93 people are killed and 147 injured.

- **December 27, 1941:** The Berlin–Warsaw express rear-ends a stationary train at the Frankfurt, Germany, station, killing 38.

- **December 28, 1941:** Fifty-six people are killed and another 50 are injured when a collision occurs on the Nantes–La Roche–sur-Yon line in La Gourge, France.

- **December 30, 1941:** Two days later, France experiences another train disaster when 50 people are killed in an accident near Hazebrouck.

- **December 27, 1942:** In Almonte, Ontario, 36 people are killed and more than 200 injured when a troop train strikes the rear of a passenger train as it is pulling out of the Almonte station.

- **January 1, 1946:** Freezing weather and a misread danger signal cause a fish train to ram the rear of a local passenger train as it waits at the station in Lichfield, England; 20 people are killed and 22 injured.

- **December 24, 1953:** The eruption of Mt. Ruapehu, a volcano near Walouru, New Zealand, destroys a traveling train, killing 151 people.

- **December 25, 1953:** The Prague-Bratislava express train, traveling at high speed, plows into the back of a local train waiting at the station in Sakvice, Czechoslovakia. A total of 186 people are killed.

- **January 1, 1958:** More than 30 people are killed and 85 injured when foggy conditions cause a collision between the Delhi–Pathankot express and a local train at the station in Mohri, India.

- **December 24, 1963:** An error on the part of an engineer results in a collision between two trains in Szolnok, Hungary. The negligent driver is sentenced to 11 years in prison for the accident, which kills 45 people.

- **December 31, 1969:** A collision between a freight train and a passenger train results in the deaths of 20 people in Theis, Senegal.

- **December 31, 1987:** Guerilla fighters ambush a train carrying 1,500 migrant workers in Mozambique. The assailants use a land mine to derail the train, killing more than 22 people, then they open fire with guns. Several passengers are kidnapped.

23 Must-Have Toys from 1950 and Beyond

*Kids write letters to Santa, asking for scads of
the coolest toys made. What are some of those favorite
toy crazes that Santa has had to deliver in the
last few decades? Well, here are some of the
best toy fads of the 20th and 21st centuries.*

1950s

1. Silly Putty was developed in 1943 when James Wright, a General Electric researcher, was seeking a synthetic rubber substitute. His silicone-based polymer was elastic, could bounce, be easily molded, and held its shape. Parents liked the fact that the putty was nontoxic and nonirritating. Since its debut as a toy in 1950, more than 300 million eggs of Silly Putty have been sold.

2. In 1943, naval engineer Richard James stumbled across an invention that would become a beloved toy worldwide. Made of 87 feet of flat wire coiled into a three-inch-diameter circle, the Slinky could "walk" down stairs when one end was placed on one step and the other on the step below. The classic Slinky really took off in the 1950s, and today more than 300 million of the simple-yet-clever toys have sold worldwide.

3. Mr. Potato Head, with his interchangeable facial features, was patented in 1952 and was the first toy to be advertised on television. But for the first eight years, parents had to supply children with a real potato until a plastic potato body was included in 1960.

4. Intending to create a wallpaper cleaner, Joseph and Noah McVicker invented Play-Doh in 1955. Initially available in only one color (off-white) and in a 1.5-pound can, Play-Doh now comes in a rainbow of colors. The recipe remains a secret, but more than 700 million pounds of this nontoxic goop have sold since its introduction.

5. The concept of the hula hoop had been around for centuries. Then, in the late 1950s, Wham-O, a maverick California toy company, rolled out a plastic hoop for swivel-hipped kids. The concept caught on, and 25 million sold in the first six months. They cost $1.98 each, and by 1958, 100 million of them had been sold around the world—except in Japan and the Soviet Union where they were said to represent the "emptiness of American culture." Ouch.

6. Barbie vamped onto the toy scene in 1959, the creation of Ruth Handler and her husband, Elliot, who along with Harold Matson founded the Mattel toy company. Handler noticed that her daughter Barbara (Barbie) and her friends played with an adult female doll from Switzerland more than their baby dolls. So, Handler came up with her "Barbie" concept, and the rest is toy history.

7. Chatty Cathy, also released by the Mattel Corporation in 1959, was the era's second-most-popular doll. Yakking her way onto store shelves, Cathy could speak 11 phrases when a string in her back was pulled. "I love you" or "Please take me with you" could be disconcerting at first, but Chatty Cathy was a '50s classic.

8. Betsy Wetsy also made a splash with 1950s-era children. Created by the Ideal Toy Company, Betsy's already-open mouth would accept a liquid-filled bottle. The premise was simple and straightforward: Whatever goes in quickly comes out the other end, helping youngsters gain valuable diaper-changing experience.

1960s

9. Since 1963, when they were first introduced, more than 16 million Easy Bake Ovens have been sold. A lightbulb provided the heat source for baking mini-cakes in America's first working toy oven. The original color was a trendy turquoise, and the stoves also sported a carrying handle and fake range top. As children, several celebrity chefs, including Bobby Flay, owned an Easy Bake Oven, which perhaps provided inspiration for their future careers.

10. Toy lovers have to salute manufacturer Hasbro for its G.I. Joe action figure, which first marched out in 1964. The 11½-inch-tall doll for boys had 21 moving parts and was the world's first action figure. Hasbro's 40th Anniversary G.I. Joe collection in 2004 included a re-creation of the original doll, his clothes, accessories, and even the packaging. Nostalgic Joe pals snapped up thousands of these new recruits.

11. Hot Wheels screeched into the toy world in 1968, screaming out of Mattel's concept garage with 16 miniature autos. The glamorous Python, Custom Cougar, and Hot Heap immediately attracted attention and plenty of buyers. Track sets were also released in the same year so that children could simulate a real auto race. Today, more than 15 million people collect Hot Wheels cars.

1970s

12. "Weebles wobble but they don't fall down . . . ." This was the unforgettable advertising slogan for these egg-shaped playthings first released by Hasbro in 1971. Each weeble had a sticker mounted on its short, fat "body" so it resembled a human or an animal. At the height of their popularity, the Weeble family had its own tree house and cottage, and a host of other characters and accessories were also produced, including a firefighter and fire truck, a playground, and a circus complete with a ringmaster, clown, and trapeze artist.

13. Also extremely popular in the '70s, the Big Wheel was the chosen mode of transportation for most young boys, and many girls too. With its 16-inch front wheel and fat rear tires, this low-riding, spiffed up tricycle was even a hit with parents, who considered it safer than a standard trike.

1980s

14. Strawberry Shortcake was the sweetest-smelling doll of the 1980s. Created in 1977 by Muriel Fahrion for American Greetings, the company expanded the toy line in the 1980s to include Strawberry's friends and their pets. Each doll had a fruit- or dessert-scented theme complete with scented hair. Accessories, clothes, bedding, stickers, movies, and games followed, but by 1985 the fad had waned. The characters were revived in the 2000s with DVDs, video games, an animated TV series, and even a full-length animated film. Sweet!

15. Xavier Roberts was a teenager when he launched his Babyland General Hospital during the 1970s in Cleveland, Georgia, allowing children to adopt a "baby." In 1983, the Coleco toy company started mass-producing these dolls as Cabbage Patch Kids. Each "kid" came with a unique name and a set of adoption papers, and stores couldn't keep them on the shelves, selling more than three million of the dolls in the first year.

16. Teenage Mutant Ninja Turtles were created by Kevin Eastman and Peter Laird, who had both studied art history. As such, they named their characters Leonardo, Raphael, Donatello, and Michelangelo. In 1984, with a mere $1,200, the Turtle creators launched the swashbuckling terrapins in a black-and-white comic book. More comics, as well as an animated television series, clothing, toys, and several full-length feature films followed, proving that the Green Team could earn some green, as well.

17. One of the biggest toy crazes of the 1980s was the brain-teasing Rubik's Cube. Created by Hungarian architect Erno Rubik, this perplexing puzzle was first introduced in 1977, and from 1980 to 1982 more than 100 million of the cubes sold. It sparked a trend and similar puzzles were created in various shapes, such as a pyramid and a sphere. The Rubik's Cube has seen a recent resurgence in popularity and retains a place of honor on many desktops.

1990s

18. From 1996 until around 1999, you couldn't escape the Beanie Baby craze. Like Cabbage Patch Kids and troll dolls of decades past, Ty Warner's Beanie Babies became a nationwide toy-collecting craze. The little plush-bodied, bean-filled animals came in dozens of different styles and colors and had special tags that included a poetic description of the character and its name. To feed the frenzy, Ty limited the release of certain Beanies and therefore sent the price of characters such as the "Blue Elephant" into the thousands. The fad died out before the millennium, but Beanie Babies still grace cubicles around the world.

19. Based on a Japanese toy called "Poketto Monstaa," Pokémon were tiny "pocket monsters" that battled each other when ordered to by their "trainer." In 1996, Nintendo adapted the Japanese characters to promote its portable video-game system, Game Boy. Pokémon trading cards and a television series were also wildly popular.

20. Undoubtedly the must-have toy of 1996, the immensely popular Tickle Me Elmo doll was based on the furry, red Sesame Street character. He'd giggle, saying, "Oh boy, that tickles," when he was tickled or squeezed. Manufacturer Tyco sold more than a million of the creatures that year, and when stores ran out of the dolls, some parents resorted to online auctions to secure one for their child.

21. Another plush gizmo, animatronic Furbies spoke their own "language" and became wildly successful in late 1998. Although they retailed for $30, they often fetched $100 or more online from desperate parents. More than 27 million Furbies sold in the first year, and a new, revamped Furby was introduced in 2005 with new features, including advanced voice recognition, so Furby can respond to questions based on its "mood."

2000s

22. The big fad toy of 2000 was the scooter, with approximately five million sold that year. These foot-propelled devices, a spin-off of the 1950s models, were made of lightweight aluminum and used tiny, low friction wheels similar to those on in-line skates. Weighing about ten pounds, they could be folded up and easily stored. Yet the scooters were relatively dangerous until opera-

tors became skilled at riding them. From January through October 2000, more than 27,000 people (mostly young males under the age of 15) were treated for scooter-related injuries.

23. Popular with kids of the new millennium (and adults too), Heelys are a brand of sneakers with one or more wheels embedded in the soles. Somewhat similar to in-line skates, Heelys enable the wearer to roll from place to place, rather than mundanely walking. As of March 2006, manufacturer Heelys, Inc., has sold more than two million of these specialty sneaks, which are available in a wide variety of styles and colors for the whole family. And for added convenience and safety, the company also sells helmets!

Strangest Christmas Movie Ever!

Santa Claus *plays fast and loose with the myth of St. Nick.*

Mexico has produced some truly bizarre movies over the years—but none more strange than *Santa Claus* (1959), a film that pits jolly old St. Nick against the forces of Satan!

And that's not the worst of it. In this surreal take on the Santa Claus legend, Santa lives not at the North Pole, but in outer space (just above the North Pole); he spies on young boys and girls in a disturbingly creepy manner; flies mechanical reindeer; and employs children instead of elves to make the toys he distributes on Christmas Eve.

One wacky story

Here's the plot in a nutshell: As Santa prepares for his annual Christmas visit, Lucifer instructs his head demon, Pitch, to travel to earth and turn the children against Santa by invading their thoughts and dreams. Pitch focuses his efforts on a little girl named Lupita, a young boy named Billy, and three other unnamed boys. He entices Lupita to be bad, but she refuses. The three unnamed brothers, however, come to believe (temporarily) that being naughty is better than being good.

Santa is made aware of Pitch's attempts at Christmas corruption, and over the course of the movie he uses a variety of tools, including magical powders given to him by Merlin the Magician, to keep the children on the path to goodness. He has several close encounters with the incompetent Pitch but manages to defeat him and successfully deliver toys to all of the world's good girls and boys.

Santa Claus did pretty good box office in Mexico, and in the 1960s an English-dubbed version was picked up for release in the United States by distributor K. Gordon Murray, who often booked it at children's matinees during the holiday season. The movie also airs occasionally on television, but don't be surprised if it gives you nightmares instead of filling you with holiday cheer.

A Tree for All Americans

*It may not be in your own home or backyard,
but the tree on the White House
grounds is a tree for all Americans.*

The first National Christmas Tree was a 48-foot balsam fir, erected by the District of Columbia Public Schools on the Ellipse south of the White House in November 1923. About 3,000 spectators gathered that Christmas Eve at 5:00 P.M. to watch President Calvin Coolidge and his wife, Grace, stroll from the White House to the tree. The President then pressed a button to activate the 2,500 electric red, green, and white bulbs on the tree, winning cheers and applause from the cold but excited crowd. Coolidge was especially pleased that the tree came from his home state of Vermont.

To cut or not to cut

Though that first National Christmas Tree was a cut tree, starting the next year and until 1953, live trees on the grounds of the White House were lit every Christmas Eve.

In 1954, the Ellipse was once again the scene of the festivities, and the event was expanded by businesspeople in Washington, D.C., into what they called the "Christmas Pageant of Peace," which included a nativity scene and live reindeer. Rather than light just one Christmas tree, that year smaller trees representing the 50 states, 5 territories, and the District of Columbia were also lit, along with the National Christmas Tree. The tree was lit earlier in the holiday season so that its lights could be enjoyed for an extended length of time. President Dwight D. Eisenhower gave a short speech thanking the people of Michigan for the tree.

A "souper" tree

Since 1973, live trees have been used for the ceremony, but that same year the tree was not lit because of the energy crisis. In 1978, the National Park Service (NPS) was looking for a live tree that could be transplanted and used year after year. They found a

Colorado blue spruce in York, Pennsylvania, at the home of Mr. and Mrs. Myers. The tree was a Mother's Day gift to Mrs. Myers, but she agreed to donate it to the White House for the National Christmas Tree. The hospitable Mrs. Myers even invited the workers who were removing the tree into her home and served them a lunch of soup.

In 1979 and 1980, President Jimmy Carter decided that the tree would remain dark in honor of the American hostages who were being held in Tehran, Iran.

Since then, the tree remains a beacon of peace to the whole world every holiday season.

"May you have the gladness of Christmas which is hope; the spirit of Christmas which is peace; the heart of Christmas which is love."

—*Ada V. Hendricks*

Letters to Santa Claus

🕯 🕯 🕯

Where do all those letters to Santa go?

Before Virginia ever wrote to a newspaper about him, children around the world wrote letters to Santa Claus. Hoping the wind would carry their wishes to the North Pole, children in 19th century Britain would burn their letters. In more recent times, children mail their letters through the post office by the thousands. But what happens to them? There's not always a court trial at which to dump the mail from the dead-letters office as in *Miracle on 34th Street.*

During the last hundred years or so, several countries have set up volunteer programs for responding to children's missives—sending gifts in some cases. In reindeer country (or Finland), paid postal workers respond to the child in their native language. France, Germany, and Canada also have large Santa letter efforts. In New York, Operation Santa Claus sprung out of the practice of United States Postal Service workers getting together and buying a few gifts in response to letters from needy kids. Volunteers could stop in and pick up letters to respond to and/or buy gifts. The program spread to other cities around the country. In Alaska, USPS responses are marked with the North Pole postmark.

Write on!

Some teachers in poor communities encourage their classes to write to Operation Santa Claus. The post office doesn't discriminate between rich, poor, or geographic location, but volunteers sift through and pick the letters they feel are deserving.

Like with many good things, a few bad apples messed things up for everyone else. Concerns for privacy led to strict changes in the Operation Santa Claus program. Children's last names were redacted for safety. Then in 2009, when a Maryland volunteer turned out to be a registered sex offender, the Postal Service almost shut down the entire undertaking.

For more information about which U.S. post offices will be participating in Operation Santa Claus, check out the USPS site.

🎥 CHRISTMAS MOVIE QUIZ

Match the line to the Christmas movie it came from.

1. "For a couple of hours out of the whole year, we are the people that we always hoped we would be!"
   a. *It's a Wonderful Life*
   b. *National Lampoon's Christmas Vacation*
   c. *Holiday Inn*
   d. *Scrooged*

2. "I fell down the chimney and landed on a flaming hot goose!"
   a. *Jingle All the Way*
   b. *Elf*
   c. *The Muppet Christmas Carol*
   d. *Mixed Nuts*

3. "Don't ever say hickory honey ham again."
   a. *Christmas with the Kranks*
   b. *The Muppet Christmas Carol*
   c. *The Nightmare Before Christmas*
   d. *National Lampoon's Christmas Vacation*

4. "Can I refill your eggnog for you? Get you something to eat? Drive you out to the middle of nowhere and leave you for dead?"
   a. *I Saw Mommy Kissing Santa Claus*
   b. *National Lampoon's Christmas Vacation*
   c. *The Muppet Christmas Movie*
   d. *We're No Angels*

5. "I speak French, but that doesn't make me Joan of Arc."
   a. *Jingle All the Way*
   b. *Miracle on 34th Street*
   c. *Elf*
   d. *White Christmas*

Answers: 1. d; 2. c; 3. a; 4. b; 5. b

Holiday Gifts for Pets

*Give your pet some special treatment
during the busy Christmas season.*

The holiday season is packed with activities, but amid the shopping, wrapping, cooking, cleaning, decorating, and entertaining, don't forget to show your pets some love! If you're looking for a great gift for a pet—whether cat, dog, bird, or boa constrictor—there's a range of "paws-ibilities."

Christmas is going to the dogs!

Everyone knows that canine pals love to play. Rather than going for plush toys (which Fido is likely to chew up in mere minutes), look for durable, interactive toys such as plastic discs, bouncy balls, and rubber chew toys that can hold treats—including peanut butter, the favorite snack of dogs everywhere! Speaking of treats, pig ears, sweet potato chews, and bully sticks make tasty gifts, but be careful about rawhide treats, as rawhide can contain antibiotics, lead, and insecticides. It's also difficult for dogs to digest.

Better yet, why not make homemade dog biscuits using all natural ingredients and Christmas- and dog-shaped cookie cutters? There's a huge variety of free recipes on the Web. Try recipes from dogtreatkitchen.com or doggiebistro.com. Another inspiring place to look for gifts is the "Pets" section of Etsy.com, a worldwide hand-made marketplace. There you'll find unique pet tags, doggie outfits, and collars and leashes made from vintage fabric. Or you can unleash your creativity and custom-make your own leash using a long strip of fabric (about five or six feet in length), an equally long piece of canvas strapping, and a metal closure. Attach the fabric to the strapping by sewing along each edge. Slide one end of the leash through the metal closure and secure with a simple stitch. On the other end, fold the leash back and stitch down to create a hand loop. Your dog will be walking in style!

Purr-fect gifts for cats

There may be nothing that kitty loves more than catnip, so try making this homemade catnip toy: Take a sock—perhaps one in a festive red, green, or Christmas print—and fill the "foot" with three parts uncooked rice and two parts dried catnip. (The rice preserves the catnip's fragrance by absorbing the oils. To refreshen, just warm it up in the microwave.) Cut off the ankle of the sock, and sew closed. Voilà! You have a toy that'll provide hours of entertainment. Instead of using a sock, you can also use two squares of fabric (sew together along three edges; fill with catnip; then sew the fourth side shut). Decorative cat bowls, scratch posts, and felt mice toys (another easy-to-make pet project: use wool felt and fill with catnip) are also great gifts. Another way to ensure your cat has a "Meowy" Christmas: Hang a stocking shaped like a paw, and fill it with all kinds of feline-friendly items: tuna flakes, catnip treats, collar charms, and jingle bell jewelry.

Tasty treats for other pets

Do you have a bird, bunny, or guinea pig? Give them the gift of a special treat. For birds, try beans, shredded wheat, or popcorn (though not microwave popcorn; it's too salty and high in fat). For bunnies, try carrot slices, a sprig of mint, or some unsweetened papaya (one slice per day; don't overdo it). Give guinea pigs up to one- or two-cup servings of cilantro, leafy greens, or red peppers. Some guinea pigs also have a thing for vitamin C tablets, so a chewable tablet or two makes an easy treat. If you own a boa constrictor, we're at a loss for gift ideas, but we do think that's pretty neat!

Personalized gifts for pet lovers

Need a gift for a pet lover? Take a photograph of a beloved pet and turn it into a mug, T-shirt, calendar, puzzle, coaster, or poster. You can even order customized stationery. Many stores' photo centers provide these services. Just make sure you allow a couple weeks to have personalized gifts or keepsakes made. You can also order photo gifts on Web sites such as Snapfish or Shutterfly.

The Toll House Mystery

One of the best things about Christmas is the smell of fresh-baked cookies. So, how did the most-beloved cookie of all come about?

In the 1930s, Ruth Wakefield and her husband operated the Toll House Inn near Whitman, Massachusetts. Wakefield was a dietitian, cookbook author, popular food lecturer, and an excellent cook.

One day, she was mixing up a batch of Butter Drop cookies, a popular sugar cookie found in recipe books dating back to the colonial days.

According to oft-repeated legend, the recipe called for baker's chocolate, but Ruth didn't have any, so she used a bar of Nestlé semisweet chocolate instead. But why would a sugar cookie recipe include baker's chocolate? Who knows? In any event, Wakefield broke up the bar and added it to the dough.

Or did she? George Boucher, who was head chef at the Toll House Inn, told a different story. According to Boucher, the chocolate accidentally fell into the mixing bowl from a shelf just above it, knocked off by the vibrations of the electric mixer. Mrs. Wakefield was going to throw out the batter, but Boucher convinced her to try baking it, and the rest is cookie history. (Doubters might wonder why the chocolate would be sitting on a shelf unwrapped, just waiting to fall into the mix, but never mind them.)

The official Nestlé version of the story states that Wakefield expected the chocolate to melt and was surprised when it didn't. But as she was an experienced cook and knew her way around a kitchen, it seems more likely that she was intentionally trying to create a new recipe and added the semisweet chocolate on purpose.

Of this there is no doubt: In 1939, Nestlé invented chocolate chips specifically for the cookies and printed the recipe on the bag. Today, Toll House Cookies are perhaps the most popular cookie in history.

Toy Story

So, we know the elves make toys—but where do the toys go from there? For almost 150 years, FAO Schwarz has been the first name in fun.

No name is as synonymous with toys as FAO Schwarz. This paragon of playtime may be a New York institution, but it actually got its start in Baltimore.

The four Schwarz brothers left Germany for America in the mid-1800s. They settled in Baltimore, where they worked for Theodore Schwerdtmann, owner of a retail store for imported goods. Henry and younger brother Frederick August Otto (the "F.A.O." in FAO Schwarz) imported toys from other countries, including Germany, France, and Switzerland, for Schwerdtmann & Co, which became Schwerdtmann & Schwarz in 1871. In 1870, Frederick left to open another branch, the Schwarz Toy Bazaar, in New York. Henry took over Schwerdtmann & Schwarz in 1872, and brothers Gustave and Richard ran their own toy stores in Philadelphia and Boston.

The brothers pooled their purchasing power to bring a wide variety of European toys and trinkets to American stores. At the time, stores that sold only toys were all but nonexistent. Most Americans gave their children handmade toys rather than store-bought playthings. There was no Toys "R" Us; instead, toys cropped up on a shelf or two at local general stores. Baltimore, however, was another story. A disproportionately large population of German immigrants lived in this shipping center. As the Schwarz clan tapped directly into that market, demand spread.

Frederick would often request specific changes from European manufacturers, making many of the toys on FAO's shelves Schwarz exclusives. This practice became a tradition, as evidenced by the unique and lavish displays in the stores, particularly the giant keyboard made famous by Tom Hanks in the 1988 movie *Big*.

The venerable American toy icon experienced financial woes at the turn of the 21st century and changed ownership several times, but its flagship New York store continues to be a must-see attraction for tourists and toy enthusiasts alike.

Aren't There Better Ways for Santa to Sneak into a House?

Except for a few sour souls, everyone loves Santa Claus. How could you not? He spends his days in an enchanted world of elves and toys, he has an awesome flying sleigh, and he has the godlike ability to watch all the world's children at the same time. Yet for somebody who is supposed to be such a magical, all-knowing being, it appears that Santa Claus possibly isn't very bright. Case in point: this chimney business.

Come on, Claus. Do you really need to shimmy down a filthy chimney to deliver your presents? And with that ridiculous diet of cookies and milk, how much longer will you fit down it?

In Santa's defense, there's a lot of tradition behind his chimney act. Even though the image of the red velvet-clad Santa known to most Americans is a fairly recent development, the figure of Father

Christmas is rooted in traditions dating back centuries. And though most people know that the Christian figure of Santa Claus is loosely based on St. Nicholas from the fourth century—St. Nick is one of Santa's nicknames, after all—most of Santa's behavior and magical powers are drawn from pagan sources.

Indeed, historians claim that not only Santa Claus, but also much of the holiday of Christmas itself is rooted in pagan

tradition. Back in pre-Christian Europe, Germanic people celebrated the winter solstice at the end of December with a holiday known as Yule. Christmas, which later supplanted the pagan winter solstice festivals during the Christianization of Germanic people, maintained many of the pagan traditions. One was the belief that at yuletime, the god Odin would ride a magical eight-legged horse through the sky. Children left food for the horse, which would be replaced by gifts from Odin, a custom that lives on today in the form of cookie bribery for Kris Kringle and his flying reindeer.

As for sliding down the chimney, folklorists point to another Germanic god: Hertha, the goddess of the home. In ancient pagan days, families gathered around the hearth during the winter solstice. A fire was made of evergreens, and the smoke beckoned Hertha, who entered the home through the chimney to grant winter solstice wishes.

It wasn't until 1822, when literature professor Clement Clarke Moore penned "'Twas the Night Before Christmas," that Santa sliding down the chimney became a permanent fixture in popular Christmas tradition. Moore's poem became even more influential 40 years later, when legendary cartoonist Thomas Nast illustrated it for *Harper's* magazine. In Nast's depiction, Santa was transformed from the skinny, somewhat creepy-looking figure of earlier traditions into a jolly, well-bearded soul. Despite Santa's physical transformation, other traits from his early incarnations linger, including the bewildering habit of crawling down chimneys.

But just because something is a habit doesn't make it excusable. The figure of Santa has morphed over the centuries, and there's no reason why he can't break the chimney routine in the future. Let's go, Santa—it's time to join the 21st century. And maybe check out the Zone Diet while you're at it.

"I stopped believing in Santa Claus when I was six. Mother took me to see him in a department store and he asked for my autograph."
—*Shirley Temple*

Index

A

Acts of the Apostles, 37
Adam, Adolphe Charles, 81
Adams, John, 262
Advent, 22, 52, 126
Advent calendars, 142
Adventures of Teddy Ruxpin, The (television), 96
Advent wreath, 144–45
Aeneas, 18
Afanasieff, Walter, 82
Afghanistan war, 160, 161
African American spirituals, 81–82
Afrikaans, 170–71
Agios Vassilis (St. Basil), 224
A. G. Spalding Bros., Inc., 271
Alabama, 195
Alaska, 139, 246
Albert (prince of England), 192, 212–13
Aldrin, Edwin "Buzz," 256
Aleut, 139
Alken, Henry Thomas, 189
"All I Want for Christmas Is You" (Carey and Afanasieff), 82
America. *See* United States.
American Colonies, 41, 187
American Greetings Corporation, 264, 292
American Red Cross, 48
Anagrams, 29
Anders, William, 256
Andersen, Hans Christian, 128
"Angels from the Realms of Glory" (Montgomery), 81
"Angels We Have Heard on High," 81
Anglican Church, 37, 38, 170–71
Anglo-Saxons, 180
Apollo 8, 256
Apollo 11, 256
Armstrong, Neil, 256
Arnold, Oren, 223
Art of Christmas, 188–89

Astrology, 31
Astronomy, 31
"Auld Lang Syne," 165
Australia, 100–101, 227
Autry, Gene, 82
"Away in a Manger," 82

B

Babbo Natale (Father Christmas), 22
Babes in Toyland (1934), 180
Babyland General Hospital, 292
Bad Santa (2003), 75, 249
Bagdasarian, Ross, Jr., 176–77
Bagdasarian, Ross, Sr., 176–77
Balder (Norse god), 19–20
Bangbelly, 194
Barbera, Joe, 283
Barbie dolls, 116, 291
Barbie in A Christmas Carol (2008), 175
Baron, Phil, 96
Barry, Dave, 186
Barton, Clarissa Harlowe "Clara," 48
Bates, Katharine Lee, 129
Baum, L. Frank, 244
Bavarian National Museum (Munich), 287
Beach Boys, 81
Beanie Babies, 293
Begin, Menachem, 47
Bell, William, 220
Bennett, Harriet M., 188–89
Bentley, Wilson A., 156–57
Bethlehem
  birth of Jesus in, 30, 122, 136
  holidays from events in, 38
  pilgrimages to, 197
  songs about, 80, 81, 211
  wise men and, 30, 39, 73, 122
Betsy Wetsy, 291
Bible, 30, 35, 45, 67, 122
Big (1988), 303
Big Apple (New York City), 208–10

Big Wheel, 292
Billboard magazine, 120, 176, 211
Birthdays on Christmas Day, 46–48
Black Christmas (1974), 26–27, 242
Black Christmas (2006), 27
Black Friday, 36
Black Pete (Zwarte Piet), 159
Blane, Ralph, 230
Blindman's bluff, 44
Bloopers (*It's a Wonderful Life*), 33
Boers, 170
Bogart, Humphrey, 46
Bolsheviks, 53, 54
Bombeck, Erma, 282
Borge, Victor, 27
Borman, Frank, 256
Boucher, George, 302
Boxing Day, 37–38
Bradley, William, 187
Brazil, 238
British Commonwealth, 105, 226.
    See also England.
British panto, 184–85
Brooks, Phillips, 81
Brooks, Randy, 82
Brown, Charles, 82
Brown, James, 94
Buffet, Jimmy, 47
Burns, Robert, 165
Burton, Tim, 48
Bush, George W., family of, 207

C

Cabbage Patch Kids, 96, 292–93
Cacophony Society, 11
Caganer ("pooper"), 117
Caga Tio (pooping log), 117
Caine, Michael, 175
Caldwell, Taylor, 127
Calloway, Cabell "Cab" III, 48
Canada, 78–79, 194
Candies, 14
Candles, 145, 152, 207
Candy canes, 138, 141, 153
Capone, Al, 109
Capra, Frank, 32, 33

Cards, Christmas
    choice of greeting on, 67
    history of, 60–62
    image of Santa Claus on, 104
    offensive, 260
    sale and delivery of, 138, 217
    White House and, 207, 217, 262–64
Care Bears, 96
Carey, Mariah, 82
Caribou. *See* Reindeer.
Caroling, 143, 221
Carols. *See also specific carols.*
    history of, 80–82
    quizzes about, 112, 172, 201, 278
Carr, Mark, 178
Carrey, Jim, 175, 280, 281
Carter, Jimmy, 297
Cassin, Henry, 102
Catalonia, Spain, 117
Catchings, Tamika, 146
Catholics, Roman
    advent wreaths and, 144
    Canadians and, 79
    Cromwell and, 107
    holidays and, 37, 38, 39
    myrrh for incense and, 91
Cats, 301
Cat's cradle ("cratch cradle"), 45
Ceauşescu, Nicolae, 93
Celebrations, 36–39
Celts, 19
Chandler, Charlotte, 103
Chaplin, Charlie, 92
Charles I (king of England), 106
Charles II (king of England), 108
Charles W. Howard Santa Claus School,
    74, 248–49
Charlie Brown Christmas, A
    (television), 198
Chatty Cathy, 291
Chesterton, G. K., 130
Children's Mass, 38
China, 31, 62, 73, 90
Chipmunks, The, 176–77, 231
"Chipmunk Song, The" (Seville &
    Chipmunks), 176–77

Chocolate truffles, 173

Chrismukkah, 39

Christ. *See* Jesus Christ.

Christianity
    beliefs of, 37
    holly legends and, 76
    Holy Land and, 196–97
    impact of Crusades on, 196
    La Befana and, 23
    mistletoe and, 20
    myrrh trade and, 73
    Nazi Germany and, 167–68
    Scandinavian, 128
    South Africa and, 170–71
    Soviet Union and, 53–55, 54–55
    tourism and, 197
    "Twelve Days of Christmas, The"
        and, 35

Christkindlein, 104

Christkindlesmarkt, 67

Christmas Album, A, 211

"Christmas Bells" (Longfellow), 130

Christmas Book (Neiman Marcus), 182

Christmas boxes, 38

Christmas Carol, A (1910), 174

Christmas Carol, A (1984), 175

"Christmas Carol, A" (Chesterton), 130

"Christmas Carol, A" (Coleridge),
    130–31

Christmas Carol, A (Dickens)
    "dead as a doornail" use in, 113
    disease and poverty in, 42–43
    drinks in, 63
    film adaptations of, 174–75
    foods in, 13, 187
    impact of, 192–93

Christmas Carol, A (television), 200

Christmas Comes but Once a Year!
    (Green), 189

Christmas Day hits (songs) by year,
    120–21

Christmas Deliveries (Aiken), 189

Christmas Eve, 29, 145, 147, 191

Christmas Evil (1980), 27

"Christmas Flintstone," 283

Christmas flower (poinsettia), 118

*Christmas in the Stars: Star Wars
    Christmas Album* (1980), 233

Christmas Island, 59

Christmas Island (Buffett), 47

"Christmas Song, The" ("Chestnuts
    Roasting on an Open Fire"), 245

"Christmas Song, The" (Cole), 82

Christmas Spectacular, 67, 208–9

Christmas Story, A (1983), 200, 241–42,
    243

Christmas Tails, 279

Christmas Tree (Warhol), 188

Christmas truce (World War I), 21

Chung, Caleb, 97

Church, Francis Pharcellus, 132, 234–35

Cinnamon, 90

Cinnamon Bear, The (radio), 215

Civil War, 48, 130, 133, 263

Clapsaddle, Ellen H., 61, 62

Clark, Bob, 26–27, 242

Clark, Elkin Donnie, 58

Clinton, Bill, family of, 206–7

Cloves, 90–91

Coca-Cola Company, 104

Cocoa beans, 66

Cole, Nat "King," 82

Cole, Sir Henry, 60

Coleridge, Samuel Taylor, 130–31

Collins, Joan, 26

Colombo, Joe, 109

Communists, 53

Como, Perry, 82, 198, 199

Continental calendar, 106

Conventions of Santa Clauses, 11–12,
    125

Cook, Captain James, 59

Cookies, 14, 302

Coolidge, Calvin, 263, 273, 296

Coolidge, Grace, 296

Corning Company, 153

Costs of being Santa Claus, 124–25

"Coventry Carol," 80

Crackers, Christmas, 226–27

Crawford, Cathy, 103

Crawford, Christina, 103

Crawford, Joan, 102–3

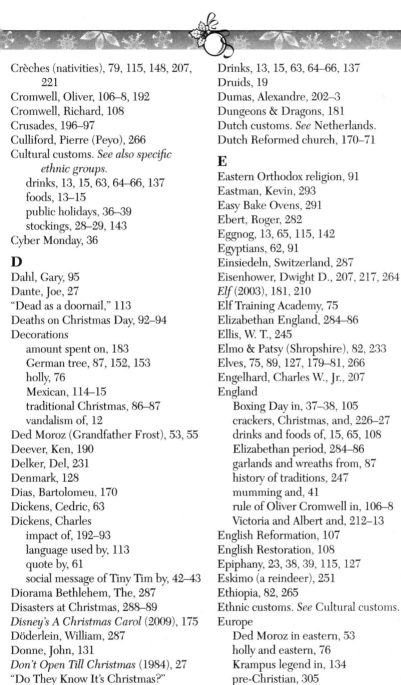

Crèches (nativities), 79, 115, 148, 207, 221
Cromwell, Oliver, 106–8, 192
Cromwell, Richard, 108
Crusades, 196–97
Culliford, Pierre (Peyo), 266
Cultural customs. *See also specific ethnic groups.*
    drinks, 13, 15, 63, 64–66, 137
    foods, 13–15
    public holidays, 36–39
    stockings, 28–29, 143
Cyber Monday, 36

D

Dahl, Gary, 95
Dante, Joe, 27
"Dead as a doornail," 113
Deaths on Christmas Day, 92–94
Decorations
    amount spent on, 183
    German tree, 87, 152, 153
    holly, 76
    Mexican, 114–15
    traditional Christmas, 86–87
    vandalism of, 12
Ded Moroz (Grandfather Frost), 53, 55
Deever, Ken, 190
Delker, Del, 231
Denmark, 128
Dias, Bartolomeu, 170
Dickens, Cedric, 63
Dickens, Charles
    impact of, 192–93
    language used by, 113
    quote by, 61
    social message of Tiny Tim by, 42–43
Diorama Bethlehem, The, 287
Disasters at Christmas, 288–89
Disney's A Christmas Carol (2009), 175
Döderlein, William, 287
Donne, John, 131
Don't Open Till Christmas (1984), 27
"Do They Know It's Christmas?" (Geldof and Ure), 82
Doyle, Jim, 200
Drac Studios, 279

Drinks, 13, 15, 63, 64–66, 137
Druids, 19
Dumas, Alexandre, 202–3
Dungeons & Dragons, 181
Dutch customs. *See* Netherlands.
Dutch Reformed church, 170–71

E

Eastern Orthodox religion, 91
Eastman, Kevin, 293
Easy Bake Ovens, 291
Ebert, Roger, 282
Eggnog, 13, 65, 115, 142
Egyptians, 62, 91
Einsiedeln, Switzerland, 287
Eisenhower, Dwight D., 207, 217, 264
Elf (2003), 181, 210
Elf Training Academy, 75
Elizabethan England, 284–86
Ellis, W. T., 245
Elmo & Patsy (Shropshire), 82, 233
Elves, 75, 89, 127, 179–81, 266
Engelhard, Charles W., Jr., 207
England
    Boxing Day in, 37–38, 105
    crackers, Christmas, and, 226–27
    drinks and foods of, 15, 65, 108
    Elizabethan period, 284–86
    garlands and wreaths from, 87
    history of traditions, 247
    mumming and, 41
    rule of Oliver Cromwell in, 106–8
    Victoria and Albert and, 212–13
English Reformation, 107
English Restoration, 108
Epiphany, 23, 38, 39, 115, 127
Eskimo (a reindeer), 251
Ethiopia, 82, 265
Ethnic customs. *See* Cultural customs.
Europe
    Ded Moroz in eastern, 53
    holly and eastern, 76
    Krampus legend in, 134
    pre-Christian, 305
    traditions of central, 37
    tree traditions and, 19

F

Fahrion, Muriel, 292
Fake Christmas trees, 228–29
Family Ties (television), 199
FAO Schwarz, 303
Ferrell, Will, 181, 210
Fast Facts, 40, 62, 85, 178, 225, 273
Father Christmas, 15, 22, 128, 205, 224
Father Christmas Letters, The (Tolkien), 89
Father Spanker, 147
Feast of St. Nicholas, 147
Feast of the Circumcision, 38
Feast of the Holy Name of Jesus, 38
Feast of the Immaculate Conception, 37, 117
Festivus, 39, 200
Field, Marshall, 110–11
Fields, W. C., 66, 93
Films. *See* Movies.
Finney, Albert, 174
Five Children Fetch Home a Very Big Yule Log (Bennett), 188
Flintstones, The, 283
Foley, Charles F., 96
Folktales. *See* Legends.
Foods, Christmastime
American Colonial, 187
Australian, 101
Brazilian, 238
Canadian, 79, 194
Dutch, 158
Elizabethan England, 286
English, 247
Ethiopian, 265
French, 147
Greek, 223
Icelandic, 253
Japanese, 191
Mexican, 115
Native Alaskan, 139
Polish, 52
Russian, 55
Spanish, 88
Swedish, 127
Texan, 88
World, 13–15

Football, 45
France
celebrations in, 147–49
chocolate truffles in, 173
Frankincense, 73, 91, 122
Fraser, Arthur, 110–11
French and Indian War, 78
Freyr (Norse god), 180
Frigga (Norse goddess), 19, 20
Frogs (Pacific Chorus), 246
Frosti (Jökul), 244
Frosty's Winter Wonderland (1976), 245
Frosty the Snowman (television), 198
Fruitcake, 14, 143
Furbies, 97, 294

G

Games, 44–45
Garland, Judy, 230
Garlands, 87
Gaudete Sunday, 145
Gävle goat (Sweden), 261
Gavlén, Stig, 261
Geisel, Theodore (Dr. Seuss), 280
Geldof, Bob, 82
George, Elector of Hanover, Germany, 99
George Fisher Show, The, 103
George I (king of England), 99
Germany
Christmas market in, 67
elves in, 180
holidays in Nazi, 166–68
legend of Krampus and, 134
tree customs in, 87, 152–53, 178
Victoria and Albert and, 212–13
G.I. Joe (doll), 116, 291
Gifts, 68–69, 142
Ginger, 90
Gingerbread houses, 14–15, 207
"Gingers," 260
"Gloria in excelsis Deo," 80, 81
Godey's Lady's Book, 266
Gold, Jack, 211
"Good King Wenceslas," 37
"Goody Santa Claus on a Sleigh Ride" (Bates), 129
Goose, roasted, 13

Gospel of Luke, 136
Gospel of Matthew, 30, 38, 122
"Go Tell It on the Mountain" (Jubilee Singers), 81–82
Grandfather Frost (Ded Moroz), 53, 55
"Grandma Got Run Over by a Reindeer," 82, 233
Grant, Ulysses S., 263
Grazer, Brian, 281
Great Britain, 15, 59. *See also* England.
Great Depression, 208
Greece
    mistletoe legend and, 18
    St. Nicolas customs and, 37
    traditions of Christmas in, 222–24
    wreaths in, 87
Green, Charles, 189
Greenaway, Kate, 61
"Greensleeves" (Jones), 80
Greeting Card Association, 138
Gregorian calendar, 54
Gremlins (1984), 27, 141
Griffin, Kathy, 235
Gruber, Franz, 81
Guerrero, Lalo, 272
Guinness World Records, 11

H
Hall, Joyce C., 50–51
Hall Brothers postcard shop, 50–51
Hallmark card company, 62, 153, 264, 274
Hallmark Keepsake Ornaments, 275
Hampton, Dave, 97
Handel, George Frideric, 98–99
Handler, Elliot, 291
Handler, Ruth, 291
Hanks, Tom, 303
Hanna, Bill, 283
Hanukkah, 39, 105
Harding, Warren G., 206
Hardy, Thomas, 131
Harper's Weekly, 104, 129, 155, 189, 235, 263, 305
Hasbro toy company, 116, 236–37, 291, 292

"Have Yourself a Merry Little Christmas" (Martin and Blane), 230–31
Heelys, 294
Heisch, Glanville, 215
Hendricks, Bill, 24
Hendricks, Diane, 24
Henricks, Ada V., 297
Henry VI, Part 2 (Shakespeare), 113
"Here Comes Santa Claus," 209
Herod, 30, 31, 38, 80, 122
Hertha (Germanic goddess), 305
Hidaka, Hiroaki, 94
Hill, Luther Leonidas, 195
Hillis, Burton, 171
Hilton, Conrad, 48
Hitler, Adolph, 166–68
Hits (songs) on Christmas Day, 120–21
Hobbit, The (Tolkien), 89, 180
Hoffmann, E. T. A., 202
Hogmanay (New Year's Eve), 164–65
Holden, Stephen, 282
Holidays. *See also specific holidays.*
    dangers to pets during, 169
    mumming and, 41
    types of, 36–39
Holiday traditions. *See* Cultural customs.
Holland. *See* Netherlands.
Holly, 76
Hollywood, 26, 32, 57
Holy Innocents Day, 38
Holy Land, 196–97
Honeymooners, The (television), 199
Hope, Bob, 160, 255
Hopkins, Anthony, 280
Hopkins, John Henry, Jr., 81, 122
Horlsey, John Callcott, 60
Hot chocolate, 66
Hot Wheels, 292
House Un-American Activities Committee, 32
Howard, Charles, 248–49
Howard, Ron, 280–82
How the Grinch Stole Christmas! (1966), 199, 279
How the Grinch Stole Christmas (2000), 280–82

Hubbard, Kin, 282
Hula hoop, 290

I

Iceland, 253, 254–55
Ideal Toy Company, 116, 291
Impersonators, Santa Claus, 58
India, 65, 90
Indonesia, 90
Industrial Revolution, 68, 87, 133, 192
International Toy Fair, 96
Internet, 36, 49, 51, 272, 277, 298, 300
Iran, 30
Iraq war, 160, 161
Ireland, 39
Irish customs, 39
Isabeau of Bavaria, 148
Islamic beliefs, 37
Israel, 196–97
Italian-American Civil Rights League,
    109
Italian American Defamation League,
    109
Italy
    food customs in, 13
    holidays of, 22, 23, 29, 37
    La Befana in, 29
    nativity scenes in, 87
    stocking customs in, 29
It's a Wonderful Life (1946), 32–33, 143,
    200
"It's Beginning to Look a Lot Like
    Christmas" (Willson), 82

J

Jack Frost, 244–45
Jack Frost (1979), 245
Jack Frost (1997), 26
Jack of Fables, 244
Jackson, Andrew, 263
James, Richard, 95, 290
Japan, 67, 191
Jefferson, Thomas, 262
Jennens, Charles, 99
Jerusalem, 30, 122, 197

Jesus Christ
    birth of, 30, 122, 126, 136
    carols about birth of, 80, 81
    Epiphany and, 39
    Feast of the Circumcision and, 38
    La Befana and, 23
Jewish Festival of Lights (Hanukkah), 39
Jews, 166–68, 196–97, 211
Jingle Bell Ball, 125
"Jingle Bells" ("One Horse Open
    Sleigh"), 16–17, 81, 211
Johan and Peewit (Peyo), 266
Johnson, Edward H., 86, 152–53
Johnson, Lady Bird, 207
Johnson, Lyndon, 264
Jökul (Frosti), 244
Jólasveinar (Yule Lads), 253, 254–55
Jones, Brian, 243
Jones, Chuck, 199
Jones, Richard, 80
Jones, W. C., 163
Jones Soda Company, 137
Joseph (father of Jesus), 136
Jubilee Singers of Fisk University, 82
Judaism, 31
Julafton (Christmas Eve), 127
Julian calendar, 54, 265
Jultomte, 127, 128

K

Karloff, Boris, 279, 280
Kataluma (inn), 136
Keepsake Christmas ornaments, 153
Kennedy, John F., 264
Kennedy, Robert F., 71
Kenner toy company, 96, 116, 258–59
Keteleeria tree, 276
Kitt, Eartha, 92
Klingon Christmas Carol, A, 240
Krampus, 134
Kris Kringel, 204
Kris Kringle
    cookies and, 305
    costs of, 124
    quotes, 177, 234

L

La Befana (the "good witch"), 22, 23, 29
La Cosa Nostra, 109
Laird, Peter, 293
Langland, William, 113
Lapland, 40, 150, 269
Lapland Vocational College, 75
Las Posadas, 114
Latin American customs, 13
Laurel and Hardy, 180–81
Lee, Brenda, 183
Leed, Robert X., 279
Legends
    Krampus, 134
    Norse, 19, 20, 134, 162, 179–80
    Rowena (Saxon), 15
    Santa Claus, 104
    Scandinavian, 19, 20, 126–27, 128
    urban, 140–41
Lenin, Vladimir, 53, 54–55
Lennox, Annie, 47
Let's Party! (Phillips), 189
Letters to Santa, 132–33, 143, 204, 298
Leyendecker, Joseph Christian, 188
Liberty Films, 32
Lights, electric, 86
Lill's Travels in Santa Claus Land and Other Short Stories, 129
Lincoln, Abraham, 263
Little Christmas, 39
Little Drummer Boy, The (television), 198
Live (magazine), 189
Logue, Eva K., 145
Loki (Norse god), 19, 134
Longet, Claudine, 71
Longfellow, Henry Wadsworth, 130
Lopez, George, 235
Lord of the Rings triology (Tolkien), 89
Los Pastores ("The Shepherds"), 238
Lost (television), 200
Lovell, Jim, 256
Lowry, Harvey, 279
Lucas, George, 116, 233, 258
Luke, Gospel of, 136
Luther, Martin, 82, 152
Lutherans, 38, 144

M

Macy's, 125, 234
Macy's Thanksgiving Day Parade, 36, 83–85, 210, 234, 250
Maeditere, Janice, 125
Mafia, 109
Magi. *See also* Three Kings; Wise Men.
    Epiphany and, 39
    frankincense and the, 91
    gifts of, 67
    identity of, 30, 122
    myrrh and the, 91
    Twelfth Night and, 38
Make-A-Wish Foundation, 125
Mall Santas, 190
Mandela, Nelson, 171
Marceau, Marcel, 174, 184
Marcus, Stanley, 182
Mardi Gras, 39, 195
Mari Lwyd ("the grey mare"), 151
Marines. *See* U.S. Marine Corps Reserve.
Marks, Johnny, 82, 163
Marshall Fields (department store), 110–11
Martin, Billy, 93
Martin, Dean, 92
Martin, Hugh, 230–31
Martin, James, 249
Marx, Karl, 54
Mary (mother of Jesus), 37, 122, 136
Marzipan, 15
M°A°S°H (television), 199–200
Mathis, Johnny, 231
Matson, Harold, 291
Mattel toy company, 116, 236, 291, 292
Matthew, Gospel of, 30, 38, 122
May, Robert L., 82, 162–63
Mayo Clinic, 140
McPherson, Miles, 146
McVicker, Joseph, 290
McVicker, Noah, 290
Medici, Gian Gastone de (grand duke of Tuscany), 98
Medrich, Alice, 173
Meet Me in St. Louis (1944), 230

Mego, 116
Meléndez, Bill, 198
Menorah, 39
"Merry Christmas!" by languages, 10, 72, 135, 232, 252
Merry Old Santa Claus (Nast), 189
Messiah (Handel), 99
Mexico
    holiday celebrations in, 114–15
    poinsettias and, 118
    tamales as Christmas food in, 88
Mickey's Christmas Carol (1983), 175
Middle Ages, 15, 19, 34, 41, 45, 144
Middle Earth, 180, 181
Military charities (U.S.), 160–61
Milk and cookies, 142
Mincemeat pies, 15, 67
Minnelli, Vincent, 230
Miracle on 34th Street (1947), 74, 84, 111, 133, 177, 234
Mistletoe, 18–20, 143
Mohr, Father Joseph, 81
Mommie Dearest (Crawford), 102, 103
Momsen, Taylor, 281
Montgomery, James, 81
Montgomery Ward, 82, 162, 163
Moore, Clement Clarke, 28–29, 130, 150, 305
Morehead, Debbie, 96
Movies. *See also specific movies.*
    Christmas horror, 26–27
    quizzes, 29, 77, 154, 257, 299
    top grossing opening Christmas Day, 57
    top highest-grossing Christmas, 268–69
    top ten worst-grossing Christmas, 268
"Mr. Christmas" (Andy Williams), 70–71
Mr. Potato Head, 290
Mrs. Claus, 129
Mulled wine (spiced wine), 64
Mumming, 41
Muppet Christmas Carol, The (1992), 175
Murray, Bill, 175
Muslims, 196–97, 205

Mynors, William, 59
Myra (currently Demre), Turkey, 28, 205
Myrrh, 73, 91, 122
Myths, 140–41. *See also* Legends.

N

Nabors, Jim, 231
Nast, Thomas, 104, 155, 189, 235, 263, 305
National Christmas Tree, 273, 296–97
National Christmas Tree Association (NCTA), 206, 273
National Community Christmas Tree, 263
National Retail Federation, 36
Native Alaskans, 139
Native Americans, 187
"Nativity: A Christmas Poem" (Donne), 131
Nativity scenes, 87, 115, 136, 142, 287. *See also* Crèches.
Nazareth, 197
Nazi Germany, 166–68
NCTA (National Christmas Tree Association), 206
Neiman Marcus, 182
Nelson, Annie Ruth, 58
Nestlé, 302
Netherlands
    Black Pete (Zwarte Piet) in, 158, 159
    Sinterklass and, 158
    stocking traditions and, 29
Nevada, Victor, 75
Newfoundland, 194
New Year's, 22, 23, 41, 151, 164–65, 222, 263
New York City, New York, 208, 234–35
New York Illustrated News, 189
New York Sun, The, 132–33, 235
New York Times, The, 104, 282
Nicholas, St. (St. Nick)
    Black Pete in Netherlands and, 159
    Ded Moroz and resemblance to, 53, 55
    evolution to Santa Claus, 104, 304–5
    Greece and, 222, 224
    image of, 155

of Myra (currently Demre), Turkey, 28, 205

North Pole, Alaska and, 204

stocking traditions in Netherlands and, 29

Nightmare Before Christmas, The (1993), 48

Nintendo Game Boy, 97

Nixon, Pat, 207

Noel, 148

"Noel" (Sandys), 80

Noel Baba (Father Christmas), 205

NORAD, 235

Norse legends, 19, 20, 134, 162, 179–80, 244. *See also* Scandinavian myths.

North America, 23, 66, 129

North Pole, 75, 139, 155, 218–19

North Pole, Alaska, 204

Not the Girl Next Door (Chandler), 103

Nutcracker, The (Tchaikovsky), 202–3, 221

Nutcracker and the Mouse King, The (Hoffmann), 202–3

Nutmeg, 91

O

"O Christmas Tree," 152

October Revolution (1917), 53, 54

Odin (northern European god), 155, 305

Off Kilter, 165

O'Hanlon, Virginia, 132–33, 234–35

"O Holy Night" (Adam), 81

"O Little Town of Bethlehem," 81

"One Horse Open Sleigh" ("Jingle Bells"), 16–17, 81

Operation Christmas Stocking, 161

Operation Phone Home, 160–61

Operation Santa Claus, 298

Ornaments, 86, 153, 183, 221, 274–75

Orthodox Church, 38

Otto, Frederick August, 303

Otto, Gustave, 303

Otto, Henry, 303

Otto, Richard, 303

"Oxen, The: A Christmas Poem" (Hardy), 131

P

Paich, Marty, 211

Pajeau, Charles, 270

Palestine, 196–97

Pancho Claus, 272

"Pancho Claus" (Guerrero), 272

PanchoClaus.com, 272

Panettone, 13, 22

Pantos (pantomines), 184–86

Papai Noel, 238

Pardo, Bruce, 58

Parker Brothers, 96

Peanuts, 198

Pease, Richard, 61

Pepita, 118

Peppermint bark, 14

Pere Fouettard, 147, 149

Pere Noel, 148, 149

Petipa, Marius, 203

Petrella, Ian, 243

Pet rock, 95

Pets, 169, 300–301

Pettit, Robert, 270

Peyo (Pierre Culliford), 266

Philips, Harvey, 220

Phillips, C. Coles, 189

Phillips, Davinia, 260

Phrygian caps, 266–67

Pierce, Franklin, 273

Pierpont, James, 16–17, 81

Pilgrimages, 197

Pitching the bar, 44

Pizzi, Romain, 251

Play-Doh, 290

Plays, 45

Playskool, 271

"Please Come Home for Christmas" (Brown), 82

Poetry of Christmas, 130–31

Poinsett, Joel Roberts, 118

Poinsettia, 101, 118–19, 183

Poinsettias (Warhol), 188

POISINDEX Information Service, 119

Pokémon, 293

Poland, 52, 53

Pomanders, 90–91

Pooper (Caganer), 117
Pooping log (Caga Tio), 117
Portugal, 238
Potter, Harry (Rowling), 111, 226
Pöttmesser, Ferdinand, 287
Prang, Louis, 60, 104, 248
Presents, 142. *See also* Gifts.
Pretenders, The, 231
Protestants, 79
Public holidays, 36–39, 165. *See also*
      Holidays.
Puerto Rican customs, 29
Puritans, 44, 106–8, 192
Pwnco, 151
Pyle, Denver, 94

Q

Quitting Hollywood card company, 260
Quizzes, 29, 77, 112, 154, 172, 201, 278,
      299
Quotes, 25, 27, 51, 61, 66, 125, 127,
      145, 163, 171, 177, 186, 200, 210,
      223, 245, 255, 282, 297, 305

R

Rabens, Neil, 96
Radio City Music Hall, 67, 208–9
Ramsey, JonBenet, 93–94
Rankin and Bass, 198, 245
Rated Xmas, 233
Ratliff, Marshall, 58, 249–50
RAW "Tribute to the Troops," 160
Red Hot Chilli Pipers, 165
Redner, Lewis, 81
Reims, France, 147
Reindeer, 40, 75, 150, 183, 225, 251, 269
Reiner, Larry, 116
Renaissance, 15
Republic of Kiribati, 59
Reyes, Richard, 272
Rickets, 43
Riding the stang, 45
"Ring Out, Wild Bells" (Tennyson), 131
Rivers, Bob, 233
Roberts, Xavier, 96, 292
Rockefeller Center, 208, 220, 221
"Rockin' Around the Christmas Tree"
      (Lee), 183

Rockwell, Norman, 188
Rooney, Andy, 51
Roosevelt, Franklin Delano, 264
Roosevelt, Teddy, 206, 273
Rovaniemi, Lapland (Finland), 75
Rowena of Saxony, 15
RTA (type-I distal renal tubular
      acidosis), 42–43
Rubik, Erno, 293
Rubik's Cube, 293
Rudolph (the reindeer), 40, 49, 162–63
"Rudolph the Red-Nosed Reindeer"
      (song), 82, 162–63
Rudolph the Red-Nosed Reindeer, 82,
      163
Rudolph the Red-Nosed Reindeer
      (television), 180, 198
Rugby, 45
Rum punch, 65
Russia, 53, 54–55
Russian Imperial Ballet, 203
Russian Orthodox Church, 54
Ruth, Babe, 123
Ruxpin, Teddy, 96

S

Sadacca, Albert, 86
Sadat, Anwar El, 47
St. Basil (Agios Vassilis), 224
St. Francis of Assisi, 87, 221
St. Knut's Day, 127
St. Lucia Day, 126–27
St. Nicholas Day, 36–37, 134, 158
St. Stephen's Day, 37
Salvation Army, 125, 141
Sandys, William, 80
"Santa Baby" (Kitt), 92
Santa Claus
    chimneys and, 304–5
    costs of being, 124–25
    depictions of. *See* Nast, Thomas
    elves and, 179–81, 266–67
    evil twin of, 134
    history of, 104
    impersonators, 58
    letters to, 132–33, 143, 204
    malls and, 190

manual, 75
reindeer and, 40, 49, 251
schools, 74–75, 124, 248–49
wife of, 129
Santa Claus (1959), 295
Santa Claus, Indiana, 221, 249
Santa Claus House (North Pole, Alaska),
    204
Santa Claus Is Coming to Town (1970),
    180
SantaCons (conventions), 11–12, 23, 125
Saturday Evening Post, The, 188
Scandinavian customs, 126–27, 128, 144
Scandinavian myths, 19, 20, 128
Schools for Santa Claus, 74–75, 124,
    248–49
Schultz, Ann, 210
Schulz, Charles, 25, 198
Schwarz Toy Bazaar, 303
Schwerdtmann, Theodore, 303
Scooter, 294
Scotland, 164–65
Scott, George C., 175
Scrooge (1951), 174
Scrooge (1970), 174
Scrooge, Ebenezer, 42, 43, 63, 174–75,
    187, 199, 200
Scrooged (1988), 175
Second Boer War, 170
Seinfeld (television), 39, 200
Serling, Rod, 46–47
Seuss, Dr. (Theodore Geisel), 199
Seven Years War, 78
Seville, David. *See* Bagdasarian, Ross, Sr.
Shakespeare, William, 39, 113
Shepherd, Jean, 242
"Shepherds, The" *(Los Pastores)*, 238
Shopping, 36, 68–69, 138, 183, 221
"Silent Night," 81
Silent Night, Deadly Night (1984), 26
Silly Putty, 290
Sim, Alastair, 174
Sinatra, Frank, 230, 231
"Sinterklaas" (poem), 104
Sinterklass, 158
Skits, 45

Slavic gods, 53
Slinky, 95, 290
Smith, Tom, 226–27
Smith, Walter, 227
Smoking Bishop (drink), 63
Smurfs, 266–67
Smurf's Christmas Special, The (1982),
    267
Snegurochka, 53
"Snow Beauties" (Bentley), 156
Snow Crystals, 157
Snowflake, Arizona, 67
Snowflake Man (Bentley), 156–57
Snowy places in U.S., 216–17
Society of American Florists, 138
Songs, 16–17, 120–21, 176–77, 239. *See
    also* Carols.
South Africa, 170–71
Soviet Union, 53, 54–55
Spacek, Sissy, 46
Space missions, 256
Spain
    foods of, 88
    holidays in, 37, 38
    hot chocolate and, 66
Special Olympics, 47
Spiced cider (Wassail), 15
Spiced wine (mulled wine), 64
Spices, 90–91
Spielberg, Steven, 27
Star of Bethlehem, 30–31, 122
Starr, Ringo, 120, 235
Star Trek, 240
Star Wars (1977), 116
Star Wars action figures, 258–59
Star Wars Early Bird Certificate
    Package, 258–59
Stewart, Jimmy, 32
Stewart, Patrick, 240
Stockings, 28–29, 143
Stoolball (baseball), 44
Stratta, Ettore, 211
Strawberry Shortcake (doll), 292
Streisand, Barbra, 211
Strina (Roman goddess), 23
Suicides at Christmas, 140

Sundblom, Haddon, 104
Superstitions, 52
Suppan, Jeff, 146
Sweden, 126–27, 261
Swedish Yule goat, 261
Switzerland, 287
Symbols of Christmas, 155

T

Tales from the Crypt (1972), 26
Tamales, 88
"Tattoo of Santa" (Warner), 49
Tattoos, 49
Tchaikovsky, Peter Ilyich, 203
Teenage Mutant Ninja Turtles, 293
Television, 174–75, 198–200
Temperance movement, 41
Temple, Shirley, 305
Tennyson, Alfred Lord, 131
Texas, 88
Thanksgiving Day, 36, 83–85, 187, 263
Third Reich. *See* Nazi Germany.
Thor (Norse god), 162, 180
Thornton, Billy Bob, 75, 249
Three Kings, 29, 39, 122. *See also* Magi.
Three Kings Day, 115
Tickle Me Elmo, 97, 294
Tinkertoys, 270–71
Tinsel, 87, 152
Tiny Tim *(A Christmas Carol),* 42–43
Tolkien, J. R. R., 89, 179–81
Toll House Cookies, 302
Tolly, A. B., 264
Tomlinson, LaDainian, 146
Tormé, Mel, 82, 231, 245
Touching Lives Holiday Program, 146
Tourism, 197
Toys, 95–97, 236–37, 290–94, 303
Toys for Tots, 24–25, 67
Traditions, 28–29, 142–43. *See also* Cultural customs.
Transco (Transcription Company of America), 215
Treats, 13–15, 173
Trees
    Chrismukkah, 39
    decorations for, 86
    fake, 228–29
    fast facts about, 178, 273
    Germany and, 152–53
    as life-giving sources, 19
    official holy, 148
    purchase and sales of real, 67, 138, 183
    thefts of Christmas, 276
    tinsel for, 87
    traditions about, 142
    White House Christmas, 206, 273, 296–97
TubaChristmas, 220
Turkey (country), 205
Turkey (food), 187
Turkish Ministry of Culture and Tourism, 205
""Twas the Night Before Christmas" (Moore), 28–29, 130, 150, 235, 272, 305
Twelfth Night, 38–39
Twelve Days of Christmas, 34, 39, 106, 127
"Twelve Days of Christmas, The" (carol), 34–35, 140
Twisted Christmas (1987 album), 233
Twister, 95–96
Tyco toy company, 294
Type-I distal renal tubular acidosis (RTA), 42–43

U

United Kingdom, 21, 59, 79, 100, 226. *See also* England.
United Service Organizations, Inc. (USO), 160
United States
    Christmas as legal holiday in, 195, 263
    games played in, 45
    military charities, 160–61
    mumming in colonies of, 41
    pantos in, 185–86
    places with significant snow in, 216–17
    restaurant Christmas dinners in, 214
    St. Nicolas customs in, 37
    stocking customs of, 29

Toys for Tots in, 24–25
trees and, 178
Urban legends, 140–41
Ure, Midge, 82
U.S. Marine Corps Reserve, 24–25, 67, 125
U.S. Postal Service, 62, 183, 249, 298

V

Valent, Tom, 74
Very Special Christmas, A (1987), 47
Victoria (queen of England), 60, 212–13
Victorian England
    drink called Smoking Bishop in, 63
    foods of, 13
    games of, 44
    impact of Dickens on, 192
    poverty and disease in, 43
Video games, 237
Vietnam War, 116
"Vision of Piers Plowman, The" (Langland), 113
"Visit from St. Nicholas, A" (Moore), 28–29, 130
Vodafone, 61

W

Wakefield, Ruth, 302
Wales, 107, 108, 151
Warhammer universe, 181
Warhol, Andy, 188
Warner, Darin, 49
Warner, Ty, 293
Warner Bros., 24
Washington, George, 262
Washington Park Arboretum (Seattle), 276
Wassail (spiced cider), 15
Waters, John, 27
Web sites, Christmas, 277
Weebles, 292
Welles, Orson, 279
Wells, Bob, 82
Westminster Abbey, 108
"We Three Kings of Orient Are" (Hopkins), 81, 122
Wham-O, 290–91

"What Child is This?," 80
"White Christmas," 221
White Christmas (snowy), 216
White House, 206–7, 217, 262–64, 296–97
Wilenow (botanist), 119
Williams, Andy, 70–71
Willson, Robert Meredith, 82
Window displays, 110–11
Winstanley, William, 108
"Winter Wonderland," 47, 198
Wisconsin Historical Museum, 200
Wise Men, 30, 31, 39. *See also* Magi.
Witch (La Befana), 22, 23, 29
Women's Christmas, 39
Woolworth, F. W., 153, 274
World of Warcraft, 181
World War I, 21, 100, 153
World War II, 84, 85, 110, 111, 208
World Wide Web. *See* Internet.
World Wrestling Entertainment (WWE), 160
Wrapping paper, 50–51
Wreaths, 87
Wright, James, 290

X

Xbox 360, 97
Xena: Warrior Princess (television), 199
Xmas, 56, 141

Y

Yankovic, "Weird Al," 233
Year-round Christmas stores, 68–69
Year Without Santa Claus, The (television), 198
"Yes, Virginia," editorial, 132, 234–35
Yule Lads (Jólasveinar), 253, 254–55
Yule log, 19, 117, 143

Z

Zoot suits, 272
Zoroaster, 30–31, 122
Zuckerman, David, 276
Zwarte Piet (Black Pete), 159

Contributing Writers:

James Duplacey has written numerous books concerning hockey. He has served as curator of the Hockey Hall of Fame and Museum and managing editor of the *Official NHL Guide and Record Book.*

Mary Fons-Misetic is a freelance writer and performer living in Chicago. Every year, her family reads Charles Dickens's *A Christmas Carol* aloud. When her husband discovered this tradition, he was horrified. Secretly, Mary thinks he loves it.

Dave Gerardi is a New York–based writer whose work has appeared in *Newsweek, ESPN,* and dozens of publications. Despite magazine articles, contributions to numerous books, and work on his MaximumAwesome.com humor site, it may surprise you that he is poor and accepts donations of food or Cadbury Crème Eggs.

Heidi Tyline King writes about holidays, travel, decorating, and home improvement. She lives in Tallahassee, Florida, with her husband and three daughters, who have yet to see snow. More about Heidi can be found at www.heiditking.com.

Yi Shun Lai is the originator of the tried-and-true stress-management technique of wallowing in warm laundry. She lives in White Plains, New York, with her dog Sprocket, and her partner Jim, originator of the horizontal filing system.

Laura Pearson is a Chicago writer and editor specializing in arts and culture. She has written for numerous publications, both print and online. At Christmas, she salutes her Scandinavian heritage by drinking ample amounts of glögg.

Michael C. Riedlinger recently graduated from the University of Wisconsin-Parkside. He is a member of the Milwaukee Press Club, a published fiction writer, and the proud father of three children who are always on Santa's good list.

Russell Roberts is an award-winning freelance writer. He has published over three dozen books, including the best-sellers *Down the Jersey Shore* and *10 Days to a Sharper Memory.* He also specializes in travel writing and public speaking.

Lawrence Robinson is a Los Angeles-based novelist and screenwriter and has contributed to several Armchair Reader™ titles. His Web site is *BritWriter.com.*

Paul Seaburn recalls that a Christmas gift of a book on comedy writing inspired him to write for *The Tonight Show, The New York Times,* numerous magazines, comedians, and many books. He's head writer for the family comedy *Taylor's Attic* and a jazz and comedy show on public radio.

Ken Sheldon is a humorist, author, and singer/songwriter. He is the award-winning creator of Frost Heaves, the most under-appreciated town in New Hampshire (*frostheaves.com*).

Donald Vaughan is a freelance writer based in North Carolina. His work has appeared in an eclectic array of publications, including *Military Officer Magazine, Cat Fancy, MAD Magazine,* and the *Weekly World News.* He always tries to get his Christmas shopping done early and feels you're never too old to sit on Santa's lap.

Kelly Wittmann has written or cowritten nine books, and her name is spelled wrong on only three of them. On one of those three, she wishes it were spelled even "wrong-er"…but hey, a girl's gotta pay the bills. She lives in Chicago.